ON CROWN SERVICE

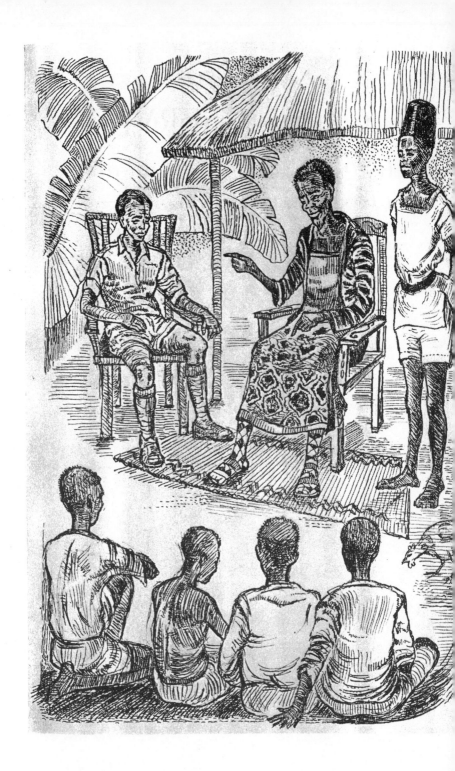

ON CROWN SERVICE

*A History of HM Colonial and
Overseas Civil Services
1837–1997*

Anthony Kirk-Greene

I.B.Tauris *Publishers*
London · New York

Published in 1999 by
I.B.Tauris & Co Ltd
Victoria House
Bloomsbury Square
London WC1B 4DZ

175 Fifth Avenue, New York NY 10010

In the United States of America and Canada distributed by
St Martin's Press
175 Fifth Avenue
New York
NY 10010

A full CIP record for this book is available from the British Library
A full CIP record for this book is available from the Library of Congress

ISBN 1–86064–260–8
Library of Congress Catalog card number available

Copy-edited and laser-set by Oxford Publishing Services, Oxford
Printed and bound in Great Britain by WBC Ltd, Bridgend

For my colleagues in the Colonial Service
and HMOCS, and for our colleagues and
successors in the national civil services
which we helped to establish.

The Queen's Message
to the Colonial Service, 1952

I desire, on my accession to the Throne, to express to all members of
the Colonial Service my warm appreciation of the ability and
devotion with which in the past they have performed their manifold
and responsible duties. The splendid traditions of the Service are well
known to me, and are rightly a source of pride to its members. I
know that I can depend with confidence on their unfailing loyalty
and on their continued and steadfast devotion to the well-being of
the peoples whom they serve.

Contents

Maps and Illustrations

Maps

Illustrations

List of Tables

List of Documents

Abbreviations

BAT	British Antarctic Territory
BDEEP	British Documents on the End of Empire Project
BIOT	British Indian Ocean Territory
BSAC	British South Africa Company
CA	Crown Agents
CAS	Colonial Administrative Service
CDW	Colonial Development and Welfare
CMG	Companion of the Order of St Michael and St George
CO	Colonial Office
CSAB	Colonial Service Appointments Board
DFID	Department for International Development
DO	Dominions Office
DTC	Department of Technical Cooperation
FCO	Foreign and Commonwealth Office
FO	Foreign Office
GCMG	Knight *or* Dame Grand Cross of the Order of St Michael and St George
GCVO	Knight *or* Dame Grand Cross of the Royal Victorian Order
GO	General Order
HMOCS	Her (*or* His) Majesty's Overseas Civil Service
HMSO	Her (*or* His) Majesty's Stationery Office
ICS	Indian Civil Service
IG	Inspector General
IO	India Office
KAR	King's African Rifles
LSE	London School of Economics
MAS	Malayan Administrative Service
MCS	Malayan Civil Service

MOD	Ministry of Overseas Development
MRCVS	Member of the Royal College of Veterinary Surgeons
OBE	Officer of the Order of the British Empire
OCRP	Oxford Colonial Records Project
ODA	Overseas Development Administration
ODRP	Oxford Development Records Project
OSPA	Overseas Service Pensioners' Association
OSRB	Overseas Services Resettlement Bureau
PRO	Public Record Office
RWAFF	Royal West African Frontier Force
SAR	Special Administrative Region
SOAS	School of Oriental and African Studies
SPS	Sudan Political Service
TAAS	Tropical African Administrative Services
TAS	Tropical African Services
VSO	Voluntary Service Overseas
WAA	Woman Administrative Assistant

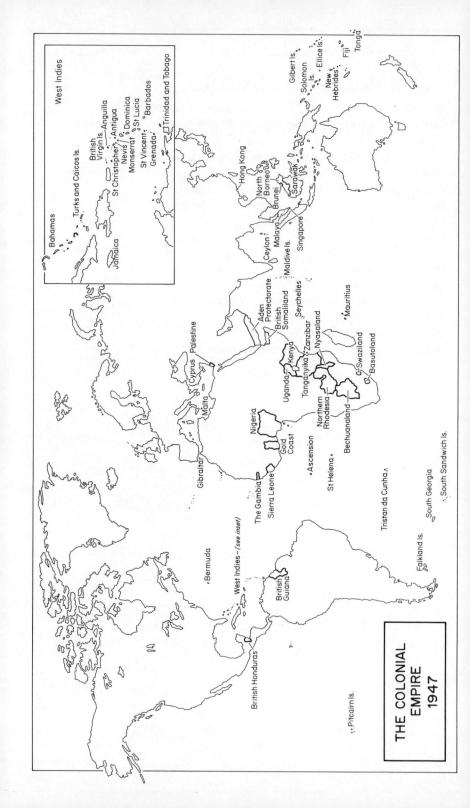

THE COLONIAL EMPIRE 1947

A Colonial Service Chronology, 1833–1997

1833	Crown Agents for the Colonies established
1837	First edition of Colonial Regulations
1854	Colonial Office separated from War Office, with own Secretary of State
1861	Annexation of Lagos
1862	First edition of the annual *Colonial Office List*
1864	Ionian Islands ceded to Greece
1867	Legal adviser to the Colonial Office appointed
	Straits Settlements transferred from the India Office
1869	Competitive examination for Eastern cadetships introduced
	Proposed scheme for interterritorial Colonial Service pensions
1874	Annexation of Fiji
1881	Report on Crown Agents for the Colonies (C. 3075)
1882	Combined examination for all Eastern cadetships instituted, allowing choice of colony
	Union of Nevis and St Kitts
1884	British Honduras separated from Jamaica
	Basutoland tranferred from Cape Colony
1885	Niger Coast Protectorate established
	Bechuanaland Protectorate established
1887	Imperial Institute opened
	Protectorate declared over Maldive Islands
1888	Seychelles separated from Mauritius
	Tobago joined with Trinidad
1890	Labuan incorporated into North Borneo
	Zanzibar became a protectorate
1892	Protectorate declared over Gilbert and Ellice Islands
1895	Joseph Chamberlain appointed Secretary of the State for the Colonies
1896	Eastern cadetships join common examination with Indian and Home civil services
	Grouping of the Federated Malay States
1897	Queen Victoria's Diamond Jubilee

1899   London School of Tropical Medicine founded
        Liverpool School of Tropical Medicine founded
1900   Selborne Report on the Colonial Service submitted to Chamberlain
        Inaugural dinner of the Corona Club
        Crown rule replaced Royal Niger Company in Northern Nigeria
        Tonga became British protectorate
1902   West African Medical Staff established
1905   Kenya transferred from the Foreign Office
        Uganda tranferred from the Foreign Office
        British Somaliland established as a separate protectorate
1906   Crown rule replaced North Borneo Company
        Joint Anglo–French administration in New Hebrides
        Swaziland came under sole British protection
1907   Nyasaland transferred from the Foreign Office
1908   *Reorganization of the Colonial Office* (Cd. 3795)
1909   Tropical African Administrative Service training courses started at
        Imperial Institute
1910   Colonial Audit Service established
        Appointment of Tropical Service Committee to consider
        assimilation of territorial services
        R. D. Furse appointed assistant Private Secretary (Appointments)
        to Secretary of State
1911   Introduction of assimilated conditions of service in tropical African
        dependencies
        Governor's Pensions Act
1913   Zanzibar transferred from the Foreign Office
1914   Cyprus established as a colony
        Amalgamation of Northern and Southern Nigeria
1916   Colony of Gilbert and Ellice Islands created
1919   Mandates for Tanganyika, Togo and Cameroons conferred on
        Britain
1920   Mandates for Palestine, Iraq and Transjordan conferred on Britain
        Report of Colonial Agricultural Services Committee (Cmd. 730)
        Report of Colonial Veterinary Services Committee (Cmd. 922)
        Report of Colonial Medical Services Committee (Cmd. 939)
        British East Africa renamed Kenya
1921   East African Medical Service established
1923   Dominion Selection Scheme for Colonial Service introduced
        Advisory committee on native education in tropical Africa established
1924   Forestry courses started at the Imperial Forestry Institute, Oxford
        Crown rule replaced British South Africa Company in Northern
        Rhodesia

Report of the Colonial Service Pensions Committee (Stevenson)
(Col. No. 1)
British Empire Exhibition at Wembley
Leo Amery appointed Secretary of State for the Colonies
1925   Agricultural scholarships established
Separation of Colonial Office and Dominions Office
1926   Tropical African Administrative Services courses started at Oxford and
Cambridge universities
Appointment of Chief Medical Officer to the Secretary of State
Survey courses started at Cambridge and at Ordnance Survey,
Southampton
Colonial Office list renamed *Dominions Office and Colonial Office List*
Report on Mr Ormsby-Gore's visit to West Africa (Cmd. 2744)
Report of West Indian Conference (Cmd. 2672)
1927   First Colonial Office Conference (Cmd. 2883)
Appointment of Economic and Financial Adviser to the Secretary
of State
Report of Colonial Agricultural Services Committee (Lovat) (Cmd.
2845)
Advisory Committee on Education extended to all colonial territories
1928   Tropical African Services courses extended to three terms
Tropical African education service course started at London University
Report of Colonial Agricultural Services Committee (Cmd. 3049)
Revised edition of *Colonial Regulations* (Col. No. 37)
1929   Report on Closer Union in East and Central Africa (Hilton–Young)
(Cmd. 3234)
Report of Colonial Veterinary Sevices Committee (Lovat) (Cmd. 3261)
Appointment of Tropical Agriculture Adviser to Secretary of State
Governor's Pensions Act
Report of Conference of Empire Survey officers
1930   Second Colonial Office Conference (Cmd. 3628)
Unification of the Colonial Services agreed
Veterinary Adviser to the Secretary of State appointed
Report of Committee on Colonial Service Appointments System
(Warren Fisher) (Cmd. 3554)
Colonial Service personnel division created in Colonial Office
Report on Colonial Films (Cmd. 3630)
1931   Report on Training of Colonial Forest Officers (Col. No. 61)
Report of Conference of Colonial Directors of Agriculture
(Col. No. 67)
Report of Conference of Empire Survey Officers (Col. No. 70)
Appointment of Inspector-General of African Colonial Forces
(RWAFF and KAR)

1932   Creation of the Colonial Administrative Service
        Incorporation of Malaya and Hong Kong (but not Ceylon) into
        Colonial Administrative Service
        End of the Eastern Cadetships entry scheme by examination
        Tropical African Service (TAS) courses renamed Colonial
        Administrative Service courses (CAS)
1933   Creation of the Colonial Legal Service
        Publication of the *Colonial Administrative Service List* (Col. No. 80)
        Revised edition of *Colonial Regulations* (Col. No. 88)
1934   Creation of the Colonial Medical Service
        Report on Colonial Service Leave and Passages (Plymouth) (Cmd.
        4730)
        Newfoundland reverted to colonial rule
        Report of the Kenya Land Commission (Carter)
1935   Publication of the *Colonial Legal Service List* (Col. No. 106)
        Publication of *An Economic Survey of the Colonial Empire* 1933
        (Col. No. 109)
        Creation of the Colonial Agricultural Service
        Creation of the Colonial Forestry Service
        Creation of the Colonial Veterinary Service
        Report of Conference of Empire Survey officers
1936   Aden transferred from the India Office
        Creation of the Colonial Prisons Service
        Report on the Widows' and Orphans' Pension Scheme (Watson)
        Publication of the *Colonial Medical Service List* (Col. No. 115)
        Publication of the *Colonial Forestry Service List* (Col. No. 122)
        Governors' Pensions Act
1937   Publication of *An Economic Survey of the Colonial Empire, 1935*
        (Col. No. 126)
        Creation of the Colonial Education Service
        First Oxford summer school on colonial administration
        Creation of the Colonial Police Service
        Women's Corona Club founded
        Publication of the *Colonial Veterinary Service List* (Col. No. 132)
1938   Creation of the Colonial Chemical Service
        Creation of the Colonial Postal Service
        Creation of the Colonial Customs Service
        Creation of the Colonial Mines Service
        Creation of the Colonial Geological Survey Service
        Creation of the Colonial Survey Service
        Second Oxford summer school on colonial administration
        Report of Conference of Colonial Directors of Agriculture
        (Col. No. 156)

	First annual publication of parliamentary report by Secretary of State, *The Colonial Empire* (Cmd. 5760)
1939	Publication of the *Colonial Audit Service List* (Col. No. 162)
	Publication of the *Colonial Police Service List* (Col. No. 168)
1940	Creation of [Queen Elizabeth's] Colonial Nursing Service
1941	Appointment of Adviser on Forestry to the Secretary of State
1943	Furse memorandum on postwar training of the Colonial Service
1944	Report of West Indian Conference (Carter) (Col. No. 187)
	Confidential report of Lord Hailey on his visit to British Tropical Africa, 1940–42
1945	Colonial Service recruitment reopened
	Creation of the Colonial Engineering Service
	Postwar Opportunities in the Colonial Service (RDW/6) issued
	West Indies Royal Commission Report published (Moyne) (Cmd. 6607)
1946	Crown rule replaced Brooke family rule in Sarawak
	Organization of the Colonial Service (Col. No. 197)
	Postwar Training for the Colonial Service (Devonshire Report) (Col. No. 198)
	Dominions Office and Colonial Office List reverted to *Colonial Office List*
	Arthur Creech Jones appointed Secretary of State for the Colonies
	Report on Inter-Territorial Organization in East Africa
	Colonial Service conference held at Oxford University
	Report on the groundnuts scheme (Cmd. 7030)
	Devonshire courses for Colonial Service training inaugurated
1947	Conference of African colonial governors
	Report of Commission on Civil Services in British West Africa (Harragin) (Col. No. 209)
	The Colonial Empire 1939–1947 (Cmd. 7167)
	First Colonial Office summer school held at Cambridge University (African No. 1173)
	Secretary of State's dispatch on local government in the colonies
	Conference on closer association of British West Indian colonies
	British Empire Forestry Conference
	Colonial Service conference held at London School of Economics
1948	Creation of the Colonial Civil Aviation Service
	Report of Commission on the Civil Services of Central Africa (Col. No. 222)
	Report of Commission on the Civil Services of East Africa (Holmes) (Col. No. 223)
	Creation of Malayan Union
	Retirement of Sir Ralph Furse as director of Colonial Service recruitment

Appointment of Police Adviser to the Secretary of State
Independence of Ceylon and Palestine
Colonial week held throughout UK
Colonial Service conference held at St Andrew's University
Report on Disturbances in the Gold Coast (Watson) (Col. No. 231 and 248)
First UN Trusteeship Council Visiting Missions to East Africa
Introduction of public service commissions in the colonial territories

1949   Unification of the Colonial Research Service
First UN trusteeship council visiting mission to West Africa
First issue of *Corona*, journal of HM Colonial Service

1950   Women's Corona Society founded
Police Adviser to Secretary of State renamed IG of Colonial Police
Report of Commission on Unification of the Public Services in the British Caribbean (Col. No. 254)

1951   Publication of *Economic Survey of the Colonial Territories* (Col. No. 281)

1952   Colonial Service appointments made since 1945 passed the 10,000 mark

1953   Federation of Central Africa established
Report on Withdrawal of Recognition from Kabaka of Buganda (Cmd. 9028)
Colonial Office conference on changes in the pattern of Colonial Service training

1954   Colonial Office conference of establishment officers from colonial territories
Reorganization of the Colonial Service (Col. No. 306) (creation of HMOCS)
Devonshire courses renamed Overseas Service courses 'A' and 'B'
Alan Lennox-Boyd appointed Secretary State for the Colonies
Report on civil services of East Africa (Lidbury)

1955   Report on East Africa Royal Commission (Dow) (Cmd. 9475)
Overseas Service Bill introduced into Parliament

1956   *Her Majesty's Oversea Civil Service* (Cmd. 9768) (Special List)
Governors' Pensions Act
Unfilled vacancies in Colonial Service approach 1500

1957   Independence of Gold Coast and Malaya
Colonial Office course for senior secretariat officers in overseas governments
Eighth Colonial Office summer conference on African administration, Cambridge University (African No. 1190)

1958   *Her Majesty's Oversea Civil Service (Nigeria)* (Cmnd. 497) (Special List 'B')

Report of Minorities Commission, Nigeria (Willink) (Cmnd. 505)

1959   Iain Macleod appointed Secretary of State for the Colonies
Reports on Hola Camp, Kenya (Cmnd. 778,795 and 816)
Report of Nyasaland Commission of Inquiry (Devlin) (Cmnd. 814 and
815)

1960   Report of Colonial Office Conference on public services
(Col. No. 347)
Final Colonial Office summer conference on African administration at
Cambridge University (African No. 1201)
Independence of Cyprus, Nigeria and British Somaliland
Publication of report on *Origins and Growth of Mau Mau* (Corfield)
(Cmnd. 1030)
Report of Commission on Central African Federation (Monckton)
(Cmnd. 1148)

1961   Formation of Department for Technical Cooperation
Technical Assistance from the UK for Overseas Development (Cmnd.
1308)
Independence of Tanganyika and Sierra Leone
First Cambridge University summer conference on colonial
government in Africa
Department of Technical Cooperation assumes responsibility for
recruitment for public services overseas

1962   *Technical Cooperation* (Cmnd. 1698)
Recruitment for Service Overseas (Cmnd. 1740)
Final issue of *Corona* journal
Independence of Jamaica, Trinidad and Tobago, and Uganda

1963   *Report of Committee on Training in Public Administration for Overseas
Countries*
HMG policy statement on above report (Cmnd. 2099)
Independence of Kenya, Zanzibar, North Borneo and Sarawak

1964   DTC renamed Ministry of Development
Independence of Malta, Nyasaland and Northern Rhodesia

1965   Independence of Singapore, The Gambia and Maldives

1966   Final edition of the annual *Colonial Office List*
Colonial Office closed and merged with Commonwealth Relations
Office as the Commonwealth Office
Independence of British Guiana, Barbados, Bechuanaland and
Basutoland

1967   Independence of Aden

1968   Creation of the Foreign and Commonwealth Office
Independence of Mauritius and Swaziland

1970   Independence of Fiji and Tonga

1973   Independence of the Bahamas

1974	Independence of Grenada
1975	MOD renamed Overseas Development Administration
1976	Independence of Seychelles
1978	Independence of Solomon Islands, Dominica, Ellice Islands
1979	Independence of Gilbert Islands, St Lucia, and St Vincent and the Grenadines
1980	Independence of the New Hebrides
1981	Independence of British Honduras and Antigua
1982	Falklands campaign
1983	Independence of Brunei, and Nevis and St Kitts
1997	Handback of Hong Kong
	Termination of HMOCS
1999	Closure of the Corona Club in its centennial year

Foreword by The Rt Hon Lord Grey of Naunton, GCMG, GCVO, OBE

The Colonial Service, with its successor Her Majesty's Overseas Civil Service, was the oldest of Britain's imperial civil services. It was the only one to be granted the title 'Her (His) Majesty's'. It was, too, the one with the widest remit, responsible at its peak for the administration of some 40 territories across the colonial empire. With the closure of HMOCS in 1997, it is right that the thousands of men and women whose careers were in Britain's largest overseas civil service should have the history of that service authoritatively remembered and recorded. From my own 30 years in the Colonial Service, I know something of the jobs they did and the lives they led. Physical hardship and family separation of a degree it is now difficult to imagine were balanced by the excitement and satisfaction of the exercise of huge responsibilities among peoples whom it was a pleasure and pride to serve, albeit that service was often exacting.

We are fortunate to have found our chronicler in Mr Kirk-Greene. From his academic base at Oxford University he has researched and written extensively about the Colonial Service over the last 30 years, his scholarship built upon his own direct experience of 15 years in the administrative service of Northern Nigeria. It is with great personal pleasure that I commend this important history whose author is widely acknowledged, both inside and outside the Service, as its leading historian.

Naunton, Glos
February 1998

Preface by J. H. Smith, CBE

Exploration and expansion have been imperatives throughout human history, beginning, as Roland Oliver, Professor of African History, has graphically described, when man outgrew Eden. That first colonization of other parts of Africa, one and a half million years ago, puts into perspective the mere century in which the men and women about whom this book is written played their role in the administration of Britain's final stage of empire. For the focus of the Colonial Service, and of its successor the Overseas Civil Service, was in an Africa rediscovered by and subject to Europeans.

Rediscovery began with the fifteenth century voyages that eventually led Europeans to every other part of the globe. Their motives were diverse and mixed, one often masquerading as another, and probably little different from those that had always stirred man to explore and expand: among them curiosity, greed, trade, escape from persecution, hope of betterment, religious zeal and the simple urge for adventure. The establishment of Portuguese trading posts along the coasts of Africa preceded settlement in the Caribbean and the Americas and the opening of sea routes for trade in exotic spices with India and China. The English followed rather than led, but the mercantile and maritime instincts of an island people combined with an early start in industrialization and stability of national government resulted in the acquisition over several centuries of the greatest empire the world has ever known. Its impact upon us and upon other peoples in every continent remains recent and pervasive.

Its beginning can be dated from John Cabot's voyage of 1497 and its end, 500 years later, in 1997 with all but total disengagement when the Hong Kong leases were surrendered to China. More romantically and more accurately, the empire spanned history from the reign of Queen Elizabeth I to the reign of Queen Elizabeth II. The settlement on Roanoke Island in 1585 was closely followed in 1603 by the landing, in search of nutmeg, on tiny Pulo Run in the Banda Islands of the Indonesian archipelago; the one the forerunner of the North American colonies, the other the forerunner of the East India Company and the Indian Empire.

Both events bear upon the story of the Colonial Service. Settlement of the North American colonies and the development of tobacco and cotton was to sustain the demand for slave labour already working sugar plantations and mines in the Caribbean and in Brazil. English merchants were also to dominate the second half of the four centuries of the Atlantic traffic in Africans, undoubtedly the greatest shame and horror of our empire.

While coastal trading posts flourished, there were few attempts to settle the tropical interior until revulsion finally led to the abolition of the slave trade. Then merchants began to seek other cargoes as industrialization in Britain encouraged both visions of new markets and a self-confident imperial mission. The formal acquisition of African colonies, in speculative competition with other European states, followed. Meanwhile, the merchant adventurers of the East Indian Company had given way to the Indian Civil Service, which in its turn became a model for the Colonial Service, which was to administer the newly acquired African colonies and others in the Far East, the Atlantic, Indian and Pacific oceans, providing intriguing threads of continuity as well as contrasts in style and procedure.

Two personal histories, less well known than they deserve, link the geography of empire, recall its succeeding stages and warn against judgements made with hindsight. Downing Street, home to prime ministers, is named after Sir George Downing, the unsavoury speculator who built it, in a career that came after, and perhaps was influenced by, his success as Secretary to the Treasury. It was Downing who established the principle of Treasury control, which in later application would determine local rather than metropolitan financing of the Colonial Service. Born in Dublin and moving to Massachusetts in boyhood, Downing was the second man to graduate from Harvard University. Yale University is named after its benefactor Elihu, one of two American colonist brothers in the service of the East India Company, whose fortune was acquired, corruptly, as governor of Madras. Nowhere in the colonial empire, except possibly in latter-day Hong Kong, could the extravagances of the British raj have been repeated. The territories were too poor. By now, too, the concept of public service had been born.

The history of American settlement, rebellion and independence, and the history of the Indian Empire have been well recorded. But it is only now that both former imperialists and former subject peoples are beginning to look back on the last stage of empire calmly and impartially. Colonial histories are appearing and it is right that among them should be a history of the Service that settled, administered and finally oversaw withdrawal from that last British Empire, often all encompassed within a single lifespan. Service to the Crown overseas drew men and women from every part of the British Isles as well as from nations whose origins lay in earlier colonial settlements: Australia, Canada, New Zealand, South Africa; and from the dependencies themselves, with, for example, West Indians serving in West Africa. These Colonial Service officers were never many in number. Their conditions of service depended on the resources of the territory to which they were appointed and varied accordingly. If the material rewards were modest, the job satisfaction was huge. Their lives, often lonely and hard, were rich in variety and offered immense responsibility at an early age. Their individual stories are told in a wealth of memoirs and novels that provide a human background to studies of colonialism and the transfer of power. In this book, Mr Kirk-Greene ably writes of the formal link between them, forester and surveyor, administrator and schoolmaster, police officer and nursing sister, wherever they served, whether on the west coast of Africa or on a Pacific island; they were members of HM Colonial Service and its successor, HM Overseas Civil Service.

We are indebted to Mr Kirk-Greene for this first history of these services, proudly commissioned by the Corona Club, their social club, to mark not only its centenary but the fitting decision to wind the club up at the end of the century that has seen the end of empire. It used to be said that the British acquired their empire in a fit of absentmindedness. Recently it has been said that nothing so became the British in their imperial mission as the leaving of it. That is a tribute that those of us who had the good fortune to be members of the Service appreciate. To a great extent we shared the aspirations of the people we served. For law and order, of course, but just as much for development — the first railways and roads were the hardest to build, the first schools and hospitals were the hardest to fill — and finally for independence. Most of us, too, learned as much as we imparted and our lives have been the richer for our close contact with other peoples and other cultures. We acknowledge our indebtedness just as we acknowledge the mistakes we inevitably made. Now, our duty done, our time is past. The future belongs to our successors in the public services of many nations. We wish them well.

John Smith
Chairman of the Corona Club
Dulverton, Somerset
January 1998

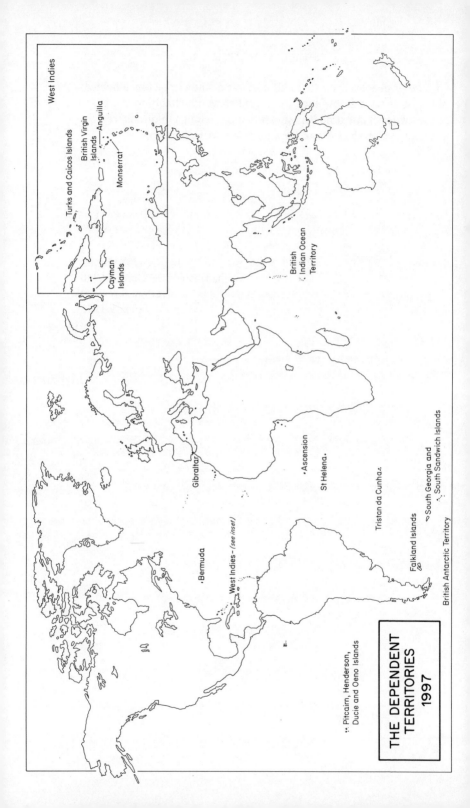

West Indies

Turks and Caicos Islands

British Virgin Islands — Anguilla

Monserrat

Cayman Islands

British Indian Ocean Territory

Gibraltar

Ascension

St Helena.

Tristan da Cunha.

Falkland Islands

South Georgia and South Sandwich Islands

British Antarctic Territory

Bermuda

West Indies – (see inset)

:: Pitcairn, Henderson, Ducie and Oeno Islands

THE DEPENDENT TERRITORIES 1997

Introduction

In 1996 the Corona Club Committee, under the chairmanship of J. H. Smith, CBE, paid me the honour of inviting me to research and write a narrative history of the Colonial Service and its successor HMOCS as part of the service celebrations arranged by a joint committee of the Overseas Service Pensioners' Association, the Corona Club and the Women's Corona Society to mark in May 1999 the closing of the Corona Club in its centennial year and the ending of HMOCS in 1997.

My original thought was to try and construct a history essentially derived from the personal memoirs and oral history of former members of the Colonial and Overseas Civil Services. It was a strategy I had adopted in working on the outline of what I hope will ultimately materialize as *The District Officer in Africa*. But that very project underlines the impossibility of having recourse to its design for the present assignment. *That* book will be focused on the colonial administrator alone and its context will be limited to Africa alone, whereas *this* book, as I have kept in the forefront of my mind as I worked on it, must be a narrative history encompassing the whole of the Colonial Service (not just the provincial administration) and the totality of the colonial empire (not just the African territories). That personalized, 'portrait' approach worked very well for the far smaller, more compact, single-territory Indian Civil Service (ICS) in the skilled hands of Philip Mason. In his *The Men Who Ruled India* (1953–54), he deliberately took a scene and a character and dwelt on each to illustrate a point before, as he explained, 'passing mercilessly — though with regret — over many years and places before the next'. But such a single-service focus could not be a viable or acceptable technique for our two services, with all their manifold variables in departments and location. The successful ICS model proved to be a non-starter here: if the nearest functional parallel to the ICS is the Colonial Administrative Service and this then became the subject of the study, more than three-quarters of the Colonial Service would be excluded from this history.

It is for this reason, of the scope of the Colonial Service precluding any single-focus chronicle, that the single territorial service histories, like those by Brown and Brown for Uganda, Chenevix Trench for Kenya and Heussler for the Malayan Civil Service (see Bibliography), are so important as a complementary contribution and a compromise solution to the otherwise too-wide-to-handle problem of trying to describe in one volume the life and work of the multifaceted Colonial Service and its successor HMOCS.

Fortunately, there is a rich literature easily to hand to 'humanize', if you like, this narrative history of the Colonial Service. One need look no further than such contemporary masterpieces as Charles Allen's *Tales from the Dark Continent* and *Tales from the South China Seas*; Arthur Grimble's *Tales of the South Pacific*, June Knox-Mawer's *Tales from Paradise* and Anne Gittins's *Tales of the Fiji Islands*; Derek Hopwood's *Tales of Empire: The British in the Middle East* and A. J. Sherman's *Mandate Days: British Lives in Palestine*; Joan Alexander's *Voices and Echoes: Tales from Colonial Women* and Joanna Trollope's *Britannia's Daughters: Women of the British Empire*; along with the literally scores of memoirs written by colonial civil servants in the 50 years since K. G. Bradley's classic *The Diary of a District Officer* (1943). Together, they provide a convincing, composite, personal portrait of the way we lived, whatever we were doing in the Colonial Service and wherever we were working in the colonial empire. What, on the other hand, the Colonial Service has so far conspicuously lacked is an institutional history of its establishment and evolution and of its successor, HMOCS, covering the 160 years of their existence. This is what I have set out to write. The last attempt at such a history dates back over 60 years. I am grateful to the Corona Club Committee for this opportunity and I trust that I have not disappointed the expectations of my co-members of the committee and the hopes of all my former colleagues in the Colonial Service and HMOCS.

In acknowledging the sources I have explored, I would like to draw attention to the only other named histories of the Colonial Service written since 1930. One is the somewhat legalistic and pedestrian course of lectures delivered at the London School of Economics by Sir Anton Bertram, a former chief justice of Ceylon, under the title *The Colonial Service*. The other is the indispensable *The Colonial Empire and its Civil Service* by Sir Charles Jeffries, together with his memoir *Whitehall and the Colonial Service, 1939–*

1956. As with Sir Charles's role in the final years of the Colonial Service, he never let us down. The sources from which the tables and documents have been derived are acknowledged individually in the text and I am grateful for permissions to reproduce, especially to HMSO for the excerpts from official publications. Whenever practicable, the documents on Colonial Service history have been left in their original format.

The extended Colonial Service chronology should prove a useful point of reference for other researchers. As a unique primary source, the Colonial Service archive built up in Rhodes House Library since the Oxford Colonial Records Project was established in 1963 under the directorship of J. J. Tawney remains invaluable. It now numbers more than ten thousand documents. The latest (1996) catalogue of manuscript collections contains more than two thousand new entries, most of them material donated by former members of the Colonial Service. The latterday vogue for Colonial Service memoirs as yet shows no sign of coming to an end, and the handback of Hong Kong to China in 1997 has already generated a strong revival of interest in the process of the end of empire and in Britain's final generation of career overseas civil servants.

My sincere thanks go to Marie Ruiz who typed the text and to Margaret Matheson who typed the tables; both have done a sterling job. I also wish to thank my editor, Lester Crook, for his encouragement and editorial wisdom, and John Smith, colleague and friend of more than 40 years, with James Hennessy for their valued textual suggestions. Finally, I wish to acknowledge the inspiration and support of my wife, who though not part of the Colonial Service life I lived for 15 years, has over the past 30 encountered and absorbed so much of its ethos, personalities and anecdotes that she now indisputably ranks as one of us.

A. H. M. Kirk-Greene
St Antony's College, Oxford
January 1998

Table 0.1: Size and Population of the Territories Staffed by the Colonial Service, 1947

	Area (Sq. miles)	Population	Crown Rule
EAST AND CENTRAL AFRICA			
British Somaliland (protectorate)	68,000	700,000	1884
Kenya (colony and protectorate)	224,960	4,200,000	1895
Tanganyika (mandate)	362,688	5,650,000	1920
Uganda (protectorate)	93,981	4,000,000	1893
Zanzibar (protectorate)	1,020	250,000	1890
Northern Rhodesia (protectorate)	287,640	1,660,000	1924
Nyasaland (protectorate)	47,949	2,230,000	1891
WEST AFRICA			
Gambia (colony and protectorate)	4,132	250,000	1843
Gold Coast (incl. Togoland) (colony)	91,843	4,095,000	1874 (1821)
Nigeria (incl. Cameroons) (colony and protectorate)	372,674	22,000,000	1900 (1861)
Sierra Leone (colony and protectorate)	27,925	1,800,000	1808
EASTERN DEPENDENCIES			
Federation of Malaya (nine protected states and two settlements of Penang and Malaca)	50,850	4,878,000	1819
Singapore (incl. Christmas and Cocos Islands) (colony)	217	941,000	1819
Brunei (protected state)	2,226	48,000	1906
North Borneo (incl. Labuan) (colony)	29,417	330,000	1946
Sarawak (colony)	50,000	500,000	1946
Hong Kong (colony)	391	1,750,000	1841
Ceylon (colony)	25,332	5,313,000	1802
MEDITERRANEAN DEPENDENCIES			
Cyprus (colony)	3,572	450,000	1914 (1878)
Gibraltar (colony)	1⁷/₈	21,000	1713
Malta (colony)	121	290,000	1814
Palestine (mandate)	10, 157	1,765,000	1923
WEST INDIES GROUP			
Bahamas (colony)	4,375	81,000	1717
Barbados (colony)	166	193,000	1662
Bermuda (colony)	21	35,000	1684
British Guiana (colony)	83,000	376,000	1814

Table 0.1 cont.	Area (Sq. miles)	Population	Crown Rule
British Honduras (colony)	8,867	59,000	1862
Jamaica and dependencies (colony)	4,846	1,308,000	1660 (1655)
Leeward Islands (colony, four presidencies)	422	109,000	1871
Trinidad & Tobago (colony)	1,980	558,000	1802
Windward lslands (colony)	821	252,000	1885
WESTERN PACIFIC DEPENDENCIES			
British Solomon lslands (protectorate)	11,500	95,000	1893
Fiji (colony)	7,083	260,000	1874
(Gilbert & Ellice lslands (colony)	333	35,000	1892
New Hebrides (Anglo-French condominium)	5,700	45,000	1902 (1895)
Tonga (protected state)	250	40,000	1900
ATLANTIC AND INDIAN OCEANS			
Falkland Islands (colony)	4,618	2,200	1833
St Helena and Ascension (colony)	81	5,000	1834
Aden (colony and protectorate)	80	81,000	1839
	112,000	650,000	
Mauritius (colony)	805	430,000	1814
Seychelles (colony)	156	35,000	1810
HIGH COMMISSION TERRITORIES			
Basutoland	11,716	556,000	1868
Bechuanaland	275,000	294,000	1885
Swaziland	6,704	184,000	1902

Source: Based on *The Colonial Empire, 1947–1948* (Cmd. 7433), 1948.

1. An Expanding Empire to Staff, 1837–99

'There are few things of which the British people are so ignorant as the Crown Colonies.' — Alfred Lyttelton, Secretary of State for the Colonies, 1905.

Britain's colonial empire had no rationalization and little coherence in its growth. What is often referred to as the First British Empire, that is to say in general terms the period of Crown government overseas between John Cabot's claim to 'the New Found Land' in 1497 — or, more viably, the pioneer permanent settlements in Newfoundland in 1583 and in Virginia along the James River in 1607 — and the acknowledged independence of the American colonies in 1783, significantly did not lead to the establishment in Britain of a separate civil service to administer the territories under the British flag — not even for the West Indies, arguably Britain's first 'jewel in the crown'. Neither the original 13 American colonies (1607–1783), or the merged provinces of upper (English) and lower (French) Canada (1791), nor the administration of the scattering of islands in the Caribbean and the Atlantic like Jamaica (1655), Barbados (1663) and Bermuda (1684), involved the formal superstructure of a home-recruited corps of British administrators and public service officers dispatched from London to manage their affairs other than, typically, the appointment of a governor by the sovereign, supported by a colonial secretary and a chief justice. For the rest, the basics of governance were taken care of by the governor's powers to appoint local staff to assist him in the administration of the colony.

With the emergence of what can be looked on as the Second British Empire, starting from 1783 and covering the period of the French revolutionary and Napoleonic wars, the substantial addition of British territory, particularly in the East with Ceylon (1802), Hong Kong (1841) and the Straits Settlements (1867), called for fresh and more formalized structures both in the metropole and in the new possessions. Whereas the previous colonies of settlement provided a resource of local population from whom a functioning public service could be drawn, the new colonies of occupation, or Crown Colonies, located in the tropics and no longer offering would-be settlers the less demanding Atlantic climate, had no such reservoir of on-the-spot manpower to which to turn. In consequence, they were obliged to create, in the East and later in Africa, what were termed 'European civil services'. Following the remodelling of the Colonial Office in the 1820s, the expanded colonial empire was divided into four groups of territories: North America, West Indies, Mediterranean and Africa, and the Eastern colonies (including at that time New South Wales). The ultimate breakthrough for the Colonial Office, which had had a Secretary of State administering the affairs of the American and subsequently Colonial Department since 1768, came in 1854 when, after 60 years of amalgamation with the War Department, the colonies at last achieved a Secretary of State for their affairs alone. In the wake of the seminal Northcott–Trevelyan report on the reform of the Home Civil Service in 1853, the Colonial Office was among the first of the Whitehall departments to institute entry through competition and to abolish recruitment by patronage.

It was in the first half of the nineteenth century, too, that the Colonial Service began to take shape. In the outline history that follows, a series of steps and stages are identified in the history of HM Colonial Service. For the newcomer to the field of imperial administration it should be stressed at the outset that the Colonial Service was always a completely separate organization, in recruitment, career and control, from either the Indian Civil Service (1858–1947) or the Sudan Political Service (1899–1955) — and from the Colonial Office, part of the UK Home Civil Service.

The initial stage of the operation of the Colonial Service may be said to have run from the first official mention of a Colonial Service, in 1837, up to 1899, when Joseph Chamberlain at the Colonial Office instituted a major review of the Colonial Service as Britain moved into an era of accelerated imperial expansion and administrative consolidation of its colonial empire. This is the period covered in Chapter 1. The second period takes the story up to 1939, marked by such interwar service milestones as the professionalization of

Colonial Service training programmes, the defining Warren Fisher report on Colonial Service appointments, and the unification of the Colonial Service. These key events form the subject of Chapter 2. Chapter 3 is focused on postwar plans for the development and expansion of the Colonial Service from 1943 to 1954 when, consequent on the constitutional advance towards independence in much of the colonial empire, it was reshaped and renamed Her Majesty's Overseas Civil Service (HMOCS). This successor service forms the theme of Chapter 4, taking the story through to 1997 when, with the handback of Hong Kong to China, HMOCS officially came to an end. In Chapter 5 I look back at the 160 years of the Colonial Service and conclude with a reflection on its part in the legacy of the British Empire. Throughout the text there runs the primary argument that the Colonial Service was a respected and sought after Crown career, aimed at and attractive to tens of thousands of British men and women in the twentieth century.

The text is illustrated with numerous tables. In addition, it is preceded by an extensive Colonial Service chronology covering the years 1833 to 1997. This offers a ready, complementary guide to the history of the service presented in Chapters 1–4. The bibliography, the first detailed Colonial Service compilation ever to be attempted, contains nearly a thousand entries, classified thematically. While researchers into Colonial Service history may appreciate the section on British government documentation (Command papers and the Colonial Office numbered series), the section on biographies, autobiographies and memoirs will be of special interest to readers who are one-time members of the Colonial Service and HMOCS.

* * *

The first identified set of Colonial Rules and Regulations, issued for the 'Information and Guidance of the Principal Officers and Others in His Majesty's Colonial Possessions', is dated 30 March 1837. As the inaugural official reference to HM Colonial Service, the Colonial Department's explanation of the need for this new document has enough historical importance to justify the reproduction of the message in full (see below). The widely held acceptance of 1837 as thus witnessing the birth of HM Colonial Service is reinforced by the fact that, within a mere decade, William Thackeray could refer in his

Introduction to Colonial Regulations

In administering the affairs of this department, Lord Glenelg has had frequent occasion to observe, that there are various regulations connected with His Majesty's Colonial Service, which appear to be inaccurately understood, and, on that account, imperfectly observed, in many of His Majesty's Colonies. To prevent, as far as possible, such misconceptions, and the inconvenience to which they have given rise, he has brought together, in the following pages, various Rules which he finds to have been hitherto dispersed through the correspondence of his predecessors. The attempt to consolidate them will probably, at first, be inaccurately and imperfectly made; but the standing regulations, now, for the first time collected together, will, at least, form a basis for future improvements; and will, probably, tend to the immediate introduction of a better method, and of greater certainty in the despatch of the duties of the Governors, and other Public Officers in the Colonial possessions of the Crown. Lord Glenelg has, therefore, instructed them to receive it as a rule for the guidance of their conduct on the several matters to which it relates.

To prevent any misapprehension upon one of the subjects discussed in the following pages, – that, namely, which relates to the settlement of the waste lands of the Crown, it is right to notice, that the regulations on that head must be regarded as provisional only, so far as respects all the minor details, and that it is not impossible that they may shortly undergo some material changes.

Colonial Department, Downing Street,
March 30th, 1837

Source: *Rules and Regulations for the Information and Guidance of the Principal Officers and Others in His Majesty's Colonial Possessions*, 1837.

novel *Vanity Fair* (1848) to the Colonial Secretary 'and the Service'. Yet, despite these two early nineteenth century references, it would be inaccurate to believe there existed anything approaching a structured, career Colonial Service for another 50 years. What took place in the second half of the nineteenth century was little more than the emergence of separate territorial civil services, each with its own procedures and character. For instance, on the transfer of Ceylon from the jurisdiction of the India Office to that of the Colonial Office in 1802, and similarly that of the Straits Settlements in 1867, each colony established its own civil service, just as Hong Kong had from 1841.

The creation of the Indian Civil Service in 1858, when the Crown took over the government of India from the East India Company, became something of a model for the Colonial Office's Eastern dependencies. Each of them insisted (Ceylon from 1855 and Hong Kong from 1861) on a formal examination for all the applicants nominated by the Secretary of State, leading in 1869 to the establishment of Eastern cadetships. From 1882, the Eastern Cadetship Scheme offered successful applicants the choice of a career in Ceylon, Hong Kong or the Straits Settlements. After 1896, the Eastern cadets had to sit the same open competitive examination as candidates for the Indian Civil Service and for Class I clerkships in the Home Civil Service. This arrangement lasted until the 1930s, when separate recruitment for the Eastern dependencies ceased and they came under the new unified Colonial Service procedures.

Appointment to a colonial governorship, however, continued to be primarily dependent on patronage, along the lines satirically featured in Thackeray's *Vanity Fair*. There, Colonel Rawdon Crawley, CB, is shamelessly — but safely — sent as governor of the aptly-named Coventry Island thanks to the intrigues of Lord Steyne so that, with her husband safely removed to a remote colonial outpost, his lordship might the better pursue his dalliance with the captivating Becky Sharp. 'We need', ran the official announcement from Downing Street on the appointment of this 'distinguished Waterloo officer' to the governorship, 'not only men of acknowledged bravery but men of administrative talents to superintend the affairs of our Colonies'.

Nevertheless, it is possible to identify from the second half of the nineteenth century the beginnings of a class of professional governors who, regardless of the patronage of their appointment, succeeded in building up a genuine record of experience and could be said to have made a career in colonial administration. This early manifestation of something approaching the twentieth century concept of a 'colonial career' can be seen in the experience of more than twenty governors, who, in the words of one authority on colonial administration in the nineteenth century, constituted a group of 'hard-core professionals who dominated the mid-nineteenth century Colonial Service'. For example, Sir Henry Barkly was, between 1848 and 1877, governor of British Guiana, Jamaica, Victoria, Mauritius and Cape Colony; Sir Alfred Moloney was successively governor of The Gambia (1884), Lagos (1886), British Honduras (1891), Windward Islands (1897) and Trinidad and Tobago (1900–4); Sir Hercules Robinson held a governorship on six occasions between 1859 and 1897; Sir James Pope Hennessy was governor of Labuan (1867), Sierra Leone (1872), Bahamas (1873) and Barbados (1875), before moving to Hong Kong in 1877 and finally Mauritius (1883–9); and between 1900 and 1925 Sir Matthew Nathan was governor of the Gold Coast, Hong Kong, Natal and, finally, Queensland.

It was the age of the new imperialism, from c.1870 and carrying over for all but a century, which was to revolutionize the way the staffing of the greatly enlarged colonial empire was managed. The outcome was what by the turn of the century could palpably be perceived as Her Majesty's Colonial Service, even though its final transformation into a single, unified Colonial Service would not occur until 1930. The catalyst was Africa, now about to emerge as the classical colonial continent, occupied by no less than seven European powers.

Following this vigorous incursion of Europe into Africa, by 1900 the demand for overseas civil servants — at this juncture principally administrators, legal and medical officers — to staff the newly acquired territories grew suddenly and hugely as Britain first increased her West African dimension, and then added an East and a Central one on to the southern African focus of her colonial empire on that continent. In 1900, Nigeria was added to the Colonial Office's older West African settlements of The Gambia, Sierra Leone, Gold Coast, Lagos and the Niger Coast Protectorate. In East and Central Africa, it was the Foreign Office which was first drawn into Uganda, the British East African Protectorate (later Kenya) and Nyasaland, while to staff the new government of the Anglo-Egyptian Sudan after its reoccupation in 1898 a separate Sudan Civil Service was formed, its political officers initially recruited from officers on secondment from the Egyptian Army along with a handful of young graduates from British universities.

Furthermore, in West, East and Central Africa alike, the Crown progressively assumed the responsibility for territorial administration from chartered companies such as Sir George Goldie's Royal Niger Company, Sir William Mackinnon's Imperial British East Africa Company, the African Lakes Company and finally, in the early 1920s, Cecil Rhodes's British South Africa Company (BSAC). While in each instance a small number of company officials might be accepted for transfer into the new territorial government services, it was how to find sufficient staff for the new colonial responsibilities that exercised the Colonial Office and called for urgent action in London in the closing years of the nineteenth century.

By 1895, the increase in Colonial Service appointments, along with the piecemeal process of recruitment and still limited career opportunities, persuaded the new Secretary of State for the Colonies Joseph Chamberlain to set up an in-house committee to discover how many serving officers might properly be ranked under the heading of Colonial Service and so help him decide whether there really was an institution that could honestly and properly be described as 'the Colonial Service'. The committee's unpublished report of 1899, which is examined in more detail in Chapter 2, gives the first real picture of what comprised the Colonial Service at the end of the nineteenth century. At the same time, what was to solidify into Britain's financial philosophy of empire, namely the belief that wherever possible colonies should be expected to pay for themselves (and hence their own civil services), was emerging. That principle of fiscal self-sufficiency was to remain in force until the Colonial Development and Welfare Act of 1940, and notably that of 1945, reversed the long-standing policy by earmarking money to fund development schemes in the colonies.

Another problem linked to exactly what was meant by the Colonial Service has been a continuing source of *prima facie* puzzlement to students of Britain's imperial history. This is because, confronted by the proliferation of Whitehall departments responsible for the management and affairs of Britain overseas, they seek to identify the centre of policy-making and to locate logic in the distribution of overseas business in the metropole. Where, they ask, should one start to penetrate the labyrinth of Whitehall responsibility for empire, amid the coexisting institutions of a Colonial Office (CO), a Foreign Office (FO), an India Office (IO), a Dominions Office (DO) and a Crown Agents (CA) for the Colonies, all handling the affairs and servicing the staffs of the official British representation overseas? As an official recruiting pamphlet in 1950 put it to British undergraduates thinking about possible choices of career in government, 'You can weigh the comparative advantages of a despatch-case in Whitehall and a cocked hat and epaulettes in Budapest, and you will be able still further to confuse your mind by also imagining yourself in a white sun helmet with a golden crest on the beaches of the Solomon Islands.'

The situation could not claim to reveal much greater clarity to the outside observer when one shifted the focus from home to abroad. Instead of the anticipated, single, empire-wide civil service, the thousands of Britons serving on permanent and pensionable terms in overseas governments took up their career in any one of a dozen separate services: the Indian Civil Service; the Indian Political Service; the All-India Services; the Egyptian Civil Service; the Sudan Political Service; the Burma Civil Service; the Ceylon, Malayan or Hong Kong Civil Service; and, of course, the notional Colonial Service, definitionally still the vaguest of them all. By the time the ultimate rationalization took place 70 years on, with the amalgamation of the Foreign Office and the Commonwealth Office into a single Foreign and Commonwealth Office (FCO) in 1968, following the prior merger of the Colonial Office and the Commonwealth Relations Office in 1966, there was no Indian Civil Service, Sudan Political Service or Colonial Service left for it to staff and service.

As late as 1948, the Colonial Office was still satisfied with its definition that '"The Colonial Service" is the term in use for the aggregate of the basic services of all the Colonial Territories for the government of which the Secretary of State for Colonies is responsible.' This was an advance on the reflection of the Secretary of State for the Colonies when, at the Colonial Office conference of 1927, he admitted to the participants that:

> Strictly speaking there is, of course, no Colonial Empire and no such thing as a Colonial Service. ... I deal in this office with some twenty-six different governments, each entirely separate from the rest, each administratively, financially, legislatively self-contained. Each, whether it deals with nearly 20m. people over an area as large as Central Europe or with 20,000 people on a scattered handful of islands, has its own Administrative Service, its own Medical Service, its own Agricultural, Public Works and other technical Services, its own scale of pay, its own pensions.

Elusive as the concept and the context of 'the Colonial Service' may have seemed to many — including, up to its unification in 1930 (see Chapter 2), many of its members — there could be no doubts about its presence on the ground around the world. Table 1.1 sets out in detail the component parts of the British Empire which the Colonial Service administered in 1947, at the zenith of its responsibilities on the eve of the independence of Ceylon and Palestine, omitting only what the Colonial Office was wont officially to describe as 'a number of islands and rocks throughout the world ... not included in any colony'.

Table 1.1 Geographical Location of the Colonial Service, 1947

Pacific (2)	Fiji (with Pitcairn Island), Western Pacific (Gilbert and Ellice Islands, Solomon Islands, Tonga and the New Hebrides)
Far East (1)	Hong Kong
Southeast Asia (5)	Ceylon, Malaya, North Borneo, Sarawak, Singapore
Africa (14)	Basutoland, Bechuanaland, Gambia, Gold Coast, Kenya, Nigeria, Northern Rhodesia, Nyasaland, Sierra Leone, Somaliland, Swaziland, Tanganyika, Uganda, Zanzibar
Mediterranean (3)	Cyprus, Gibraltar, Malta
Middle East (2)	Aden, Palestine
Atlantic (1)	St Helena (with Ascension and Tristan da Cunha)
Caribbean (7)	Bahamas, Bermuda, Barbados, Jamaica, Leeward Islands, Trinidad and Tobago, Windward Islands
Central America (2)	British Guiana, British Honduras
Antarctic (1)	Falkland Islands (with South Georgia, South Orkney and South Shetland)

Source: A. H. M. Kirk-Greene, *A Biographical Dictionary of the British Colonial Service, 1939–1966*, 1991.

One last point on nomenclature. Among all Britain's overseas civil services, only one was characterized by royal recognition in its title. This was His/Her Majesty's Colonial Service. The privilege was extended to its successor (1954) Her Majesty's Overseas Civil Service. It is to the evolution of the modern HM Colonial Service that we turn in the next chapter.

2. The Evolution of the Modern Colonial Service, 1900–39

*'Our nation has a great heritage of overseas responsibilities. ...
The men and women of the Colonial Service are the tools of our
task, the representatives of Britain overseas.'* — Arthur Creech
Jones, Secretary of State for the Colonies, 1949.

For all the evidence adduced in the previous chapter of a
certain Colonial Service presence in the nineteenth century —
the issuance of *Rules and Regulations for the Information and
Guidance of the Principal Officers and others in His Majesty's Colonial
Possessions* in 1837, the several allusions in William Thackeray's
well-read novel of 1848, the separation of the Colonial Office from
the War Office in 1854, the introduction of entry through public
examination to the Eastern cadetships in 1869, and the gradual
professionalization of the gubernatorial cadre from the 1870s — it
was not until the mid–1890s that the Colonial Service, rather than a
handful of territorial or regional institutions like those of Ceylon and
Hong Kong or the West African Medical Service, began to establish
itself both in the official mind and in public awareness.

Two major sources allow us to calculate the strength of the
Colonial Service as it reached first the silver and then the diamond
jubilee of its official recognition in the first edition (1837) of what
were later to become *Colonial Regulations*. One is the appearance in
1862 of the first *Colonial Office List* or 'General Register of the
Colonial Dependencies of Great Britain', a publication which in the
event was to appear annually right through to 1966 other than in the
war years 1941–5 and, because of the paper shortage, 1947. Planned
in 1860 and based on data compiled in 1861, it lists the name and

often the salary of every member of the civil and judicial establishment of each colony, set out under the Colonial Office's then
division into West Indian, North American, Mediterranean, and Australian and Eastern Departments. Besides reprinting a revised version
of 'Rules and Regulations for Her Majesty's Colonial Service', which
lists 37 colonial possessions (55 if one itemizes each of the Leeward,
Windward and Ionian islands), it carries a supplement of more than
1000 'persons now living who have served or are now serving under
the Secretary of State, or in the Colonies' in one capacity or another.
A number of the entries spell out employment in 'the Colonial civil
service', and several indicate employment in the Colonial Service
since the 1830s — and one who claimed to have 'entered the
Colonial Service of the Cape in 1819'.

The other invaluable source, for estimating the size of the Colonial
Service at the turn of the century, is the unpublished Selborne report
called for by Joseph Chamberlain as Secretary of State soon after his
accession to office in 1895 and submitted in 1899. In it, the strength
of the Colonial Service is recorded as 434 higher administrative
officers (approximately 100 of whom belonged to the three Eastern
Cadet Services), 310 legal officers and 447 medical officers. Just over
300 appointments were classified as 'other', giving a total of about
1500. Not all these were recruited from Britain; many were locally
appointed officers, and invariably so for posts carrying a salary of less
than £100 a year. Among the options Chamberlain went on to
consider in his search for a viable Colonial Service were the fusion of
the Colonial Service with the Indian Civil Service to form a single
British Empire civil service and an amalgamation with the staff of the
Colonial Office. In the event, neither alternative found favour.
Instead, Chamberlain decided that the Colonial Service should, in
keeping with the current expansion of empire in Africa, be enlarged
and enhanced into a career Crown service with its own identity,
attractive to and respected by all those who were keen to work in the
colonial territories in an administrative or professional capacity.

Accordingly, the Colonial Office set about in the ensuing decade
to strengthen its appeal to and its links with the universities so as to
create a public awareness of the opportunities offered by the Colonial
Service as an expanded and improved career Crown service. In 1900,
the official *Colonial Office List* carried four pages of 'Information as to
Colonial Appointments', covering a range of departments spread
across a score of territories. By 1909 it had recruited 261 adminis-

trative officers for Nigeria and 82 for Kenya in the new African territories, as well as among the older possessions 47 for the Gold Coast and 125 for Malaya. By 1910, the number of European officers serving in the West African possessions totalled: Gambia 30, Sierra Leone 150 (with a further 130 on garrison duties), Gold Coast 400, Southern Nigeria and Lagos 850, and Northern Nigeria 680. Clearly its appeal to Britain's universities was paying off as more and more graduates applied for the new opportunities in the new-look Colonial Service. The same year, 1909, also saw the Colonial Office set up a training course for new recruits to its African Administrative Services, held for two months (later raised to three) at the Imperial Institute in London. The subjects studied were colonial accounts, tropical economic products, hygiene and sanitation, criminal law and procedure, international law and Mohammedan law, elementary surveying, African languages and phonetics, and ethnology — all in no more than 12 weeks. By 1910, the new administrative staff recruited for the Tropical African dependencies had tripled over the decade to pass the 1000 mark. On the eve of the First World War, Colonial Service officers in all departments totalled 1400 serving in Africa (Table 2.1). Departmentally, the most notable initiative was the creation in 1902 of a unified West African Medical Service common to all four territories for postings, salaries, promotion and conditions of service. In 1909 this cadre totalled nearly 200 officers.

There was one more source of recruitment to the Colonial Service, especially available in the case of the administration, which was outside the standardizing pattern discussed above. It proved to be one that made a recognizable contribution to the evolving Colonial Service in Africa. This was the transfer of a number of officials from the Chartered Company administrations into the new government services when the Crown took over from company rule. This kind of cadre reinforcement took place on three major occasions during the first quarter of the twentieth century. When the British government assumed responsibility from the Royal Niger Company on New Year's Day 1900, Sir Frederick Lugard, as the new high commissioner for Northern Nigeria, was able to effect the transfer of several senior Royal Niger Company agents into the protectorate's new civil service. Some of these, such as W. P. Hewby, A. H. Festing (of the Royal Niger Constabulary) and F. Cargill (a Company medical doctor), were immediately appointed as Residents of the new provinces, while W. Wallace became deputy to Lugard

Table 2.1 Distribution of the Colonial Service in British Tropical Africa, 1914

Branch	E. Africa Protectorate	Gambia	Gold Coast	Nigeria	Nyasaland	Sierra Leone	Uganda	Total
Education	8	–	18	41	–	11	–	78
Railways	13	1	14	23	–	15	10	76
Surveys	33	1	13	31	3	2	14	97
Agriculture	6	–	6	18	5	3	9	47
Veterinary	12	–	1	2	3	1	3	22
Forestry	5	–	5	34	2	4	2	52
Medical	32	6	67	116	12	25	–	258
Marine and Transport	17	2	3	35	4	2	2	65
Public Works	17	–	55	70	4	10	10	166
District Administration	117	4	44	252	40	29	52	538
Total	360	14	226	622	73	102	102	1399

Source: Based on L. H. Gann and P. Duignan, *The Rulers of British Africa, 1870–1914*, 1978.

and acted for him when he was out of the country on leave and A. Burdon went on to become Governor of British Honduras. A few years later, similar transfers took place into the East African Protectorate (Kenya) service when the Imperial British East Africa Company was replaced by Colonial Office staff. This time, however, the principle of individual selection was less scrupulously observed, and the governor, Sir Percy Girouard, found cause to quarrel with the Colonial Office over 'the lamentable quality' of several of the administrators with whom he had been saddled. Nonetheless, among former staff of the Imperial British East Africa Company, several went on to achieve high office in the Colonial Service, among them Sir Frederick Jackson, who became Governor of Uganda, and such well-known administrators as J. M. Ainsworth, F. Hall and C. W. Hobley. The third instance of substantial lateral transfers into the Colonial Service, and in manpower the largest of the three occasions, was when the Crown took over the rule of Northern Rhodesia from the BSAC in 1924. Among them were R. A. J. Goode, who became chief secretary, and E. S. B. Tagart, the new Secretary for Native Affairs. Perhaps the outstanding officer to come in from the BSAC was R. T. Coryndon, who, having been private secretary to Cecil Rhodes and then Resident Commissioner first of Swaziland and next Basutoland, ended his career as governor of Uganda and then of Kenya.

By 1909 the expansion of the Colonial Service in Africa had been so successful that the Colonial Office set up a Tropical African Services Committee, with a brief to work out a scheme for a single, unified civil service for Africa. In this, it was invited to consider how far the West African Medical Service and the West African Frontier Force might serve as a model for an extended simulation with the services of the East African Protectorates. Given this positive trend in Colonial Office thinking towards an extension of the mid–nineteenth century Eastern cadetship service to the new Tropical (East as well as West) African service, it has been conjectured that had the First World War not intervened, the new colonial empire might have taken the shape, in Colonial Service terms, of a series of regional civil services (such as Eastern, Caribbean, Pacific), with a Tropical African Service as its largest unit. In the meantime, the case is clear for crediting Joseph Chamberlain's tenure of the Colonial Office (1895–1903) with the emergence of the modern Colonial Service.

Yet, for all the flurry of extended empire at the turn of the century and the consequent call for more Colonial Service officers to

run it, the limits of the expanded Colonial Office responsibility had
not yet been reached. With the addition of the mandates awarded by
the League of Nations at the end of the First World War to the
victorious powers to act as the administering authority in a trustee
capacity for the one-time German and Ottoman colonial territories,
the British Empire can be said to have reached its territorial peak by
1925. In Britain's case, this new responsibility included, in the
Middle East, Iraq (till 1932) and Transjordan (till 1946), as well as
Palestine; Tanganyika (the whole of German East Africa, less the
provinces of Ruanda and Urundi which went to Belgium); and in
West Africa, a proportion of the former German Togo and Kamerun,
the larger share of both mandates going to France. Together, these
added more than half a million square miles of territory, with all the
attendant staffing requirements, to the remit of the Colonial Office.
In its postwar (1921) appeal to young Britons to think about joining
the Colonial Service, the Colonial Office stressed that for the
foreseeable future vacancies in the Administrative Service were likely
to occur 'almost exclusively in the East and West African Colonies
and Protectorates'. The other major territories of Ceylon, Malaya and
Hong Kong were still recruiting separately under the Eastern
Cadetship Scheme through competitive examination. Just now and
again there might be 'a few cadetships in the Fiji and the Western
Pacific Services', but special attention was drawn by the Colonial
Office to their limitations:

> The salary is £250 with a temporary bonus. Candidates should be
> between the ages of 22 and 25. They will, in the first instance, be
> employed on clerical duties in the Secretariat, and will be on
> probation for three years, during which time they must acquire a
> satisfactory knowledge of Fijian or Hindustani or, in the
> Protectorates, pass an equivalent language test. Their subsequent
> employment, if their appointment is confirmed, will depend on the
> vacancies that may occur, and on the capacity they may have
> shown themselves to possess.

During the 1920s, and again following the world slump and
depression years of 1929–34 on to 1939, recruitment for the Colonial
Service net was spread to the Dominions. By 1930, formal schemes
were in place to attract graduates from Australia, South Africa, New
Zealand and Canada into the Colonial Service. This also fitted in well

with the Dominions' own emergent autonomy, realized in the acceptance of the Balfour formula proposed at the Imperial Conference of 1926. This enabled the transformation of the Dominions from self-governing colonies (a status also granted to Southern Rhodesia in 1923) to autonomous nations owing allegiance to the Crown. This Dominions constitutional arrangement was confirmed in the 1931 Statute of Westminster. The Colonial Office had pre-empted the change by splitting itself in 1925 into a separate Dominions Office and Colonial Office, each subsequently with its own Secretary of State but with technically interchangeable staff and, from 1926 to 1940, jointly publishing a single *Dominions Office and Colonial Office List*.

The Indian subcontinent apart, by 1925 the colonial empire comprised nearly 40 possessions. In school atlases and history books of the interwar years, a quarter of the world's population lived in lands proudly painted imperial red. The spectacular Empire Exhibition mounted at Wembley in 1924 symbolized Britain's reinvigorated pride and confidence in its empire. By then too, the Colonial Service had reached the moment of unparalleled takeoff, an expansion to be repeated (under different circumstances and with different needs) during the so-called 'second colonial occupation' of the decade 1945–55, when constitutional advance and generous Colonial Development and Welfare (CDW) funds to secure the socioeconomic basis for political independence momentarily brought more not fewer Colonial Service personnel into the field, above all in the agriculture, education, health, survey and veterinary departments.

Turning to the dramatic expansion of the Colonial Service after the First World War, the Colonial Office staff, still bound by the principle of patronage, went quickly to work to meet the indents for the expanded establishment of the territorial governments. There was, too, the need to fill the backlog of vacancies brought about by four years of non-recruitment, natural wastage and the heavy casualties among Colonial Service officers killed or wounded in action or drowned at sea. Much of that action, too, had been fought on colonial soil, largely in colonial Africa in the First World War, just as in the Second World War the brunt of the colonial impact of the fighting was to be in the campaigns in Southeast Asia and the Pacific. In 1920, 551 new appointments were made to the Colonial Service, almost twice the total of the last intake before the war (see Table 2.2). It was a principle in the years following 1918, as it was again in the immediate post–1945 period, that, in seeking government

Table 2.2 Colonial Service Recruitment, 1913–20

	1913	1919	1920
Administrative	82	108	179
Educational	19	13	37
Financial and Customs	15	27	31
Legal	10	11	21
Police	13	44	45
Medical	67	44	73
Agricultural	11	15	49
Veterinary	7	4	23
Forestry	1	4	33
Other Scientific	9	3	5
Survey and Geological	2	–	30
Other Appointments	12	22	28
	248	295	551

Source: Sir Ralph Furse, *Aucuparius: Recollections of a Recruiting Officer*, 1962

employment, preference would be given to those who had seen war-time service with the armed forces. Many of the new Colonial Service officers proudly took their wartime rank with them. The territorial Staff Lists between 1920 and 1925 regularly displayed a host of captains and lieutenants among the new entrants. In many cases, ex-officers opted to retain their wartime rank through to their retirement on the eve of the Second World War. Nearly every branch of the Service now saw a doubling of its appointments, with education, police and veterinary recruiting three times the numbers recruited in 1913. Spectacularly, and in earnest that development was now going to replace administration as the primary objective of postwar rethinking on what colonial government should be all about, appointments in agriculture, survey and forestry rose respectively from 11 to 49, 2 to 30 and 1 to 33. Only in the medical service was the increase as low as 10 per cent: not only is the profession traditionally a long-term training affair, but back in war-recovering Britain qualified doctors were as much in demand as in the colonial territories.

The 1919–21 postwar boom in Colonial Service recruitment was followed by two slump years, when the number of 'submissions' to the Secretary of State (approved applications, before any candidate withdrew of his own volition or was rejected on medical or other grounds) dropped from 703 in 1920 to 213 in 1922. To an extent, this reflected the speed with which the five wartime years' slack of unfilled vacancies, deaths and postponed retirement had now been taken up, as well as by the downturn in the postwar boom of the economy. In the next cyclical economic boom, which was to last throughout the 1920s until the worldwide slump and subsequent depression of the early 1930s, the total of Colonial Service candidates accepted rose from 232 in 1923 to 460 in 1927 and overall remained above 400 throughout the quinquennium of 1925–9 (Table 2.3). Among Britain's graduates and professional class, Colonial Service was now earning a place as an attractive, respected and competitively sought-after career. At a time when, in the 1920s, events in India, both constitutional advance and localization of the public service and of the army, as well as outbreaks of considerable violence in the Punjab and Bengal, were beginning to have an impact on how assured — or how attractive — a full career in India might be, the Colonial Office redoubled its efforts to persuade Britain's graduates that here was a viable and valuable alternative Crown career. The appeal was enhanced by the introduction in 1926 of a full year's postgraduate training course for probationers at Oxford and Cambridge.

In terms of graduate provenance, the figures for 1927–9 show how widely the idea of the Colonial Service as a career had caught the student mind (Table 2.4). While Oxford and Cambridge maintained their dominance of the administrative posts (taking 54 out of the 71 places in 1926, 79 out of 83 in 1927 — after the Tropical African Administration courses were opened there in 1926 — 84 out of 88 in 1928, and 73 out of 89 appointments made in 1929), London's medical schools were by far the largest supplier for medical appointments and Wye College for agricultural ones. The University of Edinburgh led the field in forestry appointments. For non-medical scientific appointments, the majority of candidates came from London (especially its Imperial College of Science and Technology), claiming 16 of the 71 appointments made in this three-year period, followed by Cambridge and Edinburgh with nine apiece and by Leeds and Birmingham universities on four each. For appointments in the education services, Oxford and Cambridge seemed to take it in turns to produce the greater number of candidates, with London now and again pushing one of them into third place.

Table 2.3   Colonial Service Recruitment, 1921–8

	1921	1922	1923	1924	1925	1926	1927	1928
Administrative*	90	18	67	72	85	103	101	153
Educational	43	39	30	43	46	76	64	74
Financial and Customs	21	4	12	9	10	20	18	19
Legal	10	3	8	11	12	7	16	14
Police	32	17	14	32	19	30	19	32
Medical	63	41	49	84	129	97	121	85
Agricultural	40	17	16	35	33	30	42	59
Veterinary	9	6	7	5	8	16	9	11
Forestry	25	3	10	20	16	13	11	11
Other scientific specialists	7	2	2	7	8	2	18	10
Survey and Geological	32	9	5	12	15	15	19	27
Other appointments	13	14	12	22	25	15	22	12
Total	385	173	232	352	406	424	460	507
Agricultural scholarships	–	–	–	–	16	17	15	20
Veterinary scholarships	–	–	–	–	–	–	–	–

Note: * excluding appointments filled by competitive examination for cadetships in Ceylon up to 1935, and cadetships in Malaya and Hong Kong up to 1932.

Source: C. Jeffries, *The Colonial Empire and its Civil Service*, 1938.

The global economic collapse associated with the Wall Street crash of 1929 inexorably affected the Colonial Service. Within the territories, governors were faced with the drastic and distasteful task of reducing the number of posts, selecting officers for retrenchment, and imposing cuts in salaries and allowances. In Kenya, for instance, pay was reduced by 2.5 per cent and there was a reduction in the touring and mileage allowances of 25 and 50 per cent respectively. The strength of the provincial administration, never large for so large a territory, was slashed from its peak of 145 in 1921 to 118 in 1935, a cutback of almost 20 per cent. In Tanganyika a whole department was abolished within days of the new governor's arrival in 1931.

At home, a linked shrinkage was inevitable. Colonial applications

Table 2.4   University Origins of Colonial Service Appointments, 1927–9

Cambridge	211
Oxford	198
London	108
Edinburgh	91
Glasgow	48
Trinity College, Dublin	41
Dominions and Overseas	35
Aberdeen	34
Agricultural colleges	30
Birmingham	16
Leeds	14
Liverpool	13
Belfast	12
Bristol	12
St Andrews	11
Wales	11
Durham	10
Manchester	10
National University of Ireland (and Royal College of Science for Ireland)	8
Reading	7
Sheffield	5
Exeter University College	1
Nottingham University College	1
Total, Oxford and Cambridge	409
Total, other universities	508
Grand Total	927

Source: *Report of a Committee on the System of Appointment to the Colonial Office and Colonial Services*, 1930 (Cmd. 3554).

plummeted by 50 per cent in 1931 and resulted in a low of a mere 70 appointments made in 1932, in contrast with the 507 made in 1928. Yet, on the Colonial Office's recruitment roller coaster of the mid-1930s (Table 2.5), no sooner had the recovery got into its stride in 1936 when, for the first time in six years, the total of submissions passed to the Secretary of State climbed back over the 300 mark and

Table 2.5   Colonial Service Recruitment, 1929–36

	1929	1930	1931	1932	1933	1934	1935	1936
Administrative*	115	80	20	25	36	44	67	68
Educational	62	65	18	4	1	5	9	9
Financial and Customs	15	14	11	3	9	21	22	11
Legal	11	16	8	7	8	9	17	22
Police	33	26	16	2	5	10	14	9
Medical	107	77	35	12	22	31	48	53
Agricultural	42	40	34	4	9	23	14	16
Veterinary	11	6	3	–	3	3	5	5
Forestry	13	14	7	4	6	3	9	6
Other scientific specialists	6	8	1	4	4	1	4	7
Survey and Geological	17	9	3	–	2	3	7	9
Other appointments	17	23	9	5	7	11	19	22
TOTALS	449	378	165	70	112	164	235	237
Scholarships	22	24	18	14	7	9	8	10

Note: *Excluding appointments filled by competitive examination for cadetships in Ceylon up to 1935 and cadetships in Malaya and Hong Kong up to 1932.

Source: C. Jeffries, *The Colonial Empire and its Civil Service*, 1938.

went on to pass 400 in 1938, than Britain was plunged into another crisis, the Second World War. This time, not only were bitter campaigns again fought on colonial soil, but in 1941/2 two major colonies, Malaya and Hong Kong, were overrun and remained in Japanese hands until 1946. Both their governors, Sir Shenton Thomas and Sir Mark Young, were interned. The Solomons, where Resident Commissioner William Marchant and other colonial officers like D. G. Kennedy courageously stayed behind to organize the islanders as 'Coastwatchers', and the Gilbert Islands were recovered following the epic battles of Guadalcanal and Tarawa in 1943. Yet what is clear is that between the wars the Colonial Service had overtaken the Indian Civil Service as the largest employer of British graduates among Crown civil services overseas.

Four Colonial Service milestones stand out as integral elements in the pattern of successful interwar recruitment initiatives outlined in the previous pages. These were:

(i) the formalization of Colonial Service training;
(ii) the inauguration of the Dominion Selection Scheme;
(iii) the report of the Warren Fisher Committee on the method of appointment to the Colonial Service; and
(iv) the decision to unify the various territorial civil services into a unified Colonial Service, in practice as well as in name.

The driving force behind all four initiatives was Leo Amery. He was Secretary of State for the Colonies from 1924 to 1929 and had been parliamentary under-secretary before that (1919–21). In these initiatives he was ably supported by his permanent under-secretary, Sir Samuel Wilson (1925–33), one of the very few permanent under-secretaries of the Colonial Office who had also had field service experience as a colonial governor.

Colonial Service Training

As we saw in Chapter 1, from 1908 entrants to the Colonial Administrative Service destined for West and East Africa were offered a measure of preposting training on a short course of two to three months at the Imperial Institute in London. In addition to tropical hygiene, law and accountancy, the institute staff provided instruction in what were called tropical resources. As an integral part of the expansion of the Colonial Service following the end of the First World War, the Colonial Office, determined to offer British graduates interested in the Colonial Service opportunities no less attractive than the extra year at Oxford, Cambridge or Trinity College, Dublin enjoyed by Indian Civil Service probationers, embarked on negotiating with the university authorities at Oxford and Cambridge, and in due course with the London School of Economics (LSE), to provide teaching for Colonial Service probationers. The course was to be academic rather than vocational in content, and would have a serving Colonial Service officer as its director. The courses opened in 1926. Initially called the Tropical African Administrative Services (TAAS) course, it was renamed the Colonial Administrative Service (CAS) course in 1932, when the Eastern cadets were no longer recruited through the Civil Service Commission's open competition and instead became eligible for inclusion in the Colonial Service probationers' course.

It was, perhaps, in the field of the professional services that the most far-reaching changes in Colonial Service training took place in the 1920s. Specialized committees were set up to report on the agricultural, veterinary and medical services in 1920. In 1924 a further committee recommended that in order to ensure proper and relevant training for Colonial Service agriculturists they should be sent on a postgraduate year at the Imperial College of Tropical Agriculture in Trinidad. The scheme opened in 1925. Forestry, which in terms of numbers together with veterinary had been something of a Cinderella service before the war (only four officers apiece had been recruited for the whole of the Colonial Forestry Service and the Colonial Veterinary Service in the expansionist year of 1919), saw its profile handsomely raised in 1924 when a small group of probationers were sent to the new Imperial Forestry Institute at Oxford University on a one-year scholarship. In 1927, another committee was appointed to assess the feasibility of a single colonial scientific and research service. The Colonial Veterinary Service's turn came in 1929, when university scholarships tenable for three (subsequently four) years were made available for graduates, either to qualify for the MRCVS or to undertake advanced biological training. In the Colonial Education Service, officers who had not topped their honours degree with a diploma in education were sent to the University of London's Institute of Education for a further year's training. In the course of time, too, Colonial Police cadets began to attend the Metropolitan Police College at Hendon for a year's course before assignment overseas. In the Colonial Medical Service there had long been strong links both with the London School of Hygiene and Tropical Medicine, established in 1924, which provided a five-month course for Colonial Service medical officers, and with the Liverpool School of Tropical Medicine, founded in 1899 as the direct result of an appeal by Joseph Chamberlain with the primary object of training those proceeding to the tropics in the special subjects of tropical diseases and tropical hygiene. The former institution later provided, in Sir Wilson Jameson, one of the only two chief medical advisers to the Secretary of State before 1945 who did not come from the Colonial Medical Service. The Colonial Nursing Association, dating back to 1896, recommended nurses to the Colonial Office, and by 1938 had supplied 2743 nurses for service overseas.

The Dominion Selection Scheme

Aware of the shortage of young men in Britain brought about by the heavy casualties on the Western Front and in Mesopotamia during the First World War, at the Colonial Office Leo Amery decided to explore the possibility of forging links with the Dominion universities in an attempt to persuade them to help out with the heavy postwar demand for Colonial Service recruitment. Starting with Canada in 1923, and then extended to Australia and New Zealand in 1928/9, local selection boards were convened to interview prospective candidates and then forward their nominations to the Colonial Office, in whose hands the final acceptance or rejection lay. By 1942, more than 300 persons of Dominion origin had been recruited. Further Dominions men, graduating from British universities, were also recruited through the standard Colonial Office procedure.

The Dominions Selection Scheme was to prove popular for the next 40 years. On the conclusion of the Second World War, the Colonial Office sought to step up such a valued source of recruitment by reserving for Australia 18 district officer vacancies in 1946/7, distributed between seven in Malaya, five in Uganda, two each in Kenya and the High Commission Territories, and one each in Northern Rhodesia and Nyasaland. In the ten years from 1945 to 1955, 95 Colonial Service officers were recruited from New Zealand, 80 from Australia and 75 from Canada. Of the last named, 26 took up agricultural posts, 12 medical, 8 administrative and 5 engineering. The longer-standing South African contribution, too, remained steady. It would be unusual for British Colonial Service officers recruited after 1945 not to be able to name half a dozen Antipodean or South African colleagues. In Nigeria there were at least eight Australian district officers serving in 1955. The Australian and New Zealand presence was marked in the Pacific territories, predominantly so in the veterinary service. Canadians were fewer on the ground, though as the first Dominion in which the scheme was tried out the Secretary of State made special mention of their contribution at the Imperial Conference of 1926, 'a small but steady stream of very satisfactory young candidates'. Many Dominions entrants reached senior positions in the postwar Colonial Service, including the appointment of Sir Ralph (later Lord) Grey and Sir Colin Allan, both from New Zealand, and Sir Richard Luyt (South Africa) to colonial governorships. The two most distinguished twentieth-century Canadians in the Colonial Service, Sir Gordon Guggisberg and Sir

Percy Girouard, both achieved their colonial governorships before the Dominion selection scheme was in operation. Canadians were also made the director of medical services in one colony and the general manager of the railways in another. The first chief medical adviser to the Secretary of State (1926) was Dr A. T. Stanton, who had gone from Canada to Malaya in 1907.

The Warren Fisher Committee Report, 1930

The third landmark in Colonial Service history between the wars, and arguably on a par with the contemporaneous unification scheme in its permanent and irreversible influence on the development of the modern Colonial Service, was the report of the Warren Fisher Committee submitted in 1930. It was in the same turning-point year for the Colonial Service that the second Colonial Office conference was also held. For Sir Charles Jeffries, a senior Colonial Office official long connected with the management of the Colonial Service, the report ranked as nothing less than 'the Magna Carta of the Colonial Service'. The need for fundamental reform was twofold. Following the separation in 1925 of responsibility for matters relating to the colonies from those connected with the Dominions, the whole question of the internal organization of the slimmed-down Colonial Office came to the fore. Furthermore, with the imminence of the unification of the Colonial Service, it was imperative to review the method of appointment, particularly within the continuing context of unsystematic recruitment and — given the institutionalized role of the Minister's Private Office — its risk of being, at least in theory, used as system of patronage. The committee, under the chairmanship of Sir Warren Fisher, permanent secretary to the Treasury, head of the civil service and one of the most powerful Whitehall officials of the century, was charged with examining 'the existing system of appointment in the Colonial Office and in the Public Service of the Dependencies not possessing responsible government [i.e. excluding the Dominions], and to make such recommendations as they considered desirable'.

Inevitably, consideration of the system of appointment involved the wider area of organization, at home in the Colonial Office and abroad in the Colonial Service. In the case of the former, the committee decided against the Foreign Office practice, which would have meant all or part of the Colonial Office being staffed by the Colonial Service. Instead, they recommended a regular exchange system, in which recent entrants to the Colonial Office should be seconded to colonial governments for a tour as an assistant district officer, that is posted to the field and not to a secretariat. At the same time, Colonial Service officers should, after some years' service, be seconded to the Colonial Office — always provided that their 'own' colony should not feature prominently in their portfolio. The term 'beachcomber' came into idiomatic use for the latter form of secondment.

Where the most positive and far-reaching emphasis of the Warren Fisher Committee lay was in the area of Colonial Service recruitment and staff questions. While acknowledging that the Colonial Service clearly benefited from a principle of recruitment that favoured those personal qualities — generally subsumed under the elusive but recognizable rubric of 'character', held to be of such prime importance in overseas relations — over those assessable by a written competitive examination (still being taken by those applying for the Eastern cadetship and Eastern police services), the committee found that the current recruitment system based on officially recognized patronage could not be considered satisfactory and required a thorough reconstruction. The two private secretaries (Appointments) to the minister, whose job it had been to handle Colonial Service applications according to a system which, for all its success as endorsed by governors and senior officers, was so highly personalized that it could not escape a hostile critic's charge of patronage (though the committee acknowledged that no abuse had occurred), were now replaced by permanent members of the Colonial Office staff. A new personnel division was created under an assistant undersecretary to coordinate and handle all questions of Colonial Service recruitment, promotions and discipline, hitherto the responsibility of the office's general department.

Finally, they made a recommendation dear to Amery's heart. It was one he had already aired at the 1927 Colonial Office conference. This was that the unification of each territory's public service into a single Colonial Service would not only permit a rewarding interterritorial movement of officers, particularly the professional and technical staff for whom the promotion prospect of a career in one — especially a small — territory were frequently unfavourable, but could also bring to the Colonial Service a status and prestige in the perception of the British public (and especially its undergraduate population and their families) comparable to that long enjoyed by the Indian Civil Service.

Besides the new personnel office, with its responsibility to liaise with all the standard sources of recruitment and to produce a short list of suitable candidates, an independent, standing Colonial Service Appointments Board (CSAB) was also established, which would be responsible for the final selection. Its chairman and two of its members, all of whom were required to have had experience of work in the colonies, were to be nominated by the civil service commissioners. The last link with nineteenth-century patronage (and the application forms were up to 1930 still boldly headed 'Patronage') in Colonial Service recruitment had gone for ever — or rather, all but the fresh Colonial Service application form, which coyly retained the original P in its redesigned reference of 'P1', now standing for 'Personnel' and no longer 'Patronage'.

For the key role in this major reform in Colonial Service recruitment procedures, the Colonial Office turned to an official whose lifelong work with the Colonial Service was to earn him worldwide acknowledgement and respect. This was R. D. (later Sir Ralph) Furse. Furse had been appointed (on personal recommendation, *bien entendu*) an assistant private secretary (Appointments) to the Secretary of State for the Colonies in 1910, at the age of 23. By the time of the eventful year 1930, which saw both the Warren Fisher Report and the second Colonial Office conference, Furse was already the key figure in the postwar development of the Colonial Service. He had been instrumental in putting together the Dominion selection scheme on visits to Canada in 1922 and then in 1927 via the West Indies and Fiji to Australia and New Zealand. He was, too, the driving force behind the Colonial Office's plan to involve the universities of Oxford and Cambridge in training courses for probationers in 1926, and in particular for forestry at the new institute at Oxford. Officially commended for his work on Colonial Service recruitment by the Warren Fisher Committee, Furse was now made assistant secretary in the appointments department of the Colonial Office's new personnel division. In 1948, almost 40 years after his initial involvement with recruitment for the Colonial Service, Furse retired from the Colonial Office, as director of recruitment, remaining till 1950 as adviser to the Secretary of State on training courses. Appropriately, he chose for the title of his autobiography the name Aucuparius, the famous snarer of birds in classical mythology. Within the Service itself he was often called 'The father of the modern Colonial Service'.

Unification of the Colonial Service

Amery's brainchild of a Colonial Office conference to consider empire problems and those of its Colonial Service was held for the first time in 1927 before a mixed assembly of Colonial Office officials and Colonial Service officers. Amery took the whole Colonial Service debate a critical stage further in the Colonial Office conference of 1930. From the wide-ranging agenda, one item stands out for its unique influence on the development of the service. This was the conference's decision to unify the Colonial Service. With this conference's report and the report of the Warren Fisher Committee, 1930 can truly be said to have been a turning point in the history of the modern Colonial Service, through its unification and through the reform of its system of appointment.

Amery had set out the problem succinctly at the previous Colonial Office conference, when he spoke of how in the Colonial Office he did not really deal with Colonial Service matters but rather with three dozen self-contained administrations: 'each Colonial Government and each Colonial Service has grown up on the spot by a continuous process of local evolution.' He went on to describe how 'each Governor and each Service is autochthonous, racy [sic] of the soil, adapted to local conditions, instinctive in its understanding of those conditions and in its sympathy with the population it administers.' Apart from the Audit Service, every officer was recruited for and appointed to a territorial Service, subject to its own conditions of service and, in by far the majority of cases, destined to remain in that particular service and territory for the whole of his career. Inter-territorial transfers were rare outside the top ranks of governor, chief secretary and head of department, and complicated pension arrangements did little to encourage mobility. In short, there was no such thing as *the* Colonial Service.

Under the unification scheme adumbrated at the 1927 conference, all serving officers would be eligible for transfer on promotion whenever there was a vacancy in another territory. They would equally be liable for transfer should the Colonial Office require it, as part of the new conditions of the service. In terms of Colonial Service opportunity and morale, the new strategy and structure brought a huge advantage to the service. Henceforth, when say the post of colonial secretary or director of medical services became vacant in a given territory, eligible officers serving in all the remaining colonies could expect to be considered. This, Amery reckoned, would have a

significant impact in the universities when undergraduates were
thinking of Crown service overseas, with the Colonial Service alone
in a position to offer a now literally worldwide career. The scheme
would also be of particular benefit to smaller territories, to which
officers could be seconded from larger colonies for one or two tours
without losing seniority. Finally — and this was eventually to
become a bonus of considerable value in the run-up to independence
when experience of a ministerial system of government and the
detailed processes of a transfer of power were at a premium — a
unified and interchangeable Colonial Service was able to generate a
unique pool of knowledge and comparative experience, something
that a single territory-based and territory-bound civil service could
never accumulate in its search for a precedent.

The 1930 CO conference endorsed the unification plan. The first
branch of the Colonial Service to be unified was the Administrative
Service, in 1932, allowing for the fact that the Audit Service had
always operated as a unified branch, working on a basis of regular
interterritorial transfers ever since its inception in 1910. Most of the
other branches were unified during the following decade, with the
small Colonial Civil Aviation Service and the Colonial Research
Service completing the list after the war (Table 2.6). When the
Colonial Engineering Service was formed in 1945, responsibility for
the recruitment of engineers, architects and town planners was transferred from the Crown Agents to the Colonial Office and an adviser
on engineering appointments was added.

After the triple excitements of 1930 (the Warren Fisher reforms,
the Colonial Office conference recommendations, and agreement on
the unification of the Colonial Services), and with the world economic slump beginning perceptibly to recede as the 1930s got under
way, the Colonial Service settled down to a period of rebuilding and
consolidation. Colonial service affairs within the Colonial Office
were upgraded not only by the creation of a personnel division, but
also by the formation of a series of advisory committees. An Advisory
Committee on Education in the Colonies came into being in 1929,
the same year as the Colonial Advisory Council of Agriculture and
Animal Health was constituted. A colonial advisory committee took
over the functions of the Colonial Medical Research Committee in
1931; the Colonial Survey and Geophysical Committee had its brief
enlarged in 1935; and in the same year a Colonial Forest Resources
Development Department was set up. A Colonial Empire Marketing

Table 2.6   Unification of the Colonial Service by Branches, 1910–49

Colonial Administrative Service	1932
Colonial Agricultural Service	1935
Colonial Audit Service	1910
Colonial Chemical Service	1938
Colonial Civil Aviation Service	1948
Colonial Customs Service	1938
Colonial Education Service	1937
Colonial Engineering Service*	1945
Colonial Forest Service	1935
Colonial Geological Survey Service	1938
Colonial Legal Service	1933
Colonial Medical Service	1934
Colonial Mines Service	1938
Colonial Police Service	1937
Colonial Postal Service	1938
Colonial Prisons Service	1936
Colonial Research Service	1949
Colonial Survey Service	1938
Colonial Veterinary Service	1935
Queen Elizabeth's Nursing Service	1940

Note: * Created by the removal of engineering, architecture and town planning from the Crown Agents' responsibilities.

Source: Sir Charles Jeffries, *Whitehall and the Colonial Service: An Administrative Memoir, 1939–1956*, 1972

Board was constituted in 1937. The passing of the 1929 Colonial Development Act brought into being a Colonial Development Advisory Committee.

Following the long-standing model of a legal adviser, specialist advisers to the Secretary of State were appointed for such subjects as agriculture, medicine, education, fisheries and later forestry and police. The first chief medical adviser (1929) was Sir Thomas Stanton, transferred from Malaya, and the first agricultural adviser (1929) was Sir Frank Stockdale, who came in from being director of agriculture in Ceylon. An economic and financial adviser was appointed in 1927 (Sir George Schuster) and a labour adviser (Major G. Orde Browne) followed in 1938. It is significant that many of the advisers were drawn from within the Colonial Service. Hand in hand with those initiatives, specialist subject departments, such as an economic and a social services department, were created in the Colonial Office and supplemented the traditional geographical departments. From 1938, too, the Secretary of State's regular statement to Parliament was reprinted as a separate command paper, titled *The Colonial Empire*. That for 1939 had to wait until 1947 for a comprehensive report on the war years.

Recruitment, that sensitive barometer of Colonial Service morale, had still to pull itself out of the slump. Although the *annus horribilis* of 1932 was not repeated, when for the first time since 1919 the number of appointments to the Colonial Service dropped to double figures (70) — matched only in the wartime gloom of 1942 when a mere 95 appointments were made — it was not until 1934 that the total climbed back to the 1931 level of 160 appointments. From then on the regain of ground was steady rather than spectacular, registering 231 appointments in 1935 and 249 in 1936 and rising to just over 300 in the pre-Munich crisis year of 1937. Submitting his parliamentary statement accompanying the estimates for colonial and Middle Eastern services in 1939, the Secretary of State was able to report that in 1938 the number of candidates selected for the Colonial Service was over four times as large as the number selected in 1932. This was still well behind the boom years of the 1920s, when for five successive years (1925–9) the Colonial Service recruited more than 400 men and women each year. By 1939, Europe's shadows were long enough to cast doubt upon whether this was the right moment to think of a career abroad: the number of appointments (conventionally made in the summer) dropped 20 per cent to 255. Once war broke out, recruitment to the Colonial Service was drastically curtailed (Table 2.7).

Yet even after the depression of the 1930s turned the corner and economies the world over were by 1935 beginning to pull themselves out of the mire, no colonial government could ever claim that it had enough men and women on the ground — or enough money in its budget — to undertake all the development that both it and its legislatures wanted to see implemented. Table 2.8 sets out the distribution of posts in Africa in c.1939, that part of the colonial empire that traditionally accounted for nearly three-quarters of the Colonial Service. It lends strong support to the argument addressed by one historian that the Colonial Service was truly a 'Thin White Line'. It shows that in 1936 the British government had just over 1200

Table 2.7   Colonial Service Recruitment, 1937–42

	1937	1938	1939	1940	1941	1942
Administrative	91	95	84	75	54	1
Educational	14	14	22	8	2	10
Financial and Customs	10	21	9	5	3	1
Legal	33	26	8	10	7	–
Police	19	22	11	8	10	3
Medical	47	54	54	24	25	24
Agricultural	28	23	19	15	8	15
Veterinary	7	8	18	12	5	9
Forestry	12	12	6	7	8	6
Other scientific	26	24	8	4	7	1
Survey and Geological	8	11	9	6	5	2
Other appointments	11	15	7	6	10	23
Totals	306	325	255	180	144	95

Source: Sir Ralph Furse, *Aucuparius: Recollections of a Recruiting Officer*, 1962

administrators, under 1000 police and army officers, and fewer than 200 judges and legal officers responsible for the maintenance of law and order among 43 million people spread over nearly two million square miles. Their social and developmental needs were served by merely 1000 medical officers, 800 officials in natural resources, 700 in public works and fewer than 500 in education. Even when one takes into account that at least 90 per cent of the staff of colonial governments were locally employed officials, by postwar standards of staffing and by post-independence sums of manpower budgeting, the Colonial Service between the wars was demonstrably the victim of a policy of 'Empire on the Cheap'. If the Colonial Service was at its widest in 1939, it was to be another decade before that territorial spread was translated into complementary staffing coverage.

Table 2.8 Distribution of the Colonial Service in British Tropical Africa, c. 1939

Territory	Size (sq ml)	Population	Admin	P&M	Judiciary	Medical	Education	NR	PW	Railways	Others
West Africa: Nigeria	373,000	20,477,000	386	188	37	246	109	167	235	347	333
Gold Coast	92,000	3,704,000	91	100	23	141	18	84	119	127	139
Sierra Leone	28,000	1,920,000	40	34	6	27	6	15	24	35	28
The Gambia	4,000	200,000	11	10	3	13	0	3	9	0	12
Total (West Africa)	497,000	26,301,000	528	332	69	427	133	269	387	509	512
East Africa: Kenya	225,000	3,334,000	164	164	23	162	137	163	84	89	376
Tanganyika	363,000	5,182,000	185	120	24	152	43	138	62	147	151
Uganda	94,000	3,711,000	83	72*	19	108	29	79	74	0	71
Zanzibar	1,000	236,000	20*	8*	8	22	6	11	12	0	12
Somaliland	68,000	347,000	16	21	1	5	1	2	2	0	7
Total (East Africa)	751,000	12,810,000	468	385	75	449	216	393	234	236	617
Central Africa: Northern Rhodesia	290,000	1,378,000	109	91	17	69	76	39	22	11	220
Nyasaland	48,000	1,639,000	51	37*	6	34	10	33	29	5	75
Basutoland	12,000	562,000	32	16*	3	37	9	28	5	0	39
Bechuanaland	275,000	266,000	20	51	8	27	3	36	36	0	35
Swaziland	7,000	158,000	15	26*	0	12	18	18	5	0	14
Total (Central Africa)	632,000	4,003,000	227	221	34	179	116	154	97	16	383
Grand Total	1,880,000	43,114,000	1123	938	178	1055	465	816	718	761	1512

Note: * = includes prison staff; P&M = police and military; NR = natural resources; PW = public works.
Source: A. H. M. Kirk-Greene, 'The Thin White Line: The Size of the Colonial Service in Africa', *African Affairs*, 79, 314, 1980, adapted from Lord Hailey, *An African Survey*, 1938 and from *Statesmans's Yearbook*, 1939.

3. The Expansion of the Postwar Colonial Service, 1943–54

'*An immense literature has been written about British colonial policy and surprisingly little about the men who expressed policy in administration.*' — Dame Margery Perham, 1963.

Expectedly, recruitment to the Colonial Service was not a priority during the first three dark years of the war, either in the calculations of His Majesty's Government or in the minds of the young men and women who might otherwise have been looking for a career overseas. In 1939, more than sixty men joined the armed forces before their original application to the Colonial Office had been processed. In June 1940, when Britain was virtually alone in Europe, the Secretary of State gave a special tea party to some 30 graduates who, selected for the Colonial Service in 1939, had immediately been diverted to the armed forces. Now they were pulled out of the army, in many cases unwillingly, by a desperate Colonial Office and were about to be sent overseas as civil servants. The purpose of the tea party was for the Colonial Secretary to convince them that it was the considered view of HMG that their duty was to take up the Colonial Service posting — 'I wanted you to regard this,' he concluded, 'as a definite instruction.' Total recruitment fell from 255 in 1939, already down by one-fifth from the previous year, to 236 in 1940 and, following the shock of Dunkirk, 144 in 1941. In 1942, with the Eastern dependencies of Malaya and Hong Kong occupied by the Japanese and many Colonial Service officers interned or killed in action, other manpower priorities meant that barely a hundred submissions were sent up to the Secretary of State, the least number since the nadir of the slump. Only one administrative officer was appointed in that year and for the first time since the First World War not a single appointment was made to the legal service. All in all, the Colonial Service managed to secure some 750 recruits during the war, always on the understanding that they first did six months military training and that they could be called up, returning to Colonial Service duties as early as possible.

In Winston Churchill's view, the collapse of Malaya and the fall of Singapore and Hong Kong were the worst disaster in Britain's imperial history since the American colonies declared their independence in 1776. F. C. Gimson, colonial secretary of Hong Kong, who had spent the war in Stanley internment camp and whose governor, Sir Mark Young, had been deported to Japan and humiliatingly displayed in a bamboo cage, took a bold step. Even before the arrival of the Allied fleet, he announced over the Hong Kong radio on 28 August 1945 that he and the other colonial officials who had been interned in Stanley Camp would be resuming the island's administration. Those territories where colonial governments struggled to keep a skeleton administration going during the war had their staffing problem of no new intakes compounded by the number of serving Colonial Service officers who were called up or who sought permission to volunteer. Some were granted permission while on leave, others enlisted, often serving with the expanding Royal West African Frontier Force and the King's African Rifles. Nigeria was just one of the territories whose governor persuaded the War Office to release a dozen such Colonial Service officers in the spring of 1942 and have them returned to civil duties, on the grounds that only thus could he be confident that 'an imminent collapse of the administration' would be averted. By the end of the war the Colonial Service had suffered substantial casualties, through death on active service or at sea, internment and invaliding out.

Two problems arising from the Second World War had not been experienced by the Colonial Service at the end of the First World War. First, the loss of Malaya as a major source of rubber and tin meant that in many other colonies, particularly in Africa, the colonial administration was obliged to undertake vigorous campaigns to find labour and step up the production of those vital war commodities. And second, while the First World War had often been fought on colonial soil, notably in West and East Africa, there was no precedent for the call on the Colonial Service, as in Malaya, Hong Kong, the Solomons and the Gilbert Islands, and the newly transferred North

Borneo and Sarawak, completely to rebuild the post-occupation administration and undertake large-scale reconstruction and rehabilitation. All this, too, was carried out with a huge influx of new, untrained staff, sometimes serving under senior officers who were understandably tired out after the extra burdens shouldered during the war and often had had to postpone their overdue retirement until the war ended.

What is perhaps remarkable in retrospect is how far the Colonial Office was determined even before the war was over to keep its sights on a postwar future and to look ahead with imagination. Among the boldest of such initiatives — already alluded to — was the Labour government's decision to break with the policy of the colonies' financial self-sufficiency and introduce the Colonial Development and Welfare Act of 1940, foreshadowing the generous provision of money for their infrastructural development enabled by the successor act of 1945. Several wartime events had a direct bearing on the Colonial Service. One is the secret mission undertaken by Lord Hailey in 1940–2 to evaluate the likely impact of the war on each of the African territories, with particular reference to 'the planning of future political developments'. His report, which remained a confidential document until well after the decolonization decade, was titled *Native Administration and Political Development in British Tropical Africa*. For all its insights, Hailey still saw the future lying with the traditional rulers and not in the hands of an elected elite. Inevitably, none of his recommendations could be pursued in the wartime situation, but that should not mask the boldness and vision already exercising Britain's official mind. A less comfortable event was the controversy following the signing of the Atlantic Charter in 1941, where President Roosevelt interpreted the agreement to 'respect the rights of all peoples to choose the form of government under which they will live and to see sovereign rights and self-government restored to those who have been forcibly deprived of them' as applying to colonial peoples and not only those under the Nazi yoke whom Churchill had had in mind. Both events persuaded the Colonial Office and colonial governments to give thought to the anticipated, possibly catalytic, effects of the war on their staff and on local attitudes within their territory and to consider the necessary shift in social and administrative policy. In July 1943, in the middle of the war, the Secretary of State was able to reveal to the House of Commons that he was carrying out a review of the organization of the postwar Colonial Service.

Within the Colonial Office, influential memoranda written by
G. B. Cartland and F. J. Pedler in 1946 questioning the future of the
long-standing policy of native administration were taken up by A. B.
(later Sir Andrew) Cohen in the context of replacing indirect rule
and native administration with a policy of local government. This
touched the very heart of traditional colonial administration. These
were the germs of the major policy reforms progressively argued over
and worked out during 1947: the Secretary of State's seminal
dispatch on local government issued in February, the important
summer school on African administration held at Cambridge in
August with a wide Colonial Service presence, and the strong — and
at times stormy — conference of colonial governors held at the
Colonial Office in November. It was this kind of rethinking of the
aims of colonial government in the context of an inescapably
changed postwar world that was to lead the new Labour Secretary of
State for the Colonies, Arthur Creech Jones, to declare in 1948 that
'The central purpose of British colonial policy is simple. It is to guide
the colonial territories to responsible government within the Commonwealth in conditions that ensure to the people concerned both a
fair standard of living and freedom from of oppression from any
quarter.' A new direction of policy would call for a new concept of
Colonial Service.

But it was within the Colonial Office itself that the determination
was strongest not to devote its entire energy to coping with the
present, administering emergency controls and defining war aims. In
the context of the future of the Colonial Service, nowhere was this
ability to look ahead of higher profile than in the person of the
director of recruitment, the same Major Furse who had helped to
steer the similarly strained Colonial Service through its rebirth in
1919. Conscious of what he called his 'plumbing job' at the end of
the First World War, he was soon turning his attention to how the
Colonial Service might best be reconstructed and revitalized at the
end of the Second World War. By the beginning of 1943, when the
tide of war had just visibly begun to turn through the North African
campaign, Furse had completed a long, reflective and visionary
memorandum on how the Colonial Service would be reborn,
reoriented and retrained.

The Furse memorandum of February 1943 memorably opened
with the dramatic words, 'When the [anti-aircraft] balloons come
down for good, the curtain will go up on a colonial stage for a new

act.' Gone were the days, Furse argued, 'when the most obvious task of the administrator overseas was to redress wrongs and to relieve suffering'. Furse had doubtless seen, and clearly taken to heart, the memo sent to the Colonial Office from a senior officer in the Malayan administration, H. A. L. Luckham, in which he partly blamed the loss of the colony in 1942 on complacency and the common belief that 'administration is a matter of common sense and cannot be improved by research and study'. For Furse, new problems and new issues would demand preparation for new roles for the Colonial Service, including that of economic planner. At the same time, new actors would be moving to centre stage, the university-educated men and women from within the colonial territories. There was, Furse warned, the ever-present danger of 'the Uninstructed White — and not least his womenfolk'. Reform in training was imperative: 'The Service will have to deal with a new type of coloured man and must absorb and acclimatize a new type of white officer.' Furse was of the opinion that the present system of Colonial Service training was likely to be inadequate to equip officers for the novel and more exacting responsibilities which, under the critical gaze of a much more vociferous and more sensitive international world, they would have to assume.

He put forward two plans for the enhancement of postwar Colonial Service training. One was to establish a prestigious Colonial Staff College for its senior ranks. The other was a choice of two academic strategies: either concentrate colonial studies and training in a single university or involve a combined team from the universities of Oxford, Cambridge and London in the provision of twin, interlocking, revised training courses. The first of these courses would offer Administrative Service probationers four terms at the university before proceeding overseas. The Warren Fisher Committee had in 1930 pointed to the desirability of instituting parallel Tropical African Services courses at London and Edinburgh in addition to those at Oxford and Cambridge. Furse was now keen to exploit the strong facilities available at the School of Oriental and African Studies (SOAS) by bringing the Oxford and Cambridge probationers together at the end of their year's course for a further three months of intensive language training in London. A second course, supplementary and not an alternative, envisaged that all Colonial Service officers, professional as well as administrative, should return to university at the end of their initial ('apprentice') tour of duty for a further academic year. The whole programme was Furse's pet sandwich course, 'a piece of practical meat between two slices of theoretical bread'. Confirmation of an officer's appointment would come at the end of the second course. Furse also advocated the provision of a subsequent period of training for selected officers from all branches of the service, a kind of sabbatical year where they could elect to undertake special studies.

A high-powered committee was convened in March 1944 under the chairmanship of the Duke of Devonshire, with four representatives each from the universities of Oxford, Cambridge and London, and three from the Colonial Office. Evidence was taken from a number of serving officers currently on secondment to the Colonial Office. The proposal for a Colonial Staff College was discarded in favour of a training scheme to be shared between the three universities. In accordance with the Colonial Office's preferred option, the committee examined in detail the proposals for what in the end came to be known as the First and Second (Devonshire) courses, accepting that at least in its early years the latter would have special relevance for those officers who since 1939 had gone overseas without any training. With regard to the first course, significantly they laid down that its purpose was:

To give the Cadet a general background to the work which he is going to take up; to start him with a proper sense of proportion; to show him what to look out for on his apprentice tour and the significance of some of the things he may expect to see during it; and to give him the minimum of indispensable knowledge on which to start his career.

The proposed curriculum to meet these requirements is of interest (Table 3.1). Following the Secretary of State's wish expressed when he attended one of the sessions, the committee decided to reduce the length of the recommended Second course to two terms. It was deliberately designed so that it would be attended by officers from all branches of the Colonial Service. The committee was keen to see the new academic year preceded by a short summer school for the Second Devonshire officers. They also argued that a Colonial Service club in each university would be essential as a meeting place for all those taking the course, and expressed the hope that a hand-picked serving officer would be seconded by the Colonial Office to act as supervisor of the training courses in each university.

Table 3.1   Proposed Curriculum for the First Devonshire Course, 1946

1 General Section: To be taken at Oxford or Cambridge, two full terms and one term of six weeks (October–May)

Oxford	Hours taught	Cambridge	Hours taught	Summary	Hours taught
The land, its conservation and development	40	Agriculture, forestry and animal husbandry	40	Agricultural studies	40
Interpretation of statutes, evidence and criminal law	56	Criminal law, law of evidence, interpretation of statutes	56	Legal studies	56
History of the British Empire	32	History of the British Empire including		Historical/economic studies	88
British colonial government and services	16	economic and social history and the history of colonial		Geographical studies	16
British colonial economic history and organization	16	systems of government and administration	80	Anthropological studies	56
Colonial social problems	8	Native administration	8		
International relations in the colonial field	16	Geography	16		
Geographical survey of the colonial empire	16	Anthropology including Islam	56		
Social anthropology	32				
Islam	8				
The land; systems of tenure	8				
Ethnographic survey: racial and social conditions of peoples of the colonial empire	8				
	256		256		256

II Language and regional section: To be taken at London, six months (June–December)

Source: Adapted from *Post-War Training for the Colonial Service: Report of a Committee*, 1946 (Col No. 198)

Finally, they favoured the idea that cadets posted to Africa should spend part of their first tour at Achimota College (for West Africa) or Makerere College (for East Africa) to introduce them to what was still labelled 'the educated native' and so develop mutual understanding before the British cadet 'had time to acquire prejudices'. The importance of the move by the governor of the Gold Coast in 1942 to appoint the first two African assistant district commissioners in the history of the modern Colonial Service had not been lost on the Colonial Office or on the Devonshire Committee.

The Devonshire Committee reported in 1946. In the same year, its endorsement of the First and Second Devonshire courses was taken a step further by a commission of three senior administrators from Oxford, Cambridge and London, funded by the Nuffield Foundation and dispatched to Nigeria, the largest colony, 'to enable representatives of the three universities which are likely to become responsible for the training of probationers for the Administrative Service to study the work for which the probationers are to be trained'. To a large measure, their conception of the courses derived from what they saw and heard in the districts and in the secretariats coincided with the thrust of the Devonshire Committee's thinking. They were particularly sensitive to the enhanced need to improve and sophisticate the typical district officer's 'bush' skills as he moved up the service into the secretariat where he would be required to 'master the art of administration from an office, the use of statistics, the secrets of delegating authority while retaining effective control of policy, the mysteries of public finance — in short, everything that a member of the Home Civil Service begins to absorb from the very start'. Nearly every senior officer they met, however, while accepting the need for new and improved training, was of the opinion that among all the desiderata and priorities that of getting staff out to the territory and at work in the field was second to none. Indeed, this line of argument concluded, practical experience on the job was in itself a significant element of training. Was it not Aristotle who advised that the best way to learn to play the flute was to play the flute?

The outcome of the Devonshire Committee and the Nuffield Foundation report was that while the First Devonshire course was inaugurated at the three participating universities in 1946, the Second Devonshire course was converted into Furse's third or sabbatical study leave kind of course. The original second course, planned to follow on immediately after completion of the first or apprentice tour in the field, was dropped in the recognized need to get officers onto the ground as quickly as possible. The sum of £1.5 million was allocated from the 1945 Colonial Development and Welfare Act towards subsidizing the new Colonial Service training programmes over the next ten years.

Even before the postwar plans for the fresh directions of Colonial Service training were endorsed by the Devonshire Committee in 1945, an intensive recruiting campaign was initiated by the Colonial Office following the Secretary of State for the Colonies' presentation to the War Cabinet of a memorandum on 'Staffing of the Colonial Service in the Postwar Period'. This campaign, embarked on by the Colonial Office in 1944, was directed at people serving in the armed forces who might be contemplating a Colonial Service career as the time for their demobilization came up. Temporary regional branches of the Colonial Office's appointments department were opened in Cairo and New Delhi, with other special recruitment organizations established in the Dominions and the Caribbean. A quarter of a million copies of the pamphlet *Appointments in the Colonial Service* (RDW6), dealing with postwar opportunities in the Colonial Service and recruitment procedures, were printed and distributed all over the empire together with application forms. Special notices were published in June 1945 in *Army Council Instruction* No. 631, similar notification having appeared in April for interested personnel serving in the Royal Navy and in the Royal Air Force. Following the publication in 1946 of a White Paper titled 'Organization of the Colonial Service', in which the Colonial Office set out its plan of action on the recruitment, training and structure of the postwar Colonial Service, its future shape and direction occupied a prominent position on the agenda drawn up for the conference of African governors, scheduled to meet in London in November 1947 under the chairmanship of Sir Sidney Caine.

At that conference, the governors noted with approval the plan of action's two basic assumptions, that 'the Colonial Service needs large reinforcements' and how that new-look Colonial Service

> *must provide a framework in which the right man or woman can be put in the right place, irrespective of race or colour; in which there is equality of treatment and opportunity of all on the basis of merit and efficiency; in which the 'passenger' can be disposed of*

without undue hardship; and in which the poorer Colonies stand
the best chance of getting the staff which they need.

They also welcomed the proposal to set up public service commissions and to raise the status of establishment (personnel) officers in
the colonies, and endorsed the recommendations of the Devonshire
Committee that the field for promotion to the highest administrative
appointments should be widened from within the service. They were
less enthusiastic over the Colonial Office's thinking on the pace of
independence, some of them positively pooh-poohing the idea and
Sir Philip Mitchell trenchantly dismissing the Colonial Office's plans
as comparable to 'offering the Red Indians of America their independence'. In the same year, on the eve of the independence of India,
Burma, Ceylon and Palestine, when the British Empire was at its
territorial peak, the Colonial Empire was now officially restyled the
Colonial Territories.

In November 1947, too, Furse revised his 1943 memorandum. In
extended reflections on postwar recruitment and training, he raised
the question of how the inspiration of the Colonial Service in the
rapidly changing political circumstances of a postwar empire could
be maintained. With his direct involvement and unique knowledge
of the Colonial Service recruitment and ethos reaching back to 1910,
Furse was well aware that the pace as well as the role of working in
the Colonial Service was going to be far removed from the context,
responsibilities and attitudes of 1939. The interwar paternalistic
policy of trusteeship had been anointed by Article 22 of the League
of Nations covenant, with its directive that to those 'colonies and
territories ... inhabited by peoples not yet able to stand by themselves under the strenuous conditions of the modern world, there
should be applied the principle that the wellbeing and development
of such peoples form a shared trust'. Soon to be undermined by the
world's economic crises, it had inevitably become a policy of gradual-
ism. Any thought of independence for the colonial territories — with
the exception of Ceylon — had been a long way off in the remote
realm of 'indefinite time ahead'. Indeed, until 1943 self-government
had not featured at all in any public statement of British colonial (in
contrast to India) policy. Now matters would have to change, in
speed as well as in the declared objective of Colonial Office policy as
being 'to aim progressively at self-government' within the Commonwealth for the peoples of the colonies.

The Colonial Office was determined to avoid the Colonial Service recruitment confusion of 1919. This it did by careful forward planning. Building on its 1944 initiative among those about to be demobilized, full-scale recruitment officially opened on 1 June 1945. Colonial governors sent in a preliminary indent for 2600 recruits, the equivalent of the intake for the whole decade 1929–39. The Colonial Office handled approximately 15,000 application forms between 1 June 1945 and 31 March 1947. The new First Devonshire course started in October 1946 with a record intake, 120 probationers for the Administrative Service, including men domiciled in Fiji, Malaya, West Africa and the Dominions, spending six months at Oxford or Cambridge followed by a term at London. The Second Devonshire course got off the ground in the following October, with about 100 officers attending. It was prefaced by a brief introductory summer school held at Oxford. In 1948, more than 2000 submissions were passed to the Secretary of State. All in all, nearly 4000 appointments were made between 1946 and 1948. A new class of development officer was created to enable colonial governments to implement the development plans approved and financed under the Colonial Development and Welfare Act, especially in Nigeria. While most of these officers compensated for the lack of the qualifications required for direct entry into the Administrative Service by considerable administrative experience during the war, a small number were subsequently transferred into the administration. But this was still the tail end of demobilization and a good number of applicants withdrew their candidature either before their submission reached the Secretary of State or after an offer of appointment had been made to them, or sometimes were found medically unfit. In the first five years after the resumption of recruitment, the wastage among applicants under the categories of voluntary withdrawal or failing the medical test averaged 300 a year.

Nor were women absent from this notable Colonial Service expansion, with nearly 300 posts filled every year for the period 1947 to 1952 in the nursing, education and medical services (see Table 3.2). The significance of this postwar increase is quickly understood when one compares it with the prewar figures. Between 1922 and 1943, a 20-year period, only 83 women all told were recruited for educational posts and 72 for medical posts, although as many as 2189 nursing sisters were appointed. A few women were appointed to administrative posts in the secretariat in the immediate postwar

Table 3.2   Women's Appointments to the Colonial Service, 1942–52

	1942	1943	1944	1945	1946	1947	1948	1949	1950	1951	1952
Education	5	13	54	52	49	58	69	91	109	99	118
Medical	1	4	–	8	15	13	6	7	8	11	12
Nursing	97	67	76	91	157	228	220	183	131	175	178
Misc.	1	3	6	35	7	15	6	9	7	9	8
Total	104	87	136	187	228	314	301	290	255	294	316

Source: Colonial Office, *Appointments in Her Majesty's Colonial Service*, 1953 (CSRI).

years, following the publication of a circular in Whitehall in 1944 on 'Appointments of Women: Administrative Posts in the Colonies'. The notice cautioned that such a scheme was a new departure and that appointments of women administrative assistants (WAAs) would be 'largely experimental'. In the event, the very first intakes were styled assistant colonial secretaries, but the title was not used again. WAA was later changed to woman assistant secretary, emphasizing the standard secretariat nature of the job rather than a provincial likelihood. The first two recruits, Mair Evans and Margaret Burness, were posted to work in The Gambia. Of the 1945 intake, as many as nine were sent to Tanganyika.

Overall, between 1944 and 1960 some 80 women were recruited for eight African colonies, 39 of them being posted to Tanganyika and 25 serving in Nigeria. The role of A. M. Grier of the personnel division, who was largely responsible for administering the scheme in the Colonial Office, is acknowledged in the WAAs' *War Song of the Amazons*, with its defiant chorus of 'We'll justify the Empire's call, We'll show who wears the pants!' Yet even by 1952, there were still restrictions on marriage, even though the prewar requirement of the governor's permission to bring one's wife out was no longer everywhere *de rigueur*. As the Colonial Office now explained:

> *Wherever conditions are suitable married officers are encouraged to have their wives and children with them as much as possible. In some territories officers must obtain permission from the local*

government before their wives can join them. In such cases permission is seldom refused after the officer has obtained adequate experience of local conditions. In St Helena the appointment of married officers and the encouragement of wives to accompany them in the Island, is very desirable. Where restrictions exist, they are imposed largely in the interests of the officer himself. Lack of suitable accommodation for a married man, or the need for extensive travelling in undeveloped areas may make it undesirable in a given case, that an officer should be accompanied by his wife and family.

By 1947 the strength of the Colonial Service had climbed to over 11,000. This total was divided into some 1800 posts in the administration and more than 9000 in the professional departments. Among these, about 1400 administrative officers were working in Africa, 250 in Southeast Asia, and 150 in the rest of the colonial empire. In 1950, the Colonial Service Appointments Board was still interviewing almost 2000 applicants each year who had passed the preliminary recruiting stages of references being taken up and interviews carried out by the Colonial Office staff. By 1952 the number of appointments made to the Colonial Service in the seven years since recruitment reopened had passed the 10,000 mark (Table 3.3). Leaving aside the approximately 200,000 locally employed men and women recruited directly by and working for colonial governments, the strength of the Colonial Service under the Secretary of State's control had risen by 1954 to 18,000. Of those, 2360 were in the administration, of whom the lion's share (75 per cent) were assigned to Africa. Not only had the Colonial Service never been so large; this was also its peak, for in 1957 the Gold Coast and Malaya became independent and Nigeria (with the biggest service of them all) in 1960, followed by East Africa in 1961–3 and Central Africa in 1964.

Of no less significance, given the common charge that colonial governments were interested only in maintaining law and order and had little time or money for the work of the professional services, in fact in the same peak year (1954), seven-eighths of Colonial Service men and women held posts in departmental branches, like education, health and natural resources. This important rebuttal of the 'law and order' syndrome is convincingly reinforced by a look at the huge range of departmental activities undertaken by such disparately sized governments as Ceylon in 1931 (Table 3.4a), Sarawak and Nyasaland in 1959 (Tables 3.4b and 3.4c), and Hong Kong in 1967 (Table 3.4d).

Table 3.3 Colonial Service Recruitment, 1942–52

	1942	1943	1944	1945	1946	1947	1948	1949	1950	1951	1952
Admin:											
Permanent	1	22	2	24	430	328	198	146	219	146	119
Temporary	–	6	6	79	45	16	13	12	22	7	7
Auxiliary	–	–	–	–	–	–	–	–	26	57	40
Agricultural	15	17	18	30	34	34	17	63	56	36	37
Architects/town planners	–	3	1	6	26	24	26	22	23	40	36
Audit	1	3	–	5	34	8	18	21	16	18	11
Broadcasting	–	–	–	1	21	8	4	4	9	6	4
Chemists	–	1	1	1	8	11	7	6	8	1	12
Civil aviation	3	–	1	5	21	30	17	19	6	14	12
Commerce/industry	–	–	2	2	3	5	6	8	7	–	3
Cooperation	–	–	–	2	2	6	2	4	9	14	2
Customs	–	–	–	7	19	26	1	4	10	17	11
Dental	–	–	3	8	11	6	9	6	7	8	4
Development officers	1	2	4	36	113	43	42	54	50	5	23
Economists	–	–	–	3	2	1	2	–	–	1	–
Education	10	19	62	110	197	172	190	236	233	222	258
Engineers	–	–	1	50	158	108	129	221	239	209	214
Fisheries	–	1	–	–	6	5	12	6	7	9	6
Forest	6	7	8	14	8	12	34	36	29	25	16
Geological	1	–	1	5	10	10	21	54	51	22	20
Labour	6	2	1	13	20	6	8	11	7	10	7
Legal	–	7	7	19	78	36	35	38	63	46	62
Marine	–	–	–	–	1	2	1	–	–	–	–
Medical	24	19	26	61	188	128	140	85	131	169	147
Meteorological	–	–	–	–	7	8	14	11	3	9	10
Mining	1	–	1	2	16	6	12	12	11	1	12
Personnel staff	1	–	1	–	3	1	1	–	3	2	2
Police	3	30	23	57	87	18	70	128	186	103	55
Prisons	–	–	–	3	8	13	11	6	9	4	4
Public relations	–	–	–	1	6	3	4	2	8	6	22
Social welfare	1	3	5	18	9	11	7	9	8	7	12
Statisticians	–	2	–	1	5	2	4	15	5	5	5
Survey	1	–	–	3	36	23	44	47	32	23	43
Veterinary	9	12	9	9	15	24	23	47	32	32	28
Misc. scientific	1	5	2	2	6	3	4	9	5	3	9
Misc. others	10	–	7	27	40	6	17	25	16	63	79
Subtotal	95	161	192	604	1673	1143	1143	1367	1546	1340	1332

Table 3.3 continued	1942	1943	1944	1945	1946	1947	1948	1949	1950	1951	1952
Probationerships:											
Agricultural	11	15	22	22	16	23	17	45	41	53	43
Veterinary	4	7	2	–	3	1	2	–	–	–	–
Forest	4	–	1	3	3	2	1	2	–	3	3
Total	114	183	217	629	1695	1169	1163	1414	1587	1396	1378

Source: Colonial Office, *Appointments in Her Majesty's Colonial Service*, 1954 (CSR1).

In presenting his annual statement to Parliament in July 1947, the Labour Secretary of State had taken particular pleasure in being able to report that 'Men and women secured for the Colonial Service ... were [now] drawn from a cross-section of society with varying types of educational background.' One indication of how far that educational background changed is shown in the figures worked out for the Kenya administration (Table 3.5). But the postwar rekindling of a wider interest in the Colonial Service as a career was not a matter of statistics alone. Increased recruitment depended on, *inter alia*, an enhanced knowledge among the public of what the colonies were all about. To this end, 'Colonial Weeks' were held in 1949 in the major cities of Britain with exhibitions, of which the largest was 'Facts on Colonial Progress'. There was a BBC programme titled 'Colonial Round-up' spoken by John Gielgud, a special service in Westminster Abbey, and copious free literature, the whole coming together in a Colonial Month in London, opened by the King and Queen at Church House on 21 June. The university careers offices and appointments boards were specially targeted; usefully, several of them had ex-Colonial Service officers on their staff.

At the same time, the Colonial Office directed its attention to raising awareness in the Service itself. Within the Colonial Office, an African Studies branch was created with a strong link to the academic community. It embarked on the publication of a professional journal, called at first the *Journal of African Administration* and later the *Journal of Administration Overseas*. It was envisaged as the professional journal of the Colonial Administrative Service. In 1949 a further step was taken, with the Colonial Service now having its own journal, *Corona*. Its subtitle was to change with the times, for it

Table 3.4   Not only Law and Order: Schedule of Departments in Selected Territories

(a) Ceylon, 1931

Agriculture, Department of	Land Settlement Department
Archaeological Department	Legislative Council
Attorney General's Department	Local Government Board
Boards committees	Medical College
Chief Headmen	Medical and Sanitary Services, Dept of
Civil Service	Mineralogy
Colombo Museum and Fisheries	Miscellaneous departments
Colonial Auditor's Department	Motor Department
Controller of Revenue, Office of the	Municipal Court, Colombo
Court of Requests, Colombo	Patents
Crown Proctors and Crown Advocates	Police Department
Customs Department	Port Commission, Colombo
Defence Force	Post and Telegraph Department
District Courts	Prisons Department
Education Department	Public Trustees
Electrical Department	Public Works Department
Excise Department	Railway Department
Executive Council	Registrar-General's Department
Forest Department	Secretariat
General Treasury	Solicitor-General's Department
Government Analyst's Department	Stamp Office
Government Printing Office	Statistics and Office Systems, Dept of
Government Stores Department	Supreme Court
Governor's Staff	Survey Department
Immigration and Quarantine Dept	Treasury, General
Indian Immigrant Labour, Dept of	University College
Irrigation Department	Veterinary Department

(b) Sarawak, 1959

Administrative Service	Judicial
Agriculture	Land and Survey
Audit	Land Transport
Broadcasting	Legal
Civil Aviation & Meteorological Services	Marine
Community Development	Medical
Constabulary	Museum
Cooperative Development	Posts and Telegraph
Education	Printing
Forest	Prisons
Geological	Public Works
Immigration	Secretariat
Information Service	Trade and Customs
	Treasury

(c) Nyasaland, 1959

Accountant-General	Police

Agriculture
Cooperative Development
Education
Forestry
Game, Fish and Tsetse Control
Geological Survey
Information
Judicial
Labour
Lands Section
Legal
Organization and Methods Section

Printing and Stationery
Protectorate Councils, etc.
Provincial and District Administration
Public Works
Registrar General
Relief Staff
Road Service Authority
Secretariat
Stenographers
Survey
Veterinary
Water Development

(d) Hong Kong, 1967

Agriculture and Fisheries
Audit
Civil Aviation
Civil Defence
Commerce and Industry
Education
Fire Services
Housing
Immigration
Information Services
Inland Revenue
Labour
Legal
Marine
Medical and Health
New Territories
Police
Post Office

Printing
Prisons
Public Enquiry Service
Public Works
Radio Hong Kong
Railway
Rating and Valuation
Registrar-General's Department
Registration of Persons
Registry of Trade Unions
Resettlement
Royal Observatory
Secretariat for Chinese Affairs
Social Welfare
Stores
Treasury
Urban Services

Departments that have been abolished or absorbed

Colonial Secretariat
Commissioner for Transport
Commissioner of Banking
Commissioner of Census and Statistical
    Planning
Cooperative and Marketing
Custodian of Property

Development
Director of Organizational Surveys Unit
Ecclesiastical Department
Judiciary
Magistracy
Statistics
Supplies, Trade and Industry

Sources: *Ceylon Civil List*, 1931; *Sarawak Government Staff List*, 1959; *Nyasa-land Government Staff List*, 1959; *Hong Kong Government Staff List*, 1967.

started off as the journal of His Majesty's Colonial Service (1949–51), then of Her Majesty's Colonial Service (1952–4), and finally of Her Majesty's Overseas Service (1954–62) — never, it may be noted, the correct title of Her Majesty's Overseas Civil Service (a decision

Table 3.5   Socio-educational Provenance of the Kenya
Administrative Service, 1890–1959

| (a) Schools | Entered Service | | | | | | |
	1890–1909	1910–18	1919–29	1930–9	1940–9	1950–9	Totals
Public schools (total)	12	18	28	33	57	17	164
Scottish or Irish	1	1	2	5	6	1	16
Grammar School	1	3	2	2	13	2	23
Tutored privately	1	0	0	0	0	0	1
Other	0	0	1	2	8	0	11
Total	15	22	33	42	84	20	216
No information	39	40	94	14	40	180	407
Total	54	62	127	56	124	200	623

| (a) Universities | Entered Service | | | | | | |
	1890–1909	1910–18	1919–29	1930–9	1940–9	1950–9	Totals
Oxford	10	28	21	16	37	44	156
Cambridge	3	11	18	24	31	30	137
Oxbridge (total)	13	39	39	40	68	94	293
London/Redbrick	0	0	1	2	4	15	22
Scottish and Irish	2	3	8	8	5	13	30
Africa/other Commonwealth	0	0	0	1	1	5	7
Foreign	3	0	0	0	0	1	4
Military/technical/ non-university	4	0	6	0	6	1	17
No information	32	20	73	5	40	71	241
Total	54	62	127	56	124	200	623

Source: B. Berman, *Control and Crisis in Colonial Kenya*, 1990

defended by the editor). Arthur Creech Jones had revealed his plans for a Colonial Service house magazine in his speeches to the Corona Club in 1947 and again 1948, so it was only proper that he should, as Secretary of State, contribute the foreword to the inaugural issue of February 1949. In welcoming *Corona*, he noted that 'The happy title of the journal turns to a new purpose an old word standing for the unity and association of all those who serve the peoples of the Colonial territories.' Published monthly by HMSO, altogether 14 volumes appeared. Its object was, in Creech Jones's mind, 'to establish itself as an authoritative professional journal, with as high a standing among journals of this kind as the reputation of the service which it represents'. Both its readers and its contributors were expected to come preponderantly from within the Colonial Service, although, prudently if perhaps slightly bureaucratically, each issue carried the editor's colonial regulations-like warning that 'Manuscripts submitted by Civil Servants should always be accompanied by an assurance that they have been approved for publication.' This may, it has been argued, have tended to detract from the would-be professionalism of the journal. No fee was ever paid to any Service contributor.

The first editor was K. G. Bradley, a senior Colonial Service officer who had already made a literary name for himself by his entertaining *Diary of a District Officer* (1943) — complemented, a few years later, by his wife's equally readable guidebook for Colonial Service wives, *Dearest Priscilla* (1950). For most of its life, however, *Corona* was edited by another retired Colonial Service officer, J. J. Tawney, who in 1963 went on to be an active first director of the Oxford Colonial Records Project. Nor was this the end of the era of Colonial Service reinvigoration. The Women's Corona Club, dating back to 1937, was now reconstituted as the Women's Corona Society and took on a very active role. The Corona Club, dating back to 1900 as a social dining club, went from strength to strength.

Besides the short Colonial Service summer school held at Oxford at the beginning of the academic year for officers nominated to attend the Second Devonshire course, weekend general conferences for officers of all grades and from all departments were held in the New Year, at Oxford in 1946, LSE in 1947 and St Andrew's in 1948, aimed, as the Secretary of State put it, at keeping members of the service in touch with 'the development of ideas in this country'. From 1951, spring conferences on international affairs for Colonial Service officers on leave were held at either Cambridge or Oxford.

Furthermore, the eve-of-war idea of a Colonial Service summer school was revived, with Oxford University's successful summer schools on colonial administration, so imaginatively devised by Margery Perham in 1937 and 1938 and attended by some 150 Colonial Service officers, now complemented by the Colonial Office summer conferences on African administration held at Cambridge University. The first of these took place in 1947, on the then crucial

theme of African local government, and was something of a trailer for
the Colonial Office's (in particular A. B. Cohen's) reformist policy to
replace indirect rule and native administration with local government, due for discussion at the colonial governors' conference later
in the year. Subsequent themes included agricultural development,
the role of African chiefs, African land tenure, and rural economic
development. These took place each summer until 1960, when the
university took them under the auspices of its own Overseas Studies
Committee. The themes were now widened from their Africa focus,
and for the next ten years they continued to flourish under the
inimitable directorship of Professor Ronald Robinson, with the
dynamic Sir Andrew Cohen frequently in the chair. There was a
further change of sponsorship in 1970, when the Overseas Development Administration (ODA) took charge, albeit still with Cambridge
and summer inexorably intertwined. By then academics from all over
the world had replaced Colonial Service officers as the principal
participants: the attendance roll of the Cambridge summer
conferences in the 1950s used to read like a page from the *Colonial
Office List*.

In summary — in retrospect now but often on the ground
then — it is possible to identify a number of elements in the
composition of a new-look Colonial Service created by the Colonial
Office strategies of the 1940s. An outline calendar of the intellectual
impulses in this recreation will help to indicate why and how the
postwar Colonial Service, in both its function and its personnel,
tangibly differed from its eve-of-war predecessor.

It was in October 1939 that Malcolm MacDonald, the new
Secretary of State for the Colonies, called a meeting of top Colonial
Office officials and advisers at the Carlton Hotel in London and
asked them to take a broad look at colonial policy — an opportunity
too often lost in the pressure of daily responses and *ad hoc* reactions
to colonial problems — and answer the simple question 'Where are
we going?' Although the outbreak of war prevented any practical
programme evolving, Colonial Office officials recall how the immediate outcome was 'a positive seething of thought' within the Colonial
Office. Some of the ensuing action, planned or initiated despite the
overriding national priority of winning the war and despite such
setbacks as the retreat from Dunkirk in 1940, the surrender of Hong
Kong on Christmas Day 1941, and the fall of Singapore in early 1942,
have been alluded to in this chapter.

There was the comprehensive, interventionist plan for the development of the West Indies recommended by the Royal Commission (Moyne) in 1939 (the report was withheld until 1946) set up after the devastating riots in the West Indies, especially Jamaica in 1935–8. This revealed a new element in colonial policy by emphasizing the interrelationship between economic growth and social welfare as the basis for political advance. There was Lord Hailey's secret mission to Africa in 1940, to visit every territory and report on the probable political developments there once the war was over, resulting in — at least on the Colonial Office files — an outline for five stages of legislative advance towards self-government. There was Furse's dramatic memorandum of 1943 on the postwar training for a postwar — not a revived but a reconstructed — Colonial Service, and its part realization in the professionalized Devonshire courses for the Colonial Service with both induction and 'refresher' levels. Within the Colonial Office, a major debate was taking place on native administration as a policy, with questioning memoranda written on its future.

The end of the war and the arrival at the Colonial Office of Arthur Creech Jones, an ardent Fabian and founder of the Fabian Colonial Bureau, allowed fresh concepts of colonial purpose, responsibility and personnel to advance from planning to policy. In his commitment to reform, Creech Jones was influentially supported by an outstanding Colonial Office official and fellow Fabian, Andrew Cohen (later Governor of Uganda). Defining events followed in quick succession, each destined to rethink and reshape colonial policy, its aims and its agents.

The 1945 Colonial Development and Welfare Act stood British practice on its head by replacing the hallowed economic policy of colonial self-sufficiency with large sums of grants for development and staff increases within the colonies. The 1947 local government dispatch from Creech Jones abandoned the long-revered politico-administrative policy of indirect rule and instead adopted the English-style local government model as the basis for constitutional advance at the centre. 'The key to success', he wrote, 'lies in the development of an efficient and democratic system of local government'. He spelled out the changed nature of the work of colonial administrators that this would introduce. When some of the old guard of colonial officials like Sir Arthur Richards of Nigeria, Sir Philip Mitchell of Kenya and T. R. O. Mangin of the Gold Coast warned Creech Jones that his policy was premature and to talk of 'independence within a generation' for any African territory was to be misled into thinking that 'democracy was a patent medicine', the Colonial Office quietly adopted the tactic of *reculer pour mieux sauter*.

Then, following the retirement of many of the gubernatorial old guard within the year and their replacement in 1948 by younger men, with less fixed minds and more flexible attitudes towards the postwar changes in Britain and envisaged for Britain's colonial policy, the Colonial Office appointed a new group of colonial governors such as Sir John Macpherson (with H. M. Foot as his Number 2), Sir Charles Arden-Clarke, Sir Edward Twining, Sir Maurice Dorman, Sir Percy Wyn-Harris and Sir Geoffrey Colby. By the time of the Accra riots in 1948 and the resultant commission of inquiry, it was clear that independence for West Africa was now a matter of years away, with all that that implied for the Colonial Service.

The Colonial Office summer conference held at Cambridge University in August 1947 can be seen as a shrewd stratagem to get the younger generation of middle-ranking colonial administrators on the side of the Colonial Office. For its postwar cadets, the Colonial Office had purposely set its recruitment sights on those awaiting demobilization in South Asia and Africa, young men who had not only seen something of the problems of empire and seen its underbelly but had often served with — and under — Indian commissioned officers and had learned to respect this new colonial elite as well as adopt the almost institutionalized British respect for Indian sepoys and African askaris. The series of reforms in colonial policy inevitably influenced the thinking and the attitudes of the new Colonial Service, all the way down from governor to cadet. At the same time, the dramatic expansion in the service, from fewer than 8000 in 1938 to more than 11,000 in 1947, with the Administrative Service recruiting 430 in 1946 and 328 in 1947 against 68 in 1936 and 91 in 1937, constituted a further influence in its own right.

The intellectual impulses of postwar colonial thinking needed — and found — their outlet in a Colonial Service willing to replace the old concept of paternalistic trusteeship with one of partners-in-development and to substitute self-government for law and order as the primary aim of Britain's postwar colonial policy. If different purposes require different people, or at least people with different attitudes, nowhere was this truer than in colonial administration after the war.

Yet, with the Colonial Service at its numerical maximum in 1954, one further radical change was, however imperceptibly, already taking shape in the official mind. Though few in the Colonial Service outside the governor's office were aware of it, at the very moment the Colonial Service could point with pride to the tide of numbers applying to join as proof of its career popularity and its active and attractive engagement in the policy of accelerated colonial development, which had characterized the years immediately following the end of the war, the culmination of two year's philosophizing and planning in the Colonial Office was about to take place in the corridors of Whitehall. The outcome was to spell goodbye to Her Majesty's Colonial Service and replace it with a fresh role, structure and title. It is with the introduction of Her Majesty's Overseas Civil Service (HMOCS) that Chapter 4 deals.

4. Reshaping a Successor Service: HMOCS, 1954–97

'[HMOCS] carries on into the new era the status and the traditions of the Colonial Service as one of the great Services of the Crown' — Oliver Lyttelton, Secretary of State for the Colonies, 1954.

In the summer of 1954 a sudden and silent revolution swept through the Colonial Service, barely noticed by the British public and its implications only gradually comprehended by those involved. On the night of 17 June, some 15,000 British men and women went to bed as members of Her Majesty's Colonial Service; the following morning they woke up to learn they would now become members of Her Majesty's Oversea (the 'Overseas' came later) Civil Service. If 'what's in a name?' was the most popular reaction within the Service to this instant metamorphosis, the answer was to be a matter of internal debate and institutional modification for several years to come. The Colonial Service's transition was not finally completed until 1962.

Not that the new nomenclature and its implications were in themselves conjured out of the air in a trice. In 1948 the first of the British colonies became independent, Ceylon, and much thought was given to just what this would mean for its Colonial Service staff, especially for those who had come in after the provisions recommended by the Donoughmore Commission in 1929 (namely before the unification of the Colonial Service took effect) on pensions, salaries and conditions of service had been incorporated into the 1931 constitution. Recruitment to the Colonial Service continued in top gear after the independence of Ceylon in 1948, still within the framework of offering a full and satisfying career to all new entrants to the unified Colonial Service.

Within the Colonial Office, however, thought was being quietly given to the longer-term questions of what provision should be made for the career security of those whom it was still actively — and expandingly — recruiting. It was an issue on which the up-beat 1946 White Paper 'Organization of the Colonial Service' had been noticeably thin in thought and coverage. One idea explored — albeit in no way a new one on the Colonial Office files — was the possibility of merging the Colonial Office and the Colonial Service staffs into one joint service. Another was to undo the unification of the Colonial Service, approved in 1930 and completed by the unification of the Colonial Research Service in 1949 (see Table 2.6), and revert to a scheme which had been in the official mind since c.1910, namely of creating integrated regional Colonial Services: for West Africa; for East and Central Africa; for Malaya and Borneo; and for Fiji and the Western Pacific. A fifth Service would comprise the remaining territories, scattered rather than regionally coherent, and could perhaps be managed not by the deunified Colonial Services but by the Colonial Office itself. For each of the four regional services, the key principles would be those of interchangeability in staffing and uniformity in conditions of service.

Other ideas to ensure security of tenure came up against the underlying difficulty inherent in the Treasury view that the only contractual relation officers selected by the Secretary of State had was with the territorial government they were serving and not with the Secretary of State — who nevertheless had made the initial appointment. Constantly in the background loomed HM Treasury, conscientiously alert to any danger of HMG being involved in having to pay from British taxpayers' money the pensions of Colonial Service officers should a territorial government default on its obligations. Yet it was precisely on the matter of pensions that the greatest disquiet would soon be felt among Colonial Service officers, anxious for a specific guarantee by the British government.

Eventually, an outline scheme proposing that officers should now enjoy a contractual relationship with the Secretary of State as well as with their employing territorial government, including a proposal that they would be guaranteed a full career or, if this were not possible, adequate compensation for loss of career, was sent out to all colonial governors for comment at the end of 1948. The Colonial Office then recast its 1948 proposals for a new contractual relationship between Colonial Service officers and the Secretary of State in the light of governors' replies. The revised plan was sent to governors in 1950 for further comment, in the hope that it might come into effect in 1951. This proved too optimistic a timetable. Dispatches shuttled between the Colonial Office and territorial governments in 1951 and 1952 and, as further problems were raised, fresh redrafting was undertaken. But by now it was becoming apparent that the complexities were too great in the Colonial Office plan for a Colonial Service that would be at once under the general authority of the Secretary of State yet whose members were employees of territorial governments from which the Secretary of State's control was being progressively withdrawn. In the opinion of a senior Colonial Office official who was at the centre of the 1948 guarantee scheme, Sir Charles Jeffries, what had been conceived as an uncontroversial administrative operation, not involving political issues, had been caught up in the general turmoil of constitutional development. The Colonial Office now decided to abandon its guarantee scheme and accepted that the best that could be hoped for was to rely on writing safeguards into each territorial constitution as the occasion arose, for it was when a territory became independent that the practical issues would arise. Governors were informed of this decision in May 1953.

At the same time, the Colonial Office was coming under increased pressure 'to do something' from many quarters, including the Colonial Service itself through the representations of the Colonial Civil Servants' Association. This had been formed in 1946 and now had some two dozen watchdog territorial associations. In particular, Colonial Service staff in the Gold Coast and Nigeria were anxious about their future as they saw the pace of constitutional development quickening in the two territories, which together employed a large proportion of all the administrative officers in the colonial empire. Triggered by this worry, the Colonial Office, having abandoned its guarantee scheme, took up another proposal, aired by Sir Charles Jeffries in 1952 when it became clear that the original guarantee scheme was not going to take off. 'I painted,' this tireless architect of a dignified rundown of the Colonial Service wrote, 'a depressing picture of the future of the Colonial Service as a series of transfers of officers from one untenable post to another slightly more tenable, until in the end the Administrator of Tristan da Cunha would remain as the sole inheritor of past glories — in short, a kind of tontine'. The new tack was to set up what at this incipient stage was labelled a 'British Overseas Service', whose members would be appointed as British civil servants. Their pay scales would be analogous to those of the Home Civil Service, with appropriate allowances paid when they served abroad. They would serve wherever the Secretary of State required.

This fresh direction of thought was not long confined to the Colonial Office. Several members of Parliament called for the creation of a 'Commonwealth Service'. Correspondence in the national press emphasized the need for some kind of new service, maybe a 'Commonwealth Civil Service', which would provide a corps of experts so needed by the developing countries. This time, the Colonial Office maintained close consultation not only with colonial governors but also with the Commonwealth Relations Office and with the Foreign Office in exploring the possibility of a 'British Overseas Service'. Despite a mixed reaction among the colonial governors, a working party, including the critical Treasury, was set up in 1953. While in the early 1950s neither the Colonial Office nor the Colonial Service could have foreseen that within the next 15 years some two dozen British colonies would be independent, it was already apparent that they would need to take account of the fact that within the next 20 to 30 years (that is to say the likely career span of junior officers and those currently being recruited by the Colonial Service) most of the larger territories would achieve independence.

Perhaps the central difficulty lay in trying to solve two problems by the creation of a new service: the concern among current members of the Colonial Service as the career uncertainties of independence embroiled them, and the longer-term staffing needs of the new nations. With regard to the former, the morale of the Colonial Service and the sudden decline in attractiveness as a career after its flourishing in the immediate postwar years were manifest in the percentage of posts remaining unfilled when set beside the number of appointments made. In 1951, despite 1396 new appointments, 988 posts were still unfilled. In 1952, the corresponding figures were 1378 and 1055 and for 1953, 1227 and 1048. Half the approved Colonial Service posts in West Africa and 40 per cent of all those in East and Central Africa were unfilled in 1953. The single comprehensive solution, of creating a new British Overseas Service, offering every Colonial Service officer the chance to transfer into it, and thereafter to recruit only into it, involved too open a commitment for it ever to have been on the Colonial Office cards that ministerial, parliamentary and Treasury endorsement could be secured.

So, once more it was back to the drawing board for the Colonial Office. With the Colonial Service described by the high commissioner in Malaya, Sir Gerald Templer, as being 'in the doldrums', and a mood of alarm painfully palpable within the Nigerian administration, the Colonial Office was directed by Secretary of State Oliver Lyttelton to work out a new package deal for the Colonial Service. This time it was to encompass a triple objective: to make it easy, politically as well as financially, for territorial governments to employ British staff; to enable experienced officers to stay on if they wanted; and to offer new recruits a satisfactory prospect of a career. This package deal was delivered to the Treasury at the end of 1953. Once more, the Colonial Office met with rigid opposition to the concept of a British Overseas Service. It was invited to draft yet another scheme to form the basis for further discussion. This now took the radical form of a positive deunification of the Colonial Service, by drawing up two lists of officers. The first list would comprise those officers who had been appointed by the Secretary of State to one of the unified branches of the Colonial Service. They would be given six months to indicate whether they wished to be included in the new service. The second list would consist of other serving officers who were recommended for enrolment by their governor and were accepted by the Secretary of State. No officer would be included in either list unless he applied. It was assumed that locally domiciled members of the Colonial Service would not want to join the lists, as they would expect to continue in their own public service following future constitutional changes.

It was from the Nigerian end that the new corporate name for the officers to be included in the list was to come. Subject to the Queen's approval, the new service would be known as Her Majesty's Oversea Civil Service. The unenthusiastic Governor of Tanganyika thought that an improvement would be 'Her Majesty's Civil Service Overseas'. While the Treasury was still adamantly opposed to any scheme that might be seen as accepting that officers should be recruited into the putative HMOCS as direct employees of HMG for assignment overseas on loan by the Secretary of State, it did authorize reference in the forthcoming parliamentary statement to current calls for the idea of some future British Overseas Service or Commonwealth Service.

With some positive progress thus achieved after six years of planning, consultation, drafting and redrafting, the Colonial Office called for an early statement by HMG on the important matters on which agreement had at last been secured. It was now March 1954. At the beginning of April, the Colonial Service featured prominently in a debate in the House of Commons on the future respective spheres of responsibility between the Commonwealth Relations Office and the Colonial Office in an era of accelerated and expanded transformation from colony to independent state. The Colonial Office now fine-tuned its draft statement on the reorganization of the Colonial Service, giving governors the deadline of the end of May to comment on the latest proposals. They were well aware that it would not be difficult for a cynic to argue that, apart from a cosmetic change in name, the blueprint of the would-be HMOCS offered little that was new for the Colonial Service. In the end, it was on 18 June that the Secretary of State made a brief statement in the House of Commons on the White Paper published simultaneously, 'Reorganization of the Colonial Service'. On the same evening, however, he expounded at length on the HMOCS proposals at the annual dinner of the Corona Club.

The Corona Club had been founded in 1900 by Secretary of State for the Colonies Joseph Chamberlain to provide an opportunity for Colonial Service officers on leave to meet their colleagues from other territories and officials from the Colonial Office and the Crown Agents. Its annual dinner was frequently marked by the Colonial Secretary taking the Colonial Service into his confidence and addressing some matter of policy. On this occasion, 300 officers of the Colonial Service and Colonial Office officials were present. It was a truly major statement (the press were allowed to be represented), in which Oliver Lyttelton set out the fundamental reason for the re-examination of the structure of the Colonial Service arising from constitutional developments in the territories and the resultant reduction in his own powers of control: 'A territory cannot be given self-government and the Colonial Secretary retain the strings in his own hands.' He stressed that in replacing the unified branches of the Colonial Service with the new HMOCS the change was far more than one in mere name alone. Transfer into HMOCS would not be

automatic and eligible officers would be required to apply individually for acceptance. 'The new service,' the Colonial Secretary
maintained, 'is a definable body, differing from the much more
loosely defined body such as is the Colonial Service today.' At the
same time, he conceded, 'it carries on into the new era the status and
traditions of the Colonial Service as one of the great Services of the
Crown.' Lyttelton gave the assurance that, once enrolled, each
member of HMOCS would be kept on the books and could be
considered for any suitable employment the UK government might
be able to offer: 'Her Majesty's Government will continue to have an
interest in his career and in his welfare.' He ended by saying that the
creation of HMOCS did not rule out the widely discussed ongoing
debate on the possibility of some entirely new Commonwealth or
British Overseas Service, despite the difficulties inherent in any such
institution. For now, Oliver Lyttelton concluded, the new step taken
'at least clears up the present position of the Colonial Service',
providing a vantage point from which the wider implications of the
wider proposals could be studied. HMOCS, he assured his audience,
offered 'a firm foundation upon which members of the unified
Colonial Service can build their future careers'.

Her Majesty's Oversea Civil Service would technically come into
being on 1 October 1954. What had hitherto been known as the
unified services would be renamed Branches of HMOCS. The Colonial
Audit Service would now become the Oversea Audit Service, and the
Colonial Legal Service was to be restyled the Legal Branch of HMOCS.
Only the Queen Elizabeth's Colonial Nursing Service would retain its
distinctive title, albeit as part of HMOCS. In the course of time, the
title of the Service was quietly revised in 1956 to become 'Her
Majesty's Overseas Civil Service', the Colonial Office's preference for
the use of 'overseas' as an adverb and never as an adjective having
been overcome. The White Paper, while emphasizing that the 'loyal,
devoted and efficient work of the men and women in the Colonial
Service ... is far from over', spelled out a number of assurances
which officers could now expect. These were, in summary:

1. The government of the territory concerned was not to alter terms
    of service so as to make them less favourable than those on
    which the officers were already serving.
2. The pensions and other benefits were to be similarly safeguarded.
3. They would continue to be regarded as members of Her Majesty's

Service and be eligible for consideration for transfer or promotion to any posts by the Secretary of State.

4. The government by which they are employed was to preserve their existing pension rights on transfer.
5. There was to be adequate notice of any intention to terminate their employment in consequence of constitutional change and HMG would endeavour to find them alternative employment should they so desire.
6. In the event of premature retirement resulting from constitutional changes, they were to receive compensation from the government of the territory concerned.

While the following months were occupied with translating the White Paper into action by preparing lists of officers who wished to be enrolled in HMOCS, the staffing position in the colonies continued to deteriorate. By 1955, only 17 per cent of the established Administrative Service posts in West Africa were filled and the departments were running at 50 per cent below strength. Nor was the position much more reassuring in East and Central Africa, where the administration was two-thirds below strength and the departments again reduced to 50 per cent. If the staff position in the Gold Coast was desperate, that in Nigeria was critical. The Governor-General, Sir John Macpherson, impressed on the new Secretary of State, Alan Lennox-Boyd, on his visit to Nigeria that for his purpose HMOCS was insufficient a measure to retain his staff. Unless a UK-based service were created, the governor-general acknowledged that he might be unable to prevent a breakdown of administration in the Federation of Nigeria caused by the steady haemorrhage of Colonial Service staff, in particular from its Eastern region.

Yet again the Colonial Service division in the Colonial Office was sent back to the drawing board. A number of schemes were considered (for instance, the payment of a gratuity to officers who were willing to stay on rather than take early retirement with compensation), most of them encountering the stumbling block of local political resistance in Nigeria to anything hinting at a subsidy designed to retain expatriate officers or facilitate their employment. Because the HMOCS scheme seemed to be working well outside West Africa, the Colonial Office was reluctant to disturb the new organization. Instead, following a visit to the Colonial Office by a deputation of senior Nigerian officials in June 1955, the idea took shape of a 'special division' within HMOCS, whose officers would be in the direct employment of HMG in the United Kingdom. In the course of time, this special division was to emerge as the Special List. Unlike the earlier scheme for a British Overseas Service, this special division would be situated within the framework of HMOCS. Furthermore, membership would be offered only to officers in territories approaching self-government. The Treasury's willingness to go halfway towards setting up a Special List within HMOCS for which HMG would accept a special responsibility was flatly rejected by Sir James Robertson, the new governor-general in Lagos, as totally inadequate to stem the fatal exodus of his staff. For his part, the permanent under-secretary of the Treasury stood firm. 'My concern,' he minuted, 'is where we are going to stop.'

Progress was stalled until the governor-general and the three regional governors of Nigeria came to London in October 1955 to review arrangements for the promised grant of regional self-government in 1956. Deputy Under-Secretary of State Sir Charles Jeffries drew up a new formula for HMOCS, but this was dismissed by the Nigerian governors on the grounds that it encouraged officers to leave rather than to stay. What they were looking for was the provision for their officers to transfer to the service of HMG. This was the last thing the Treasury was prepared to contemplate, adding yet another civil service to the Home Civil Service and Foreign Office for which HMG was responsible. So yet another plan was thrashed out and, in November, Alan Lennox-Boyd sent it to the Chancellor of the Exchequer, R. A. Butler. A sharp correspondence now ensued between the Chancellor, who refused to accept anything that could be interpreted as an infinite financial liability and rejected the scheme, and the Colonial Secretary, who in the end felt he would have to take the issue to the Cabinet's Colonial Policy Committee.

A fortunate — for the Colonial Office — reshuffle in the Cabinet in December 1955 suddenly meant that Butler was replaced as Chancellor by Harold Macmillan. Macmillan had had previous experience of the Colonial Office during 'a brief but lively spell', in the words of a senior official who had served under him there as parliamentary under-secretary in 1942. Although he, too, questioned parts of the new scheme, he eventually agreed to it being formulated as a basis for consideration by the Cabinet. At last the Colonial Office had got rid of the bogey of a seemingly perpetual Treasury veto. With extra pressure building up from Nigeria, where not a single administrative recruit had been obtained since 1954, Lennox-Boyd decided to go ahead without waiting for Treasury agreement and took his plan to the Colonial Policy Committee. In this, he was probably further pushed by the constitutional conference on independence for Malaya held in London in January 1956, where much time was given over to the question of the future of the public service. The Malayan nego-tiations strengthened the Colonial Office's hand, to date seemingly Nigeria-forced, for a Britain-based pool of skilled officials available for lending to overseas governments as required. It was this longer-term, constructive aspect of the Colonial Office's latest scheme that seems to have impressed the Colonial Policy Committee when it met in February 1956. It was now a Cabinet decision: 'to instruct officials of the Treasury and the Colonial Office to prepare at once a detailed scheme to give effect to our decisions'. There were more disagree-ments and disappointments, but eventually the Colonial Secretary persuaded the Chancellor that the new scheme should be applied forthwith to Nigeria, and later to other territories as and when this might be desirable. Approved by the Cabinet's Colonial Policy Committee on 15 May, the Colonial Secretary just had time to make his statement before Parliament rose. A White Paper, 'Her Majesty's Oversea Civil Service: Statement of Policy Regarding Organization', was issued on 17 May. Once more, the Secretary of State took the opportunity of the Corona Club dinner to unveil what he described as his 'revolutionary' plans for a Special List.

While part of the White Paper dealt with the intention of HMG to draw up a list (the 'central pool' concept) of people with special qualifications for secondment to overseas governments as required, who would be ready to accept such service and who might, should the demand rise to substantial proportions and regular employment for a number of years be foreseen, be taken into the regular employ-ment of the UK government, its essence lay in the introduction of a Special List for Nigeria. Specifically, it provided that there would now be a Special List of officers from within HMOCS. These would be in the service of HMG, for secondment to the employing govern-ments. On eventual retirement, members' pensions would be paid in the UK by HMG, who would recover the money from the employing governments. The Colonial Office hoped that, 'in the ordinary way', continuous employment would either be found for all officers on the new Special List up to at least the age of 50, or that they would

continue to be paid for up to five years while efforts continued to
find them alternative employment.

It might seem that the establishment of HMOCS in 1954,
modified by the establishment of a Special List in 1956 to handle the
staffing crisis in Nigeria, would have smoothed the ultimate transition from Colonial Service to HMOCS and the attendant anxieties of
serving officers over security of employment and their future. But,
for all the labyrinth of Whitehall interministerial negotiations and
colonial governments' misgivings over the effect of the various
schemes on the morale of their staff, HMOCS was not yet safely
under way. It was not until June 1957 that the necessary agreements
were signed with the Nigerian governors, and officers in the four
Nigerian services could be invited to join the Special List. The delay
brought the whole problem of the exodus of serving officers once
more to the fore. In a nutshell, the Special List concessions had come
too late. When the returns of officers wanting to join the Special List
were counted in May 1958, it was found that fewer than 400 of the
2000 officers eligible to join had applied to do so. Most of these were
in the Federal government and the Northern region; hardly any of
those serving in the Eastern and Western regional services took advantage of the inducement to stay on. Lump-sum compensation proved
more attractive. There was, too, a widespread feeling that since one
was in any case going to have to leave at some date in the future, the
sooner one got home and started looking for a job the better.

'A desperate situation called for desperate remedies,' noted a
senior Colonial Office official — and rapid ones, too. The gloomy
count of so few takers for the Special List (less than 20 per cent of
those eligible) stimulated frenzied activity in the tireless Colonial
Office's resolution to look after its Colonial Service, a determination
in which it was inspired by the equally caring leadership of its
Secretary of State, Alan Lennox-Boyd. Within a matter of weeks, yet
another White Paper on HMOCS was published, again specifically
relating to Nigeria, with other territories not ruled out in future
should a case be made. Issued in July 1958, it set up another special
list, this one called Special List 'B', to complement the original one,
now retitled Special List 'A'. This offered much more attractive terms
to officers appointed before August 1957 who were willing to stay on
in Nigerian service, whether they were members of the original
Special List or not, by granting them an immediate advance of the
lump-sum compensation for which they would eventually be eligible

on retirement, along with the opportunity for 'freezing' the amount of compensation at its maximum age point.

Every HMOCS officer in the Nigerian service was now called on to select an irrevocable option: to remain in the public service without joining Special List B; to remain in the public service and join Special List B; to join Special List A or, if previously joined, to remain on it; or to retire immediately. Implemented in 1959, Special List B elicited a good response (unlike Special List A) from the Nigerian services, and many more experienced officers transferred to the Nigerian government service at independence in 1960 than had ever seemed possible during the previous six years. By March 1959, some 1200 officers had been admitted to Special List 'B'.

In the event, the hastily improvised Special List 'B' was never introduced for HMOCS officers in any of the other colonial territories. Not until 1960 did the three East African governments discontinue the recruitment of expatriate officers on permanent and pensionable terms, while Tanganyika went further by introducing two-tour contracts for overseas officers. Instead of extending the Special List 'B' provisions, a comprehensive review of how well HMOCS had worked out in its first five years was undertaken. The UK government then issued a statement in 1960, 'Service with Overseas Governments'. In it, HMG finally came round to accepting responsibility for the 'inducement' (earlier 'expatriation') element in an officer's salary. It also accepted liability for part of his pension as well as paying education and children's allowances at Home Civil Service rates. Implemented under the provision of the Overseas Aid Act of 1961, the terms can be said to have been generous.

The establishment of HMOCS had helped to raise the level of new recruitment at a time when additional staff were urgently needed to execute the development plans generated by the Colonial Development and Welfare Acts. Paradoxically, this funding meant that in the last decade before independence, more and not less Colonial Service and HMOCS staff were needed on the ground, leading some critics to talk of 'the second colonial occupation' of Africa, especially when the accelerated promotion of Africans to posts in the senior service was held to be a priority. In the ten largest Colonial Service departments, annual recruitment rose by nearly 50 per cent, from 680 in 1947 to 983 in 1957, with the annual rate of appointments boosted by the establishment of HMOCS in 1954. The principal difference between HMOCS and its predecessor Colonial

Service now lay in the distribution of manpower between branches. Whereas in 1947 the biggest intake was into the Administrative Service, in 1957 266 appointments were made to the medical service and 329 to the educational service against 128 and 139 respectively in 1947. Only 109 administrative officers were appointed in 1957, compared with twice that figure in 1947.

In addition to the Colonial Office's responsibility for, broadly speaking, recruitment to Colonial Service posts requiring a degree or full professional qualifications, the Crown Agents for Oversea Governments (as they had now become) were busy with appointments that called for technical qualifications or experience. In the same year, 1957, they made approximately 1350 Colonial Service appointments, including engineering inspectors of works, radio and telecommunications technicians, agricultural superintendents and livestock officers, railway and marine technicians, accountants, health inspectors, assistant meteorologists and hydrological inspectors. The recruitment of women administrative secretaries (changed from assistants) also underwent expansion in the 1953–60 period, with a large group — all graduates — posted to Nigeria between 1953 and 1957 and others posted to Tanganyika, Uganda and Northern Rhodesia between 1956 and 1960.

By 1960, HMOCS numbered about 20,500 officers, a measurably higher figure than that achieved by the Colonial Service at its peak in c.1954 on the eve of its reconstruction as HMOCS. Of these, 14,000 were pensionable members of HMOCS, of whom about 7000 were serving in East Africa and 2200 in Nigeria and Sierra Leone. Of the 6500 officers on contract, 2000 were in East Africa and about the same number in the two West African territories. The Colonial Office's scheme of 1956 to form a central pool of experts never came off, just as nothing came of its earlier 'grand design' for converting the old Colonial Service into a centrally managed organization to provide the territories with the staff they needed, contracted and redeployed as necessary.

The 1960 statement on 'Service with Overseas Governments' concluded that the creation of the long pressed-for home-based Secretary of State's service would not comprehensively solve the problem of the future prospects of HMOCS, whose members seemed to be in good shape. HMOCS would continue in being. In 1961 the Colonial Office transferred to the new Department of Technical Cooperation (DTC) responsibility for recruitment for the overseas public services. A year later the DTC — subsequently restyled the Ministry of Overseas Development (MOD), then the Overseas Development Administration (ODA) and today the Department for International Development (DFID) — which had taken over the advisory and recruitment services from the Colonial Office in 1961, issued a statement 'Recruitment for Service Overseas'.

By then HMOCS recruitment had fallen away from its peak, as of course had also the number of territories requiring overseas staff. Appointments dropped from some 1300 in 1957 and a similar total in 1958 to approximately 1000 in 1959 and again down to half that number in 1961 (see Table 4.1). Recruitment, the 1962 statement concluded, would now be based on the principle that service overseas would be for limited periods and as part of a career structure based primarily in Britain. There would no longer be any regular establishment, only a series of contract or loan appointments. The old basis of a lifetime career in HM Colonial Service on permanent and pensionable terms had now given way to opportunities for specialist men and women to serve overseas for limited periods only. Indeed, under an imaginative arrangement entered into by the independent government of Northern Nigeria, between 1961 and 1963 a handful of Voluntary Service Overseas (VSO) young men were sent to the Northern Region to work as assistant district officers for a year. A few moved on to contract terms with HMOCS. The story of Britain's technical assistance programmes lies outside the scope of this history. This is, however, an appropriate moment in this history of the evolution of the modern Colonial Service and its reconstruction as HMOCS to summarize (Table 4.2) the essential recruitment figures for the often golden but equally switchback years 1913 to 1957.

Amid the service shifts in planning for the postwar Colonial Service and the seemingly endless battle between the Colonial Office and the rest of Whitehall (notably the Treasury) that occupied the whole of the 1950s, three wider political events in rapid succession were to reshape the empire scene. One was the fiasco of Suez in 1956, when for a moment it seemed as if Britain wished to relive its imperial days of gunboat diplomacy and, against all its postwar deeds and declarations of decolonization, impose its hegemonic will by armed force on a third world country — one which, furthermore, had already experienced its period of British overrule. The second, coming just a year later and showing the very opposite direction of

Table 4.1 HMOCS Recruitment, 1957–61

	1957	1958	1959	1960	1961
Administrative	109	77	53	56	35
Agricultural	60	65	48	49	20
Architecture and Town Planning	37	29	26	18	6
Audit	15	24	22	3	1
Biological	5	10	8	6	5
Broadcasting	2	4	8	4	5
Chemical	8	7	2	1	2
Civil Aviation	12	6	15	1	14
Cooperation	2	3	4	–	3
Customs	3	5	6	–	1
Dental	7	6	3	7	3
Education (men)	210	181	158	96	107
Education (women)	119	119	92	72	61
Engineering (civil)	147	144	72	49	34
Engineering (electrical/mechanical)	35	35	21	14	11
Fisheries	3	8	5	4	1
Forestry	19	26	18	23	12
Geological survey	21	23	11	16	18
Income tax	38	10	19	13	2
Labour	12	11	7	6	3
Legal	26	28	26	20	17
Medical	105	119	100	90	47
Medical auxiliaries	26	20	15	15	10
Meteorological	5	3	3	1	2
Mining	4	2	7	2	1
Nursing	135	140	131	100	66
Police	47	95	71	35	22
Postal	11	8	11	3	1
Prisons	11	20	7	–	6
Public relations	13	9	3	2	6
Quantity and building surveyors; valuation	21	24	22	21	10
Social welfare (men)	4	–	4	3	1
Social welfare (women)	9	6	4	3	2
Statistics	6	3	3	6	–
Survey	21	19	17	12	17
Veterinary	28	19	24	17	11
Miscellaneous	31	27	37	58	18
Totals	1367	1335	1083	816	581

Source: *Recruitment for Service Overseas: Future Policy*, 1962 (Cmd. 1740).

Table 4.2   Profile of Colonial Service Recruitment, 1913–57

Branch	1913 (prewar)	1920 (boom)	1922 (slump)	1928 (boom)	1932 (slump)	1938 (recovery)	1946 (renewal)	1950 (expansion)	1953 (decline)	1957 (reduction)
Administration	82	179	18	153	25	96	553	246	108	109
Education	19	37	39	74	4	14	193	207	222	329
Finance and customs	15	31	4	19	3	21	16	9	?	41
Legal	10	21	3	14	7	26	77	52	50	26
Police	13	45	17	32	2	22	81	188	47	58
Medical	67	73	41	85	12	54	180	114	133	266
Agricultural	11	49	17	59	4	23	48	136	62	65
Veterinary	7	23	6	11	0	13	18	33	36	28
Forestry	1	33	3	11	4	12	8	30	14	19
Other Scientific	9	5	2	10	4	24	1	(under agriculture)		?
Survey	2	30	9	27	0	10	46	74	64	42
Other	12	28	14	12	5	15	494	429	252	?
Total	248	551	173	507	70	325	1715	1510	1227	983

Source: A. H. M. Kirk-Greene, *A Biographical Dictionary of the British Colonial Service, 1934–1966*, 1991.

imperial intent, was the portentous memorandum from Prime Minister Harold Macmillan, dated 28 January 1957. In this he asked the Cabinet Secretary to draw up a possible political timetable along with a profit and loss account of the cost of maintaining the British Empire. Reading between the lines, it was not hard to see that colonial withdrawal was now irreversible. 'It would be good', Macmillan minuted as he elaborated his call for the Colonial Policy Committee's estimate of the probable course of constitutional development and the years ahead, 'if Ministers could know more clearly which territories are likely to become ripe for independence over the next few years — or, even if they are not ready for it, will demand it so insistently that their claims cannot be denied — and at what date that stage is likely to be reached in each case'. As for the profit and loss account for each of the colonial possessions, this would enable the Cabinet to 'be better able to gauge whether from the financial and economic point of view, we are likely to gain or lose by its departure'. This would, of course, need to be weighed against political and strategic considerations.

The third political event impinging on the Colonial Service came in 1959/60. Culminating in his celebrated 'wind of change' speech on the need to take note of the hurricane of nationalism that was sweeping through the continent of Africa, Macmillan had shown he was on course for exchanging any last longing for empire for early entry into the European Economic Community. In this acceleration of Britain's withdrawal from its African empire, the last of these political events impacting on the Colonial Service is situated. This was the accession of Iain Macleod to the Secretaryship of State for the Colonies on the retirement of Alan Lennox-Boyd in October 1959. In contrast with both Lennox-Boyd and his predecessor Oliver Lyttelton, who believed that Britain should not simply 'cut and run' from Africa in the face of internal and external pressures and reckoned that the pace and temper of local anti-colonial nationalism could at least be controlled, Macleod, sensitive to the imperatives of UK domestic politics, committed himself to what he called 'the policy of the lesser risk'.

Rather than Britain staying on too long in its colonial possessions, with the risks of rising anti-colonial hostility, of a breakdown in law and order, and of an appeal to communism for international support in the 'struggle for liberation', Macleod argued for a rapid transfer of power, leaving the new nations grateful and friendly rather than sullen and ill-disposed towards a Britain they would thus be happy to retain as a welcome trading partner. That Macmillan found it easier to carry with him the governor-general of Nigeria than the governors of the East African territories, who at a meeting at Chequers in January 1959 had been reluctant to do more than pencil in target dates for independence sometime in the 1970s, is well illustrated in an extract from his memoirs. Passing through Nigeria *en route* for South Africa a year later, he discussed the problem of the timing of independence and the concept of 'the lesser risk' with Sir James Robertson:

> *After attending some meeting of the so-called cabinet, or council, I said, 'Are these people fit for self-government?' and he said, 'No, of course not.' I said, 'When will they be ready?' He said, 'Twenty years, twenty-five years.' Then I said, 'What do you recommend me to do?' He said, 'I recommend you to give it to them at once.' I said, 'Why, that seems strange.' 'Well,' he said, 'if they were twenty years well spent, if they would be learning administration, if they were getting experience, I would say wait, but what will happen? All the most intelligent people, all the ones I've been training will all become rebels. I shall have to put them all in prison. There will be violence, bitterness and hatred. They won't spend the twenty years learning. We shall simply have twenty years of repression, and therefore, in my view, they'd better start learning [to rule themselves] at once.' I thought that was very sensible.*

In the last few years of the Colonial Service and in the initial years of HMOCS, officers found themselves assuming roles and responsibilities unheard of in the prewar colonial possessions, often exciting but rarely those for which they had had any training on the postwar Devonshire courses (renamed Overseas Service courses in 1954). Contemporary staff lists reveal such novel positions as development officer, labour officer, government statistician, cooperatives officer, public relations officer, adult literary organizer, palm oil development officer, fertilizer campaign officer, principal of an institute of public administration, director of a housing corporation, and chief broadcasting executive. None of these was known to their predecessors in bush and *boma*; now all — and more — were mushrooming on the coat-tails of Colonial Development and Welfare funds and of constitutional advance. The accelerated pace of constitutional change inaugurated by A. Creech Jones's influential dispatch of 25 February 1947, with its credo of 'The key to success lies in the development of an efficient, democratic [subsequently altered to 'representative'] system of local government' as the basic solution to the problem of African administration, set in motion new directions for the Colonial Service and generated its own group of posts to handle the legislative, electoral and local government process. These included chief electoral officer, clerk to the legislature, secretary to the Executive Council, secretary to the Public Service Commission, localization officer, and Speaker of the House. But members of HMOCS, mindful of their predecessors' reputation as jacks of all trades, were nothing if not versatile.

Once elections had led to the introduction of a ministerial system of government, yet another set of responsibilities opened up for Colonial Service officers, with appointment as Secretary to the Cabinet and the whole Whitehall range of permanent secretary, under secretary, and private secretary to ministers. All these posts were initially filled by Colonial Service officers, departmental as well as generalist. By the time HMOCS came into being in 1954, admin-istrators were beginning to look more like Sir Humphrey Appleby than the legendary Sanders of the River. More than one admin-istrative officer was heard to murmur in mild protest that this was the very Home Civil Service set-up he had joined the Colonial Service to escape on graduation. Nor did professional officers always find it easy to adjust to the ministerial system, either because of having to spend more time on the administration of a ministry structure than in practising their profession, or else finding the post of director (later adviser) of medical or veterinary services, of public works and so forth, being subordinated to the control of a permanent secretary, often drawn from the generalist Administrative Service.

In step with Britain's progressive withdrawal from its colonial empire after the final African transfer of power in 1968 (Swaziland), through the Caribbean and Mediterranean possessions in the 1960s and the Pacific in the 1970s (Table 4.3), the core of HMOCS pro-gressively located in Hong Kong. Though in land size it had never ranked high among the colonies, its population, strategic and commercial importance, together with the calibre of its civil service, had long assured its place among the leading colonial governorships. It had surrendered to the Japanese on Christmas Day 1941. After the return of the British in 1945, Hong Kong experienced rapid growth

Table 4.3 Independence: A Colonial Service Calendar, 1947–77

1947	(India)
1948	Ceylon, Palestine
1956	(Anglo-Egyptian Sudan)
1957	Gold Coast, Malaya
1960	Cyprus, Nigeria, British Somaliland
1961	Sierra Leone, Tanganyika
1962	Jamaica, Trinidad and Tobago, Uganda
1963	Kenya, Zanzibar, Sarawak, North Borneo
1964	Malta, Nyasaland, Northern Rhodesia
1965	Singapore, The Gambia, Maldives
1966	British Guiana, Bechuanaland, Basutoland, Barbados
1967	Aden
1968	Mauritius, Swaziland
1970	Fiji, Tonga
1973	Bahamas
1974	Grenada
1976	Seychelles
1978	Dominica, Solomon Islands, Ellice Islands
1979	St Vincent and the Grenadines, St Lucia, Gilbert Islands
1980	(Southern Rhodesia), New Hebrides
1981	British Honduras, Antigua
1983	St Christopher (St Kitts) and Nevis, Brunei
1990	(Namibia)
1997	Hong Kong

Note: Countries in parentheses are included as markers in the chronology of independence in the British Empire. They were not staffed by the Colonial Service.

and the number of its government departments expanded proportionately. By 1961, there were no less than 40 departmental establishments and more than 70 government councils, committees and boards staffed by the civil service. Only in the more rural New Territories could a Hong Kong administrative officer share the sense of being the archetypal district officer of the classic Colonial Service, in contrast with the secretariat and departmental context of being a cadet in the highly urbanized central district. The Hong Kong Civil Service, which had grown from about 700 at the turn of the century to almost 3000 on the eve of the Second World War, numbered nearly 80,000 in 1970. The Hong Kong staff list, with names in Chinese characters as well as Roman letters, totalled 690 pages. Management consultants were called in to reorganize the Hong Kong Civil Service in 1973. At about the same time the localization of the Cadet Service became a priority. Because of the war, the scheme had not got under way until 1948, when the first Chinese was appointed to the administrative grade. By 1970, the cadre included 43 Chinese administrative officers and, by 1974, local officials predominated in the 1000 permanent posts (point 46 in the master pay scale). Anson Chan, who in 1993 was the first Chinese (and the first woman) to be promoted to the post of chief secretary of the colony, had joined the Hong Kong Civil Service in 1962.

With such a large public service, and with Britain's dependent territories otherwise reduced to a handful of islands, it was inevitable that Hong Kong should become the final destination of the last serving members of HMOCS. On the eve of the handback of Hong Kong to the People's Republic of China, it was estimated that there were still more than 750 members of HMOCS in the Hong Kong government service. Some of them made the headlines by exercising an old Colonial Service right to return home by sea on retirement, and 53 sailed back to England on the *Oriana* in March 1997. Others opted to continue to serve in Hong Kong after it became a special administrative region (SAR) of the Peoples' Republic of China in July 1997, in the same way as so many HMOCS officers had in the 1960s happily elected to stay on after independence in the government of the new states, particularly in Africa. That landmark year of 1997 was also to see the end not only of Hong Kong after 156 years as a colony but also, after a similar period of 160 years, the end of the Colonial Service in the form of its successor HMOCS.

The replacement of the Colonial Service in 1954 by HMOCS eventually — after much crisis, confusion and confrontation over the issues of career security, early retirement, lump-sum compensation (in cash or in kind by way of continuing employment under HMG) — succeeded in achieving a viable balance between its dual objectives of, on the one hand, the moral responsibility of HMG for 'looking after' the interests of the permanent and pensionable officers whom it had recruited for overseas service in the expectation of a full career and who now found it cut short through no fault of their own, and on the other of enabling the new states to receive, as HMG put it, 'the assistance of officers with exceptional administrative or professional qualifications' whenever and for as long as they wanted it. Yet it would be premature to accept that the end of the HMOCS on the transfer of Hong Kong back to China on 30 June 1997 will *ipso facto* mean the end of concern by the last members of HMOCS over their complex pensions and retirement benefits. The continuing disquiet over the pension arrangements of officers who had transferred to the Central African Federation in 1953–63 furnished a precedent. A reading of the proceedings of any annual general meeting of the Overseas Service Pensioners' Association (OSPA) over the past ten years immediately dispels the hope of such a tidy climax to the stroke of midnight on 30 June 1997. Even beyond that, a residual responsibility remains for those HMOCS officers who continue to serve in Hong Kong now that it is an SAR of the Peoples' Republic of China. While there were no HMOCS officers serving outside Hong Kong in 1997, closure of HMOCS and the transfer of power there in that year cannot be taken as quite the end of the Colonial Service story. The epilogue is yet to come.

In following on the internal — and sometimes less than exciting, save to those whose security of office and pensions were at stake — dynamics of the transformation of the Colonial Service in 1954, the hiccups of the emerging HMOCS, and its attendant Special Lists 'A' and then the panic 'B', sight must not be lost of the equally dramatic reorganization of the Colonial Office. At the macro level, its changing structure to handle the changing nature of its responsibilities between *c.*1928, the heyday of the long-time geographical departments, through 1938 and 1948, when subject departments were the dominant structure, up to 1958 when the Colonial Office was substantially beginning to shed its territorial responsibilities, is shown in Table 4.4. Even when the fact is accepted that the Colonial Service and the Colonial Office were two distinct and differently recruited Crown services, the relationship between the two tends to remain complex to the outside observer. In an attempt to reduce the apparent contradiction, the argument might be advanced that while the Colonial Office initially selected, appointed, trained, dispatched, and in due course promoted and sometimes transferred members of the Colonial Service, it was the territorial governments that paid and posted them, organized their career and, in the end, pensioned them off.

The Colonial Office's prewar personnel division (the creation of the Warren Fisher Report of 1930), with the dual structure of a recruitment and training department and a Colonial Service department,

Table 4.4 The Changing Structure of Colonial Office Business, 1928–58

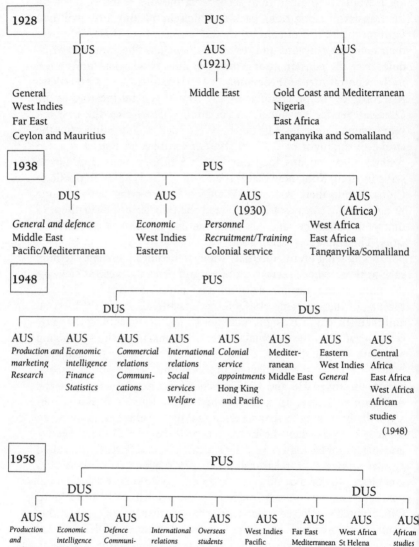

1928 — PUS

DUS | AUS (1921) | AUS

General
West Indies
Far East
Ceylon and Mauritius

Middle East

Gold Coast and Mediterranean
Nigeria
East Africa
Tanganyika and Somaliland

1938 — PUS

DUS | AUS | AUS (1930) | AUS (Africa)

General and defence
Middle East
Pacific/Mediterranean

Economic
West Indies
Eastern

Personnel
Recruitment/Training
Colonial service

West Africa
East Africa
Tanganyika/Somaliland

1948 — PUS

DUS | DUS

AUS — *Production and marketing* *Research*
AUS — *Economic intelligence* Finance *Statistics*
AUS — *Commercial relations* Communi-cations
AUS — *International relations* Social services Welfare
AUS — Colonial service appointments Hong King and Pacific
AUS — Mediter-ranean Middle East
AUS — Eastern West Indies *General*
AUS — Central Africa East Africa West Africa African studies (1948)

1958 — PUS

DUS | DUS

AUS — *Production and marketing Research*
AUS — *Economic intelligence Finance Statistics*
AUS — *Defence Communi-cations Intelligence*
AUS — *International relations Social services*
AUS — *Overseas students*
AUS — West Indies Pacific
AUS — Far East Mediterranean
AUS — West Africa St Helena
AUS — *African studies* Central Africa East Af

Source: J. M. Lee with M. Petter, *The Colonial Office, Ware and Development Policy*, 1982.

whose schedule included conditions of service, promotions and transfers, discipline and honours, was restructured as soon as peacetime
recruitment reopened. In 1946, the structure of the new appointments division, still headed by Sir Ralph Furse, now with the title of
director of recruitment, was split into departments 'A' and 'B', the
former responsible for training as well as recruitment from the armed
forces and the latter responsible for submissions, allocations and the
Colonial Service Appointments Board. At the same time, a Colonial
Service division was created, again subdivided into two departments,
'A' looking after promotions, honours, petitions, the appointment of
colonial governors and the preparation of the annual *Colonial Office
List*, and 'B' responsible for pensions and conditions of service
generally. Within a few years, the Colonial Service division had
grown, *pari passu* with the expansion of the Colonial Service, into no
less than five departments, the principal change being the distribution
of Colonial Service appointments, transfers and promotions among
three departments each of which had its own schedule of business
for those departments of the service allocated to it (Table 4.5). In
addition to the responsibility of the Colonial Service division for
Colonial Service matters, individual departmental matters were
regularly kept under review through an extensive system of Colonial
Office advisers and advisory committees, the latter numbering as
many as 27 in 1958 (Table 4.6).

In 1961, the Colonial Office absorbed responsibility for staffing
the High Commission Territories (HCTs) of Bechuanaland, Basutoland and Swaziland, for which it had been making appointments
since 1945. By the time the British Antarctic Territory and the British
Indian Ocean Territory (BIOT) were added to the Colonial Office
schedule in 1962 and 1965 respectively, the Colonial Office had
already given up most of its traditional responsibility for recruiting a
Colonial Service to administer Britain's overseas possessions. Following an intensive inquiry into the future distribution of Whitehall
responsibilities overseas in a post-imperial context, the Colonial
Office was closed down in 1966, a reflection as well as a symbol of
imperial demission. Its residual functions were transferred to the
Commonwealth Office, the 1947 successor to the Dominions Office.
During the 112 years of its history as a separate department of state,
it had nearly 60 secretaries of state, of whom about half held office in
the twentieth century (Table 4.7). Some of them spent months rather
than years in office, while others, like Joseph Chamberlain (1895–

Table 4.5   Distribution of Colonial Service Matters in the Colonial Office, 1954

Department 'A'

Recruitment policy and procedure, Colonial Service training courses

Department 'B'

Conditions of service, discipline, pensions, honours, precedence, uniforms, ceremonial
Head of Department: K. W. Blaxter, CMG

Department 'C'

Appointments, transfers and promotions: Administrative (including finance, economics and commerce and industry), agriculture, audit, biological, fisheries, forestry, immigration, police, statisticians and miscellaneous
Head of Department: A. D. Garson, CMG

Department 'D'

Appointments, transfers and promotions: Architects, broadcasting, civil aviation, chemical, engineering, geological, marine, meteorological, mining, postal, public relations, public works, railways, rating and valuation, survey, town planners
Head of Department: R. A. Whittle, CBE, MC

Department 'E'

Appointments, transfers and promotions: Cooperation, dental, education, income tax, labour, legal, medical, nurses, printing, prisons, social welfare, Treasury, veterinary, women's appointments
Head of Department: E. R. Edmonds, CMG

Source: *Colonial Office List*, 1954

1903), Leo Amery (1924–9), Philip Cunliffe-Lister (1931–5), Arthur Creech Jones (1946–50) and Alan Lennox-Boyd (1954–9) notably held office for four or more years. While it is not possible to claim with authority which of the Secretaries of State were the most popular within the Service (and, as Lugard himself experienced, individual Colonial Office relationships could at times be disastrous), at the risk of generalization a case could be made out that few surpassed Alan Lennox-Boyd in personal popularity among the 'rank and file' of the Colonial Service. He endeared himself by leading the fight in the Cabinet over fair pension arrangements for loss of career consequent on self-government, and again after his retirement by his

Table 4.6 Colonial Office Advisory Committees, c.1954

Agricultural research	Local government
Agricultural machinery	Medical
Agriculture, animal health and forestry	Medical research
Colleges of art, science and technology	Native law
Cooperation	Pesticide research
Economic research	Products
Education	Research
Higher education	Road research
Falkland Islands Dependencies	Social development
scientific committee	Social science research
Fisheries	Treatment of offenders
Geology and mineral resources	Tsetse fly and trypanosomiasis
Housing and town planning	University grants
Labour	Welfare of colonial students in the UK

Source: *Colonial Office List*, 1955.

dedicated welfare work as president of the Overseas Service Pensioners' Association. At the top, of course, each governor had his most (and on occasions least) liked Secretary of State. As to which Secretaries of State exercised the widest influence on the Colonial Service, it is likely that Chamberlain, Amery and Creech Jones could, as these chapters have revealed, claim credit for the most far-reaching reforms of the service, though Iain Macleod's policy of the lesser risk through accelerated decolonization inevitably affected many members of the Colonial Service without always earning him a comparable amount of warmth or respect.

The Colonial Office had also been well served by its permanent under secretaries, 21 in all, and its nine deputy permanent under-secretaries of state between 1931, when the post was created, and 1965 (Table 4.8). Among these distinguished civil servants, it is noteworthy that only one of them had come in from the Colonial Service. This was Sir John Macpherson, who became governor-general of Nigeria after a career in the Malayan Civil Service. Two other permanent under secretaries had had field experience as a colonial governor. Sir John Anderson's career in the Colonial Office was interrupted by the governorship of Malaya, and Brigadier-General Sir Samuel Wilson had been governor of Trinidad and Tobago and then of Jamaica before moving to Whitehall. Sir John Maffey (later Lord Rugby) had had the field experience of having

Table 4.7   Secretaries of State for the Colonies, 1895–1966

1895, 28 June	Joseph Chamberlain
1903, 9 October	Alfred Lyttelton
1905, 11 December	Earl of Elgin and Kincardine
1908, 16 April	Earl of Crewe
1910, 7 November	Lewis Harcourt
1915, 27 May	A. Bonar Law
1916, 11 December	W. H. Long
1919, 14 January	Viscount Milner
1921, 14 February	Winston Churchill
1922, 25 October	Duke of Devonshire
1924, 23 January	J. H. Thomas
1924, 7 November	L. C. M. S. Amery
1929, 8 June	Lord Passfield
1931, 26 August	J. H. Thomas
1931, 9 November	Sir Philip Cunliffe-Lister
1935, 7 June	Malcolm MacDonald
1935, 27 November	J. H. Thomas
1936, 29 May	W. G. A. Ormsby-Gore
1938, 16 May	Malcolm MacDonald
1940, 13 May	Lord Lloyd
1941, 8 February	Lord Moyne
1942, 23 February	Viscount Cranborne
1942, 24 November	O. F. G. Stanley
1945, 3 August	G. H. Hall
1946, 7 October	A. Creech Jones
1950, 2 March	James Griffiths
1951, 27 October	Oliver Lyttelton
1954, 30 July	Alan T. Lennox-Boyd
1959, 19 October	Iain Macleod
1961, 16 October	Reginald Maudling
1962, 17 July	Duncan Sandys
1964, 17 October	Anthony Greenwood
1965, 23 December	Earl of Longford
1966, 6 April	Frederick Lee

Source: *Colonial Office List*, 1966.

Table 4.8   Permanent and Deputy Permanent Under-Secretaries of State in the Colonial Office, 1825–1966

a) Permanent under-secretaries of state for the colonies

1825	Robert William Hay
1836	Sir James Stephen, KCB
1847	Herman Merivale, CB
1860	Sir Frederic Rogers, Bt, GCMG
1871	Hon. Sir Robert G. Wyndham Herbert, GCB
1892	Hon. Sir Robert H. Meade, GCB
1897	Sir Edward Wingfield, KCB
1900	Sir Montague F. Ommanney, GCMG, KCB, ISO
1907	Sir Francis J. S. Hopwood, GCB, GCMG, GCVO, KCSI
1911	Sir John Anderson, GCMG, KCB
1916	Sir George V. Fiddes, GCMG, KCB
1921	Sir James E. Masterson Smith, KCB
1925	Brigadier-General Sir Samuel H. Wilson, GCMG, KCB, KBE
1933	Sir John Maffey, GCMG, KCB, KCVO, CSI, CIE
1937, 2 July	Sir Cosmo Parkinson, GCMG, KCB, OBE
1940, 2 February	Sir George Gater, GCMG, KCB, DSO
1947, 1 February	Sir Thomas Lloyd, GCMG, KCB
1956, 20 August	Sir John Macpherson, GCMG
1959, 20 August	Sir Hilton Poynton, GCMG

(b) Deputy permanent under-secretaries of state

1931, 15 August	Sir John E. Shuckburgh, KCMG, CB
1942, 18 March	Sir William Battershill, KCMG
1945, 13 April	Sir Arthur Dawe, KCMG, OBE
1947, 1 February	Sir Sydney Caine, KCMG/Sir Charles Jeffries, KCMG, OBE*
1947, 6 April	Sir Charles Jeffries, KCMG, OBE
	Sir Charles Jeffries, KCMG, OBE*
1948, 5 August	Sir Hilton Poynton, KCMG
	Sir Hilton Poynton, KCMG*
1956, 1 July	Sir John Martin, KCMG, CB, CVO
	Sir John Martin, KCMG, CB, CVO*
1959, 20 August	Sir William Gorell Barnes, KCMG, CB
1963, 1 June	Sir John Martin, KCMG, CB, CVQ
1965, 26 January	A. N. Galsworthy, CMG

Note: * Appointments held jointly with the person immediately below.
Source: *Colonial Office List*, 1966.

served in the Indian Civil Service and as governor-general of the Anglo-Egyptian Sudan before his elevation to head the Colonial Office.

A further — and final — Whitehall reorganization took place in

1968, when the Commonwealth Office was merged with the Foreign Office to form the new Foreign and Commonwealth Office (FCO). Over the ensuing 30 years, HMOCS affairs were handled by the FCO and then, to an increasing extent, by the ODA. After the transfer of Hong Kong in 1997, Britain's Dependent Territories, which number 13, remained an FCO responsibility. In 1998, they were renamed British Overseas Territories, with new proposals for citizenship rights. For the most part island territories, they include the Falkland Islands, six dependencies in the Caribbean, and St Helena and its dependencies, all at one time staffed by the Colonial Service, and the newer groupings of the British Antarctic Territory (BAT) and the British Indian Ocean Territory (BIOT). The tradition of appointing an officer from the armed forces to the governorships of the 'fortress colonies' of Bermuda and Gibraltar (and of Malta before its independence in 1964), with a Colonial Service deputy, has now been replaced by both diplomatic service and political appointments. The last Colonial Service governor of Hong Kong was Sir David Trench (1964–71), his successors over the next quarter-century coming from the Foreign and Commonwealth Office (Lord MacLehose, Sir Edward Youde and Lord Wilson) and, Hong Kong's last governor, the politician Christopher Patten. Refusing to don the official uniform, he was sworn in wearing a business suit. He was similarly dressed, too, on the night of 30 June 1997, when in the presence of the Prince of Wales the colony of Hong Kong was handed back to China: the only British farewell to empire that did not end in independence and the only transfer of power that left a colony in a state of unique and unbelievable economic prosperity yet which, again uniquely, was not marked by a greater measure of democracy than before.

For all the media hype about the handback of Hong Kong marking the end of empire, the truth is that to a considerable extent the classic British Empire is in retrospect better seen as having ended 50 years earlier, when India became independent, and the essential Colonial Empire 40 years earlier, when the Gold Coast, the first of the African colonial territories, and Malaya gained independence. Hong Kong, dramatic as the event was, is better viewed as the end of the end of empire. On 30 June 1997, the colonial empire, which in 1937 had numbered almost 60 million inhabitants in an area of over 2 million square miles, was reduced to a handful of islands carrying a total population of under 200,000 (Table 4.9). Ironically, among them is

Table 4.9   Britain's Dependent Territories, 1999

1. Anguilla	Settled 1650; Crown rule 1653 (1969); formerly administered with St Kitts; population 7500
2. Bermuda	Settled 1609; Crown rule 1684; population 60,000
3. British Antarctic Territory	Claimed 1919; uninhabited
4. British Indian Ocean Territory	Crown rule 1976; formerly administered from Seychelles and Mauritius; uninhabited
5. British Virgin Islands	Settled 1666; Crown rule 1713; population 17,000
6. Cayman Islands	Crown rule 1679 (1959); formerly administered from Jamaica; occupied 1765 (1833); population 26,000
7. Falkland Islands	Crown rule 1841; population 2100
8. Gibraltar	Settled 1632; Crown rule 1633; population 30,000
9. Montserrat	Settled 1632; Crown rule 1633; population 12,000
10. Pitcairn, Henderson, Ducie and Oeno Islands	Settled 1790; Crown rule 1838; population 53
11. St Helena, Ascension, Tristan da Cunha	Settled 1661; Crown rule 1834; occupied 1815; Crown rule 1922; occupied 1816; Crown rule 1938 (all administered from St Helena)
12. South Georgia and South Sandwich Islands	Claimed 1775; Crown rule 1908 and 1917; formerly administered as the Falkland Islands Dependencies; uninhabited
13. Turks and Caicos Islands	Settled 1678; Crown rule 1766; until 1973 administered from Jamaica and Bahamas

Britain's oldest colony, Bermuda, founded in 1609 (population 60,000), which in 1995 rejected a referendum option of independence.

On 30 June 1997, too, Her Majesty's Overseas Civil Service also came to an end. The claim to have been the last British district officer in the empire belongs to David Browning, whose first posting, as an administrative cadet in Northern Rhodesia in 1960, was followed by the New Hebrides. He transferred to Hong Kong in 1980 and in 1995 was the final British DO of Sha Tin in the New Territories. In the event, outside Hong Kong there had been no HMOCS officer serving anywhere since 1995.

5. Envoi

'The splendid traditions of the service are well known to me, and are rightly a source of pride to its members' — HM the Queen, 1952

The year 1997, while marking the end of Her Majesty's Overseas Civil Service and its immediately anterior Her Majesty's Colonial Service, cannot be allowed to mark the end of the story of these two Crown civil services. A number of prominent questions and considerations remain to be addressed, and where possible answered, by those keen to know more about a Crown service which, for more than 150 years under one or other of its royal titles — an honour not granted to any of its sister overseas services such as the Indian Civil Service or the Indian Political Service, nor constitutionally possible for the comparable Sudan Political Service — had offered a respected, demanding and rewarding opportunity (today's 'work experience') for tens of thousands of British (and some Dominions) men and women in search of a Crown career overseas.

Three questions are invariably asked by those for whom a Colonial Service career was never an option, that is to say more or less any one born after 1935. First, what was the work of the Colonial Service and what was the life like? Second, what kind of people joined the Colonial Service and how did they get into it? Finally, how were people appointed to the so-called plums of the service, the colonial governorships? These questions seem set to continue to arouse interest as long as the mechanisms and modalities of how the Colonial Service was constructed and how it operated remain the subject of historical discourse. In the case of the post-1954 HMOCS, where the idea of a permanent career was deliberately discounted in favour of a series of overseas assignments from a UK base (other than for those who, on its inauguration, had opted to transfer into it from the permanent and pensionable cadres of the Colonial Service), the procedures were necessarily so shot through with the element of short-termness and *ad hoc* consideration that they are different enough to call one day for separate treatment. In any case, the circumstances and conditions of the 1970s and 1980s were often very unlike those that obtained in the 1950s and even less comparable with those of the 1930s. Above all, the HMOCS new entry of the 1970s never had the opportunity to experience life and work in what might be looked on as the classic Colonial Service territories: Ceylon, Malaya and the whole of Africa (the 'colonial' continent *par excellence*), where the last of the territories staffed by the Colonial Service achieved independence in the mid–1960s.

The first question, what did the Colonial Service do and what was the life like, has to a large extent been handled by members of the Colonial Service themselves. A glimpse into answering that question is given in Document VIIId, but it must be said that even another whole book could not begin to answer it to the satisfaction of all — least of all by those who have lived the Colonial Service life. Because of the huge range of work (there were 20 different professional branches) in which the Colonial Service was involved, and because of the utterly different countries in which it operated (almost 40 territories spread across ten continents, oceans and seas), there is no way of meaningfully writing of an agriculturalist's life in Africa and an administrator's in the Pacific under the same descriptive rubric as a doctor's work in the Atlantic and a nurse's in Southeast Asia, let alone setting the Hong Kong experience beside St Helena or Cyprus beside British Guiana: 'my' Aden was nothing like 'his' Bermuda or 'her' Ceylon. One man's colonial paradise might be another man's colonial purgatory. It is here that individual territorial service chronicles, like those already written on the Malayan, Kenyan and Ugandan services, are so important (even though they have so far been restricted to the administration) in helping to fill the gap. So extensive and so rich, too, is the autobiographical literature published by members of the Colonial Service over the past quarter of a century that the record — the insider's memories, perceptions and reflections — is readily and amply to hand. For ease of reference in answering, then, this first ongoing question, the principal sources are sketched briefly in the Introduction and set out in detail in the Bibliography.

Turning next to what kinds of people joined the Colonial Service and how were they recruited, the very size of the service has militated against the validity of any overall statistical research. In 1957 alone, there were 18,000 members in the Service — and the Service was by then almost 120 years old, with an establishment of more than 1000 posts in 1900, more than 7000 in 1937 and more than 10,000 in 1947. And that is not the only definition of 'size'. From 1930 the Colonial Service comprised, as we have seen, 20 different professional branches, each of which could produce its own profile of the kind of people who opted for this career. Again, none of those branches was a static body in its recruitment requirements: administrative officers in the 1930s — and even more so in the 1950s — needed very different qualities from those sought in the first decade of the century, and the qualifications of legal or medical staff recruited in the 1890s were not those looked for in the 1950s. What work there has been on the kind of person who aspired to a career in the Colonial Service tends to be focused on the Colonial Administrative Service, concentrating on the common denominator of educational background (see, for example, Table 3.5). Once more, the Service (in its tens of thousands) was too vast to allow the scrupulous statistical analyses available for the Indian Civil Service (in its thousands, fluctuating between 850 in 1859 and 1300 in 1939, nearly half of whom by 1947 were Indian officers), and the Sudan Political Service (in its hundreds, barely reaching a total of 500 in its whole 56-year history). Another grave limitation has been that the factual particulars of Colonial Service officers are not available to the researcher to the same extent as those of Britain's other imperial services, thereby restricting the amount of accessible educational and familial data available for analysis.

The kind of general picture that emerges is that of the Colonial Administrative Service (CAS) as predominantly — at least until 1945 — a public (and later grammar) school-derived and university-educated elite. Though the unified CAS from 1930 had its share of academic 'Firsts' and athletic 'Blues', there were proportionately more intellectuals among the ICS (after all, they sat the same rigorous civil service examination as the Home Civil and the Diplomatic Services), while more of the top university athletes went for the SPS. By far the most common degree was a good second class (honours). The introduction of probationers' courses at Oxford and Cambridge in 1926, and later at the LSE, meant that even those cadets who (especially in

1945–9) did not have a degree spent a year at university. Forest probationers went mostly to Oxford, agricultural ones to Cambridge (and then Trinidad), and education officers to London. In its recruitment for the Administrative Service, the Colonial Office accepted a degree in whatever subject the candidate had chosen to study (not excluding theology, science and agriculture), and no premium was put on economics, politics or even public administration. Current research suggests that history, English and modern languages were the most popular subjects, with classics characterizing the earlier intakes.

The spread of schools attended is wide, notably including many in Scotland. No school was recognized as *the* school for potential colonial administrators in the way that Haileybury had once been for the ICS, not even the eponymous Imperial Service College. Similarly, no public school had a separate Colonial Service class in the same way as before 1939 many leading public schools had an Army class. If the family ties were not so tight or so generational as in India, where Indian Army and East India Company family names often continued into the ICS, a fair number of Colonial Service officers followed a father, an uncle or a brother into the Service. 'Son of father' on a Colonial Service application form, meaning that the candidate's father was or had been in the Service, was a testimonial in itself.

In family terms, the real link should perhaps be looked on as one of imperial Crown service rather than of Colonial Service, for after the First World War the Colonial Service began to recruit an increasing number of graduates whose fathers or friends in the ICS seemed less confident about the prospects of a career in India. It is interesting how in the 1930s CAS candidates often applied for the SPS as well, and some to the ICS too. In terms of English social class, there is some evidence to support the generalization that over the first half of the twentieth century the Colonial Administrative Service largely comprised the sons of the (upper) middle and the professional class, with fathers who for example were clergymen, bank managers, civil servants, lawyers and doctors. Sons of the landed gentry and of the aristocracy were few (though they were there): primogeniture had long meant that younger sons joined the professions, notably the army and the church, and later the imperial civil services, while the family estate went to the eldest son.

As to motivation — for the Colonial Office a more significant factor in the make-up of colonial civil servants than educational background or familial provenance — preliminary research reveals that the reasons for joining run a remarkable and at times irrational gamut: they even include the proverbial candidate who, in answer to whether he had any preference in territory, replied that he was attracted by the Pacific because on his map Fiji appeared to be as far away as possible from his future mother-in-law. Such a reply is paralleled, in reverse order of rank, by the incoming Secretary of State who told his staff that, no, he did not know where the Virgin Islands were but presumed they were well removed from the Isle of Man. Documented responses include a search for adventure, a desire to see the world, a wish to help those less fortunate and the prospect of early responsibility. Others have listed family ambience or connections, the influence of undergraduate friends who joined a year or two earlier, a career suggested by a college tutor or recommended by the University Appointments Board, and the wish to get away from a Whitehall kind of office routine or to escape the 8.27 commuter herd into London Bridge. A distinguished administrator, after coming down from university, rationalized his choice as the only career he knew where he would not need to sit another examination. Besides the impact of history and geography lessons at school, one should not discount the influence of cinema (*Sanders of the River* is often mentioned by those who joined in the 1930s), of novels by G. A. Henty or later of stories by Arthur Grimble, and even the Stanley Gibbons stamp catalogues and cigarette card collecting. Nor was it then unfashionable or 'naff' to talk of a sense of service or the wish to serve the Crown. Insofar as there is something approaching a would-be final word on why so many well-educated men applied for the Colonial Administrative Service and who they were in the British social milieu, it is encapsulated in (though in no way restricted to) the reflection of K. G. Bradley, an administrator in prewar Northern Rhodesia who went on to become a well-known writer on and propagandist for the Colonial Service. 'We were,' he reflected, 'the younger sons of the professional, middle class, and had been given a Sound Old-Fashioned Liberal Education in the Humanities at preparatory and public schools, ending with an arts degree from one of the older universities.' In his estimate, the Colonial Service recruitment process favoured those who had the qualities

which the tough character-training of the boarding school and then the broad training of the mind provided by the older universities

combined to foster ... who had learned at school the elements of
leadership and to carry a little responsibility, and who had, at the
university, learned to be sympathetic with the other man's point of
view and yet to be detached and self-reliant.

As for Colonial Service recruitment, apart from the separate competitive examination for the Eastern cadets until unification in the
early 1930s, its essence was that it eschewed any formal entrance
test. 'There is no written examination, and no entrance fee,' pro-
claimed the official literature, *Appointments in HM's Colonial Service.*
'Candidates are selected,' it went on, 'by competitive selection based
on record and personal interview.' Account was taken of general
educational attainment, intellectual ability, health, character and
personal fitness and, where applicable, professional qualifications,
civil employment and war record. For professional, scientific and
technical classes of appointment, a degree or the appropriate
professional qualification was required. For other classes, the qualifications were more 'elastic'. A second-class honours degree was the
norm aimed for. Whatever the case, 'a high standard of general
intelligence' was expected.

Applicants were required to apply in writing to the director of
recruitment for an application form. Once their references had been
obtained, usually from their schoolteachers, headmasters, college
tutors and, especially after 1945, commanding officers, and their
records were considered to be sufficiently suitable, they were
required to attend for one or more personal and searching interviews
at the Colonial Office. Prospective candidates were warned — in
bold type — that the Secretary of State would not be prepared to give
reasons for his decision on any application, and that 'attempts to
influence the selection through Members of Parliament or other
persons who are not personally well acquainted with the candidate
are useless'. Indeed, such a move would be interpreted by the
Colonial Office as 'indicating that the candidate does not consider his
qualifications sufficiently good to justify his appointment on his own
merits'. Every candidate who got through the preliminary interviews
was required to pass a medical examination by one of the consulting
physicians to the Colonial Office. It is in this well-practised recruitment process that the Colonial Office resorted to the term
'submission' to describe the final documentation that went up to the
Secretary of State. A submission was a well-defined document, made

up of three parts: the top sheet, setting out a summary of the factual particulars of the candidate's career; a second sheet, quoting pertinent extracts from the reports received on the candidate and from minutes of the personal interviews held at the Colonial Office; and a third sheet, summarizing the appointments staff's estimate of the candidate. The complete submission would carry on its top sheet the title of the post in question and its initial salary, followed by the staff officer's entry 'I submit Mr X' and concluding '? appoint'.

For certain classes of appointment there would be a final interview before the Colonial Service Appointments Board. Tales of the Colonial Office interviews have become part of Colonial Service anecdotal lore and are still amusingly added to in latterday memoirs. Those who passed this were sent a formal offer of appointment in a letter from the Secretary of State setting out the terms and conditions of service attached to the post to which they were nominated. Applicants for the larger services, especially the Administrative Service, were permitted to name the three territories in which they would most like to serve, qualified by the caution that in no circumstances could their choice be guaranteed. To fit in with the academic year in the UK, most vacancies were filled in July and August, calling for initial applications to be made in the first six months of the year. Since candidates had to be 21 before they could take up an overseas appointment in the Colonial Service, they were advised not to submit an application before their twentieth birthday. In the 1930s, the names of successful candidates and their schools were sometimes published in *The Times*. No announcement was ever made of the number of vacancies available, and the Colonial Office's recruitment staff was proud of its reputation that it would rather leave a vacancy unfilled than appoint a misfit or a dud.

While professional qualifications lent themselves to ready assessment, it was in the selection of candidates for the Administrative Service that the less tangible qualifications of 'character and personal fitness' were at a premium. The Warren Fisher Committee of 1930 had laid down its desiderata in the *beau idéal* administrative cadet: 'Vision, high ideals of service, fearless devotion to duty born of a sense of responsibility, tolerance and, above all, team spirit'. The legendary Sir Ralph Furse, whose influence was far-reaching and unequalled, used to talk of his 'hunches', and it was often said that for him the ideal candidate was a house prefect who had also been captain of the school XI.

Another way of identifying 'the right type' is to consider, from a Colonial Office confidential memorandum on appointments, the attributes that the new Colonial Service officer must *not* display. 'He must above all not be infected with racial snobbery. Colour prejudice in the colonial civil servant is the one unforgivable sin.' An internal 1948 handbook went on to talk about the old school of the colonial administrator 'who liked the primitive people but could not get on with the educated native'. The time for that kind of attitude had gone for ever. 'The European whose prejudices will not allow him to accept the educated classes of colonial communities as social equals as opposite numbers in negotiation, and even as official superiors may be an admirable person but he should seek another vocation.'

While the philosophy of emphasis on personality and character subjectively evaluated by references and interview might find it hard to justify itself in the eyes of the c.v.-driven and professional personnel staff of the second half of this century, for the most part the individualistic Fursian system did deliver the goods. In retrospect, more and more former officers have been prepared to argue that no other method, and no one but Furse, could have produced such pre-eminently successful results. It was not only colonial governors but — far harder to please — Service seniors and peers who expressed continuing satisfaction with the calibre of the new entry.

If that, in outline, was the way the Colonial Service was recruited on entry, with its emphasis on 'character' rather than examinations, the procedure was no more cut and dried when it came to appointments to its top, final level. During the interwar years there were some 40 colonial governorships to be filled, normally for a five-year term and rarely beyond the age of 55. Yet, though a governorship constituted the peak of a Colonial Service career, the appointment was not always made from within the ranks of that Service. Three, the 'fortress' colonies of Gibraltar, Malta and Bermuda, were reserved for appointment from the armed forces. Given the huge variation in the size of territory, say between Tanganyika (363,000 square miles) and St Helena (81 square miles), in population (Nigeria with 22 million in 1947 and Fiji with 260,000), or in their primary strategic (Bermuda, Gibraltar, Malta, Cyprus, Aden) and economic (Malaya, Hong Kong, Gold Coast) importance, obviously not all governorships could be considered equal in status and salary.

The Colonial Office took to categorizing its colonial governorship into four grades (see Table 5.1), with the possibility of the grade

Table 5.1 Classification of Colonial Governorships, 1939

Dependency	Title of Post	Class
Aden	Governor and Commander-in-Chief	III
Bahamas	Governor and Commander-in-Chief	III
Barbados	Governor and Commander-in-Chief	III
British Guiana	Governor and Commander-in-Chief	II
British Honduras	Governor and Commander-in-Chief	III
Ceylon	Governor and Commander-in-Chief	I
Cyprus	Governor and Commander-in-Chief	II
Falkland Islands	Governor and Commander-in-Chief	IV
Fiji	Governor and Commander-in-Chief	II
Gambia	Governor and Commander-in-Chief	III
Gold Coast	Governor and Commander-in-Chief	I
Hong Kong	Governor and Commander-in-Chief	I
Jamaica	Captain-General and Governor-in-Chief	I
Kenya	Governor and Commander-in-Chief	I
Leeward Islands	Governor and Commander-in-Chief	IV
Mauritius	Governor and Commander-in-Chief	II
Nigeria	Governor and Commander-in-Chief	I
Northern Rhodesia	Governor and Commander-in-Chief	II
Nyasaland	Governor and Commander-in-Chief	III
Palestine	High Commissioner and Commander-in-Chief	I
St Helena	Governor and Commander-in-Chief	IV
Seychelles	Governor and Commander-in-Chief	IV
Sierra Leone	Governor and Commander-in-Chief	II
Somaliland	Governor and Commander-in-Chief	III
Straits Settlements	Governor and Commander-in-Chief	I
Tanganyika Territory	Governor and Commander-in-Chief	I
Trinidad and Tobago	Governor and Commander-in-Chief	I
Uganda	Governor and Commander-in-Chief	II
Windward Islands	Governor and Commander-in-Chief	IV
Zanzibar	British Resident	(IV)

Note: The governorships of the 'fortress colonies' of Bermuda, Gibraltar and Malta were at that time reserved for members of the armed forces. In the High Commission Territories of Basutoland, Bechuanaland and Swaziland, the title of the post was Resident Commissioner. For pension purposes, the British Resident of Zanzibar did not rank as a governor.

Source: C. Jeffries, *The Colonial Empire and its Civil Service*, 1938.

being altered in the light of constitutional change, as happened for example in the 1950s with Nyasaland and the three regional governorships of Nigeria. While the nineteenth-century practice of appointing politicians and military officers to colonial governorships beyond the reserved 'fortress colonies' continued to an extent into the middle of the twentieth century (for instance, Northey, Grigg, Byrne and Air Chief Marshall Brooke-Popham, all to Kenya between 1919 and 1937, along with the 'Emergency' appointments of General Templer to Malaya in 1953 and Field-Marshal Harding to Cyprus in 1955), by then the majority of governors were drawn from within the ranks of the Colonial Service.

The entry of the experienced professional administrator onto the colonial governorship scene in the 1860s had by the 1930s become the norm. From time to time a Colonial Office official was appointed to a colonial governorship, for example Sir John Anderson to the Straits Settlements in 1904, Sir Gerald Creasy to the Gold Coast in 1948 and Sir Andrew Cohen to Uganda in 1952. The political appointment, never completely out of the scene, staged a spectacular re-entry as the final governor or governor-general of a territory before or at its independence, for example Viscount Soulbury in Ceylon, the Earl of Listowel in Ghana, Malcolm Macdonald in Kenya and Chris Patten in Hong Kong. Table 5.2 offers a composite profile of the provenance of colonial governors appointed between 1919 and 1960.

Leaving on one side individual political and military appointments, gubernatorial promotions from within the Colonial Service were handled by the compilation of two lists in the Colonial Office. List 'A' was made up of names of officers under 55 to be considered for promotion to a governorship when a vacancy occurred. Serving governors eligible for promotion to a senior governorship also appeared on this list. List 'B' performed a similar function for younger officers, usually high-flyers, thought suitable for appointment to a colonial (Colony) or chief (Protectorate) secretaryship, normally the testing ground for those who might make List 'A'. Six months before a vacancy occurred in either category, a small Colonial Office committee would draw up a short list from the relevant list 'A' or 'B', supported by comments on competing claims made by the personnel department and, where necessary, an explanation of why other names had been omitted. It was the permanent under secretary in the Colonial Office who made the final recommendation to the Secretary of State. Sometimes the latter had strong views of his own. Sometimes, too, the prime minister had a personal

Table 5.2   Profile of Career Antecedents of Colonial Governors, 1919–60

	Total appointed 1919–39	Total appointed 1940–60
1. Full-time career in Colonial Service (or associated work) excluding war service:		
(a) as eastern cadet, MCS, or Ceylon	16	20
(b) in tropical Africa	20	49
(c) in other colonies	15	6
(d) as aide-de-camp or private secretary	3	3
2. Began in other careers. Appointed to Colonial Service below rank of governor:		
(a) formerly army	22	4
(b) formerly home civil (CO)	3	1
(c) formerly Home Civil Service, other departments	3	2
(d) formerly Egypt, Sudan, or ICS	4	1
(e) legal profession	–	5
(f) all other	5	4
Appointed directly to governorship		
(a) from politics	5	2
(b) from army	6	3
(c) from Home Civil Service	1	3
(d) from diplomatic service	–	1
(e) all other	–	6
Total	103	110

Source: Based on A. H. M. Kirk-Greene, 'On Governorships and Governors', in L. H. Gann and P. Duignan, *African Proconsuls*, 1978, in turn derived from J. M. Lee, *Colonial Development and Good Government*, 1967, and K. E. Robinson, *The Dilemmas of Trusteeship*, 1965.

interest in the filling of the vacancy. Finally, of course, the sovereign's approval had to be obtained.

How extensively colonial governors could move around the empire is documented in Table 5.3. The governorships of what became

Table 5.3 Migration Among African Colonial Governors, 1900–65

Transferred from	Appointed to
Aden, 2	Tanganyika, Uganda
Barbados, 2	Northern Rhodesia, Tanganyika
Basutoland, 2	Nyasaland, Uganda
British Guiana, 2	Kenya, Nigeria
British Honduras, 2	Gold Coast, Nyasaland
Ceylon, 2	Gold Coast, Uganda
Cyprus, 2	Northern Rhodesia, Nyasaland
Dominica, 1	Uganda
Falkland Islands, 2	Gambia, Sierra Leone
Fiji, 1	Kenya
Gambia, 6	Barbados, British Guiana, British Honduras, Gambia (2), Fiji
Gold Coast, 12	British Guiana, Hong Kong, Jamaica, Malaya, Malta, Nigeria, Northern Rhodesia, Nyasaland, Sierra Leone (2), Tanganyika
Hong Kong, 2	Gambia, Nigeria
Jamaica, 1	Nigeria
Kenya, 17	Ceylon, Gambia (3), N. Rhodesia, Nyasaland, Sierra Leone (2), Somaliland (2), Tanganyika, Uganda (3), Windward Islands, Zanzibar (2)
Malaya, 4	Gold Coast, Kenya, S. Nigeria, Sierra Leone
Malta, 1	Sierra Leone
Mauritius, 1	Northern Rhodesia
Nigeria, 6	Ceylon (2), N. Rhodesia (2), Nyasaland, Tanganyika
Northern Nigeria, 6	Gambia, Hong Kong, Kenya, Leeward Islands, Northern Nigeria, Uganda
S. Nigeria, 5	British Guiana, Gold Coast, Southern Nigeria, Sierra Leone
Western Nigeria, 2	Zanzibar
Eastern Nigeria, 2	Bahamas, Eastern Nigeria
North Borneo, 3	Gambia, Sierra Leone, Tanganyika
N. Rhodesia, 6	Ceylon, N. Rhodesia, Sierra Leone, Somaliland, Trinidad, Uganda
Nyasaland, 7	Gold Coast, Jamaica, Mauritius, N. Rhodesia, Nyasaland (2), Zanzibar
Palestine, 2	Tanganyika, Zanzibar
St Helena, 2	Gambia, Zanzibar
St Lucia, 2	Gambia, Sierra Leone
Sarawak, 1	Gold Coast
Seychelles, 1	Sierra Leone
Sierra Leone, 11	Barbados, Cyprus, Gambia (2), Gold Coast (2), Kenya (2), Leeward Islands (2), Malta
Somaliland, 13	British Honduras, Nyasaland, St Helena, Somaliland (6), Tanganyika, Uganda (2), Zanzibar
Sudan, 3	Nigeria, Northern Nigeria, Tanganyika
Tanganyika, 11	Aden, Hong Kong, Nigeria, Eastern Nigeria, Palestine, Somaliland, Sudan, Trinidad, Uganda, Zanzibar
Trinidad, 3	Gambia, Sierra Leone, Zanzibar
Uganda, 6	Fiji, Kenya (2), Nigeria, N. Nigeria, Sudan
West Indies, 1	
Zanzibar, 4	Aden, Western Nigeria, Trinidad, Zanzibar

Note: Column 1 allows for promotions to as well as transfers within governorships.
Source: A. H. M. Kirk-Greene, 'The Progress of Proconsuls', *Journal of Imperial and Commonwealth History*, VII, 2, 1979.

Britain's dependent territories after the FCO took over responsibility in 1968, properly lies outside the scope of this study. For the most part, once the penultimate and final governorships of the residual territories had been filled by former Colonial Service officers now members of HMOCS — for instance those of Fiji, the Seychelles, and the Gilbert and Ellice Islands — the latterday posts of governor (for example, Anguilla, the British Virgin Islands, and the Falkland Islands) and administrator (for example, Ascension and BAT) generally went to FCO staff or to non-career appointees.

With the closure of the Colonial Office in 1966, it will soon become possible to construct meaningful career profiles of the holders of these top posts in the dependent territories. There is a neat service satisfaction about the way in which a small group of officers who had left the Colonial Service or HMOCS in the 1950s and 1960s and were accepted into the diplomatic service still ended up in Government House. Among them were Sir Roger du Boulay in the New Hebrides, Sir Richard Posnett in Bermuda, Sir James Hennessy in British Honduras, and Sir Rex Hunt in the Falkland Islands. The appointment of Sir Richard Luce to Gibraltar in 1996 was of particular interest in latterday Colonial Service history. Not only had his father been a colonial governor (Aden, 1956–60), but he himself had momentarily been a district officer in Kenya (1960–2) before turning to a career in politics, which in the 1980s brought him the post of Minister of State in the FCO with responsibility for the dependent territories.

If these three principal lines of enquiry rounding off this outline history of the Colonial Service and its successor were largely matters of established procedure, the next represents something of a palpably transitory character. This is, following premature retirement from the Colonial Service or HMOCS occasioned by the imperatives of localization and the advent of independence, consideration of what kinds of employment former members of these Services obtained. While it is still too early for a complete analysis of 'second careers', particularly with the last but large wave (compared with the smaller ripples from the Pacific in the 1970s and 1980s) of ex-HMOCS officers returning from Hong Kong yet to be absorbed, it is nevertheless important to include some reference here to such a final chapter in the history of the surviving members of the Colonial Service and HMOCS.

The key step in their rehabilitation and re-entry into the British employment market was the establishment by the UK government of the Overseas Services Resettlement Bureau (OSRB), eventually located within the Overseas Development Administration of the Foreign and Commonwealth Office. The agency was opened in 1957 as the Malayan Services Re-Employment Bureau. Administered by a small group of former HMOCS officers, its primary function was to match up applicants with prospective employers, the bulk of whom were in commerce and industry. In putting them in touch with public and private sector recruitment agencies and career consultants, the OSRB also offered guidance on such matters as how to prepare what it called 'viable personal history formats' (today's ubiquitous and inescapable c.v.). It issued a series of *Guides* for returning HMOCS personnel and *Notes* on being interviewed and on training courses. The services offered were free, and there was no compulsion for retired officers to seek such employment only through the OSRB. Many found new jobs at their own initiative. As serving officers had always anticipated when they studied the various early retirement schemes discussed in the previous chapter, those in the higher age brackets proved the hardest to place.

By the end of its first five years of work (1957–62), the OSRB had successfully placed most of its applicants in four main fields of employment. Some 38 per cent had found employment in business, either in the UK or abroad, and 19 per cent went into education, again both at home and overseas. The largest proportion, 46 per cent, took up government and quasi-government work, 27 per cent of them in the UK and 19 per cent returning to overseas employment. In the same year (1962), the bureau still had nearly a thousand names on its books from all the principal branches of the Colonial Service (Table 5.4). Ten years later, with decolonization completed in central and southern Africa, administrative officers on permanent and pensionable terms had dried up as the largest group of job hunters and it was education officers who comprised the single largest category on the OSRB's books as HMOCS staff began to return to the UK on the expiry of their contracts. In 1970 there were still 2500 career staff (that is not on the contract terms offered to new entrant HMOCS officers) in service, half of them on the Hong Kong establishment. By 1976, however, with the exception of 1216 pensionable officers in Hong Kong, there were no more than 161 HMOCS staff serving in other territories and by 1995 none. The OSRB's success rate was high. Even in its third quinquennium, when contract officers from HMOCS had replaced career officers on

Table 5.4   Overseas Service Resettlement Bureau: Applications
Outstanding by Colonial Service Branch Categories, 1962

Accountants	37
Administrative officers	188
Administrative auxiliaries	132
Agriculture and Forestry	88
Customs	16
Education	62
Engineering (professional)	58
Engineering (technical)	135
Legal	12
Medical	22
Police or Prisons	168
Railways and Marine	55
Storekeepers	15
Surveyors	17

Source: OSRB records (unpublished).

permanent and pensionable terms as its chief clients, it was still
finding jobs for more than 400 former overseas officials each year
(Table 5.5). It is interesting to see how former Colonial Service and
HMOCS officers found themselves, as it were, 'recalled to the
colours' from time to time, sometimes on commissions of inquiry
such as those of Devlin (1959), Fairn (1959), Monckton (1961) and
Pearce (1972); sometimes as election monitors in, for instance,
Uganda and Angola; and, most notably and on a grand scale, for the
Zimbabwe general election of 1980, when more than 50 ex-district
officers found themselves back in the field as election supervisors.

While the matter of the 'second careers' of one-time Colonial
Service and HMOCS officers is a finite one, in that once the last
officer retires from his post-service occupation the issue shifts from
actuality to history, there are two further matters of relevance to this
account of the Colonial Service and its successors that cannot be
ignored. One may be called definitiveness, the other legacy.

Even though the Colonial Service came to an end in 1954 and its
successor HMOCS terminated in 1997, there is no possibility of
anything like the definitive history of either service being written for
a number of years to come. After all, the present volume is one of
only a handful of studies with 'Colonial Service' in their title to

Table 5.5   Overseas Service Resettlement Bureau: Re-employment
of HMOCS Officers, 1972–6

	1972	1973	1974	1975	1976
1. Commerce and industry	130	144	164	99	101
2. Government and quasi-government (except education)					
(a) In UK	94	70	67	64	31
(b) Overseas	126	130	120	124	109
3. Education (home and abroad)	54	225	62	64	88
4. Other	68	86	63	52	66
Totals	472	545	486	403	395

Source: OSRB records (unpublished).

appear in the twentieth century. Following the publication in quick
succession of Anton Bertram's *The Colonial Service* in 1930 and
Charles Jeffries's *The Colonial Empire and its Civil Service* in 1938,
there appeared in 1949, as part of the stimulated postwar
reawakening of interest in the Colonial Service as a career, Jeffries's
shorter second volume, *Partners for Progress*, subtitled *The Men and
Women of the Colonial Service*, along with Kenneth Bradley's official
recruiting call *The Colonial Service as a Career* (1950), revised in
1955 as *A Career in the Oversea Civil Service*. Both were prepared by
the Colonial Office and the Central Office of Information. Robert
Heussler's *Yesterday's Rulers*, with its subtitle of *The Making of the
British Colonial Service*, was the first — and last — full-length
academic study of recruitment to the Colonial Administrative Service
to be undertaken — all of 36 years ago. In other words, even when
there was a Colonial Service in being, there was not enough interest
in it by the British public to justify much literature about it. The
present volume owes the largest part of its inception to its
anniversary (or, more literally, memorial) nature, commissioned as it
has been to mark the end of the HMOCS and its forebear the
Colonial Service after 160 years of existence and the closure of the
service's own Corona Club in its hundredth year.

A principal reason why there cannot be a definitive history of the
colonial period, and hence of the work of the Colonial Service, lies in

the fact that not all the records and documentation are yet in the public domain. The Public Record Office (PRO) statutorily observes a 30-year rule (reduced from 50 years in 1967 and 100 years only in 1958) whereby researchers cannot have access to official files before 30 years beyond the relevant file date. Nor is there any undertaking that the records will be opened after 30 years: the closure regulation can be extended should the files involved be deemed to warrant it. Thus, for example, the official correspondence on the handover of Britain's last major colony, Hong Kong, will not under present regulations be open for consultation before the year 2027 — if then. Finally, as the PRO registers reveal, large numbers of files relating to Colonial Service matters have been destroyed under statute during the regular weeding out process of which files to keep and which to destroy. Files retained on the Colonial Service do not constitute a single major block. In any case, no personal files are ever open for consultation. Thus, the brakes on any definitive history of the Colonial Service based on public records are obvious and off-putting.

To an extent, this vacuum in the public record of the Colonial Service has been compensated by the considerable effort put into preserving the private papers, diaries and correspondence of colonial officials since the inception of the Colonial Records Project at Oxford University (1963–72) and its successor Oxford Development Records Project (1977–84). Together, they built up a unique colonial archive, now housed in Rhodes House Library. Related retrieval schemes, often concentrating on Colonial Service oral history, have helped to create important collections in the National Library of Scotland and at the new Empire Museum in Bristol. The late Hong Kong episode could well generate another round of Colonial Service archival collection.

The concept of definitiveness of a Colonial Service history, however, also encounters a geographical and actor limitation. The contemporary British documents on the end of empire project (BDEEP), with its admirable range of intimate documentation of the conduct of colonial affairs since 1925, remains just that — a detailed and richly documented record of the official papers of the British government but of no colonial government. The current flow of memoirs by former colonial civil servants makes its own eye-witness contribution, always provided the researcher is alert to the pitfalls as well as the rewards of autobiography as a source. The genre of gubernatorial and Secretary of State biography and autobiography provides another valuable historical source. Yet all of this can *ipso facto* illustrate no more than half the story of the Colonial Service, the British actors.

For the whole picture, we need documented studies by Asian, African, Caribbean and Pacific writers of how they saw, experienced and interpreted the Colonial Service with which they came in contact. For definitiveness we need, too, more memoirs by those local civil servants who, in that unique generation of the transfer of power, worked with two sets of masters, first under, then alongside and finally over Colonial Service officers. Again, we have much to learn from insights into the Colonial Service on the ground from the traditional and the nationalist leaders of Asia and Africa. Even more revealing, yet far less likely to come about, would be the recorded views of ordinary people in the colonies — subordinate government and native administration staff, peasants and petty traders, locals and immigrants — on how they perceived the Colonial Service, both on and off duty. The British character was, at least in the colonial period, one in which reserve in relations with others could often be mistaken for aloofness and determined detachment. Such a hesitation to display warmth probably explains what lay behind the anecdotal pan-colonial lament of 'Yes, you gave us law and order, you gave us schools, hospitals and roads ... but how often did you give us your hearts?' Only when we know what 'they' thought of 'us' and what *they* thought we were doing in relation to what *we* thought we were doing, can the definitive story of the Colonial Service be acceptably presented.

Such reservations over a definitive Colonial Service history lead into the second field of enquiry, that of the colonial legacy. What was the impact of the colonial period, above all — in the context of this study — in the achievement and attitudes of the frontline representatives of the colonial governments (the men and women of the Colonial Service), on what have since emerged as the new nations, predominantly in the Third World? This is a far more profound question than the prompt, off-the-cuff assessment of good or bad, of fair-to-middling, or a mixture of both. It will have to be the judgement of history; and that means not of mere decades, where we are today, or even of generations, but more likely of centuries. Today, and for years to come, the colonial period is far too near for any objective evaluation to be convincingly claimed. Yet it is perhaps a pointer to the shape of things to come that, after half a century of younger Britons often distancing themselves from the colonial period and decrying — or at least down-playing — the work of the Colonial Service, with untutored talk of unremitting 'oppression' and unrelieved 'guilt' from the severest critics of empire, the tide is beginning to turn. Scholars are willing once again to look at both sides of the debate.

In the context of the imperial legacy, Roman Britain may offer a valid comparison. The Romans left Britain 1500 years ago, after a 500-year occupation lasting approximately from 55 BC to AD 407. That is a period three times longer than the existence of the Colonial Service and nearly ten times the length of British rule in colonial Africa. Today, in the healing perspective of time, it is not the burden of Roman occupation that Britons remember but the positive, practical artefacts of the legacy: the towns and roads and public baths, the law and numerals, and, albeit often quite unconsciously, the vigorous and lasting carry-over of Latin on the shaping of standard English at virtually every turn of the language, whether it be literally Latin or Latin in root and structure. Maybe we shall have to wait till the British colonial period is as remote as the Roman Empire is from us today before any would-be final balance sheet of credit and debit can be drawn up and the legacy be evaluated, in the round and definitively.

While in the age of modern technology and design, coupled with the impact of tropical climates, the infrastructural survival of colonial architecture and roads is less likely to be a relic of the colonial contact than it has been for Britain in the Roman case, in the long-term future there is a fair chance that, besides the lasting gift of the worldwide English language (today the language of the web and of tertiary education, and of international air navigation, too), the legal and higher educational systems in the new states and maybe their civil service structure may carry recognizable evidence of the British colonial era. So far, it has been the Indian empire rather than the generality of colonial empire that reflects what an Indian scholar, brought up under the Raj and today looking back on half a century of independence, has called 'the unintended consequences' of colonial rule — if not democracy itself, then the essential conditions for democracy, namely the law and the courts, a non-political army, a professional civil service and a free press.

Many observers of the colonial scene also single out with particular emphasis the contribution of the Colonial Service to training local cadres to succeed it and to manage the administration of the

new independent governments. However retarded the implemen-
tation of that policy, it may prove to have been their final and their
finest contribution to new nationhood. This, according to Sir Hugh
Foot (later Lord Caradon), constituted the principal objective of the
modern Colonial Service. 'We of the Colonial Service,' he declared as
he looked back on his own career, 'were engaged in creating and
working many different institutions — parliaments, municipalities,
rural councils, courts, schools and universities, hospitals, agricultural
stations and the whole range of departmental services — but none of
our tasks was more important than that of building up civil services
capable of taking the strain when independence came and making
the institutions of government work.'

Some colonies had a better (in the sense of longer) record of this
initiative than did the African ones. In Malaya, the subaltern Malayan
Administrative Service (MAS), created as far back as 1910, was to
provide a valuable reservoir of trained talent when the time came for
the Malayanization of the Malayan Civil Service (MCS), and the
localization of the Hong Kong Civil Service was well in train 30 years
before independence. On the other hand, in the Gold Coast it was
only in 1942 — 15 years before independence — that the first two
Africans were appointed as assistant district commissioners. In
Northern Nigeria, only 30 per cent of the provincial administration
posts were held by Northerners on the eve of independence. In
Nyasaland, the first such local appointments occurred only four years
before independence and there was none to the super-scale class
until six years after independence. Now and again, the foot dragging
was that of the traditional, legislative or political leadership, and not
solely that of the colonial administration.

Yet, in retrospect, there is much to be said for pointing to the
slow and sometimes unimaginative pace of the localization of the
bureaucracy as an opportunity missed or mishandled. The British did
more than the French, and both went far further than the Belgians, in
preparing and training local cadres to succeed them. Nevertheless, if
there is a single area in which the colonial administrations were
culpably slow (Malaya apart, with its special junior MAS cadre), it
was in the tardiness of initiatives for localization and subordinate
cadres. Only in the final decade was colonial Africa characterized by
priority programmes for the localization of the civil services, often in
new institutes of public administration (that at Zaria in Northern
Nigeria was the pioneer) staffed by specially selected Colonial Service

officers with a remit to train the new cadres of the provincial administration. Nothing could be calculated to give the Colonial Service
more pleasure and more pride than to have made its mark in such a
crucial way as training its successors to take over from it.

Impact is, however, a two-way affair. Besides those who inherit a
legacy, there have to be those who bequeath it. Whatever the
ultimate judgement on the work of the Colonial Service and of
HMOCS, whether within generations or in centuries to come, there
can be no doubt of the impact of that work on those who performed
it. Whatever the original motivation that prompted well-educated
men and women to join the Colonial Service, the final reflection was
nearly always a sense of satisfaction at a job worthwhile and well
done. Few if any of them shared the reaction of St Augustine and his
missionary monks in their protest to Pope Gregory at being
dispatched to Britain in AD 597, pleading that they were 'appalled at
the idea of going to a barbarous, fierce and pagan nation of whose
very language they were ignorant'. Ask anyone who chose a career in
the Colonial Service about his or her time there, and in nine cases
out of ten the answer is likely to incorporate the overriding
sentiment of 'the best years of my life'. There is, too, nearly always
expressed the follow-up semi-nostalgic reflection: here was a
worthwhile, sought-after and respected Crown service career which
can no longer be offered to or experienced by their children or
grandchildren. Lord Lloyd had not been wrong when, as Secretary of
State for the Colonies, he had told the last batch of Colonial Service
cadets recruited before the Second World War, 'When all is said and
done, you are going out to a grand life.'

While critics of empire may seem to be somewhat out of place in
a history commissioned to mark the end of the Colonial Service and
its 'offspring' (as the Colonial Office fashionably styled it in the
period of transition), the HMOCS, it would be dishonest and
unscholarly to pretend that they did not exist. Two groups will be
noted here — Britain's post-colonial critics of imperialism and those
whose voices came from within the Colonial Service.

In generational terms, the post-end-of-empire 1960s and 1970s
engendered a wave of rejection of empire and of — to have recourse
to a seafaring analogy — 'all those who served in her'. It revealed a
display of instant dislike unknown to those Britons belonging to
prewar generations and its accusations were unrecognized by those
who had actually participated in empire. A generation on, it is now

possible not only to discuss the work and ethos of the Colonial Service in an objective way, but also to find historians of the mid-1990s reversing the condemnatory *a priori* judgements of their immediate predecessors. One can actually sense a turnaround in historical interpretation. 'After half a century in the doghouse,' notes one imperial historian in his comment on the phenomenon of a positive about-turn, 'the Empire's reappraisal is palpably beginning to turn away from the doctrinaire anti-colonialism of Marxist revisionism towards a more balanced reassessment of not only what the men and women of Empire did and why they did it, but also, in the light of the headlined chaos and collapse of so many former colonial possessions, of how they did it.'

It is a matter of fact, not of coincidence, that major studies of the colonial record from James Morris's *Farewell the Trumpets*, 1978, published in the run-up to 100 years after the imperial extravaganza of Queen Victoria's diamond jubilee and on the eve of the handover of Britain's last major colony (Lawrence James's, *The Rise and Fall of the British Empire*, 1994; Trevor Royle's, *Winds of Change: The End of Empire in Africa*, 1996; Robin Neillands's, *A Fighting Retreat: The British Empire, 1947–1997*, 1996; and John Keay's, *Last Post: The End of Empire in the Far East*, 1997), emphasize the same message: it is time to stop automatically rubbishing the achievements of colonial rule and disparaging its executive Colonial Service. Instead, the time has come to 'stop apologizing for the British Empire' (James) and to highlight the positive features of the imperial record. Keay points to a continuum of economic growth and goes so far as to argue that, in the Far East, 'Empire may take some credit for the "Asian miracle".' Concluding that British administration was generally 'decent and fair', Trevor Royle notes of the Colonial Service how 'those ideals inspired the many men and women who enriched their own lives and the lives of the people they served'.

In the mid-1990s, in contrast with the 1960s, the commanding heights of morality are no longer occupied by the anti-colonial critics. A combination of the healing properties of time and the sorry decline of a number of one-time colonial territories (conspicuously in Africa) into the political scientists' new, sad category of 'collapsed states', has brought a sobering rethink and a recognition of the credit as well as the debit side of colonial administration. Today's interpreters of empire, still rigorously devoid of the slightest wish to see a return to empire (other than through self-indulgent nostalgic reconstruction in film or fiction), are prepared to accept the implications of the unacceptable paucity of Colonial Service personnel (and, of course, of funds) on the ground and to recognize the accuracy of its description as 'the thin white line'. Few students of the modern state in the Third World can fail to grasp the significance of the curbs imposed by the fact that, for example in 1913 the government of the major colony of Malaya had only 129 administrative officers, 68 medical officers, 64 officers in public works and 14 in education on its establishment, or that in 1926 Britain's premier possession in Africa, Nigeria, comprising 373,000 square miles and 20 million inhabitants, had a Colonial Service staff of only 2200 officials (see Table 5.6).

Table 5.6   Distribution of Colonial Service Posts in Nigeria, 1925

Agriculture	39	Mines	7
Audit	17	Nigeria Regiment	233
Colliery	27	Police	61
Customs	28	Political Administration	368
Education	101	Post and Telegraph	76
Forestry	40	Printing	6
Geological survey	9	Prisons	18
Governor's office	3	Public works	252
Judicial and magistracy	9	Railway	462
Lands	3	Secretariat	47
Legal	6	Survey	38
Lieutenant Governor's office	2	Treasury	25
Marine	132	Veterinary	17
Medical and sanitary	204		

Source: *The Nigerian Handbook*, 1926.

In the context of the focus of this book, it is a second level of criticism of empire that is the more interesting. This is the instances of lack of sympathy towards colonial rule coming not in the post-colonial period, like the cases above, but during the interwar colonial years and, most interestingly of all, occasionally from within the Colonial Service. The principal criticism within Britain, expressed above all by the Fabian Colonial Bureau to whose socialist ideals a number of Colonial Service officers subscribed, was that of the class-based exclusivity of Colonial Service recruitment. This was especially so in the case of the Administrative Service, with its dominant interwar preference for the public schools and for Oxford and Cambridge. It was a line of attack which, 50 years on, the Fabian Society was to follow up in its criticism of Britain's recruitment into the officer corps of the armed forces in 1997.

Hand in hand with this attack on the social background and upbringing of many of the administrators, went accusations of aloofness, authoritarianism and paternalism in their relations with the local people. The bureau's pamphlet *Downing Street and the Colonies* (1942) called for a positive redesigning of the sources and system of postwar recruitment to the Colonial Service. A parallel attack came from an influential professor at the London School of Economics, H. J. Laski. In a stinging assault on 'The Colonial Civil Service', which appeared in the *Political Quarterly* in 1938, he dismissed the fashionable nobility of 'trusteeship' as 'too flattering to the results obtained' and declared that the result had been the degeneration of the colonies into 'the slums of empire'. Like the Fabian Colonial Bureau, he concentrated his criticism on the administrative branch of the Colonial Service: it was drawn from too narrow a source, it preferred the 'sound' man to the imaginative innovator, it was running the empire on the cheap, and it did not welcome criticism. In endorsing Professor W. Macmillan's contemporaneous belief that the Colonial Service was now, as he put it, like the ICS, 'acquiring an equally high reputation for intellectual ability, integrity and devotion to duty', Laski added his own qualifying conclusion that it was also acquiring the same characteristic defects of complacency, lack of imagination, and absence of sympathy for the local educated classes. 'Taking the service as a whole,' he lukewarmly concluded, 'it is probably fair-minded and moderate. ... The best that can be said is that many officials do, as individuals, devoted and zealous work despite the insuperable difficulties under which they labour.' But they were up against too many handicaps and restrictions. Above all, for Laski, they could never rise above their status as 'servants of a purpose which denies the hope that trusteeship may be fulfilled even while it proclaims its devotion to it'.

There was, too, a decade later, Field-Marshal Montgomery's disdain for the calibre of the Colonial Service at the end of his tour to the African colonies in 1947, as he wondered whether the 'burnt-out' colonial governors who had spent 20 to 25 years in Africa could cope with his own 'grand design' for colonial development. 'As regards

brains,' he bluntly opined, 'there is a marked lack of men of real
ability in our African colonies.' What was required, he declared, was
'men of vision, who will think big, who will take risks, and who are
good judges of men'. From the Colonial Office, Creech Jones had no
hesitation in minuting to the Cabinet, 'I emphatically disagree with
[his] assessment of the Colonial Service.'

No less interesting are the criticisms of the Colonial Service from
within itself. Here rejection derived not from prior antipathy or
ideology — for such, the Colonial Service was unlikely to have been
a voluntarily chosen career — but from personal experience which,
on occasion, expanded into a wider anti-colonialism. It may well be
that some of these were square pegs in round holes. That would, of
course, test the fallibility of the recruitment process, whose exacting
thoroughness in weeding out misfits and general success in selection
have already been commented on. It may also be that some of the
square pegs soon found the hole rounder than they had imagined
and felt they were unable to fit in. Besides the 'rebels', there were
other junior officers (among them at least two postwar cadets whose
fathers had been colonial governors) who soon tendered their
resignation — with less panache — because they realized they simply
did not like the job or felt that it was not turning out to be what they
expected. Others left because the Service, which set store by an
annual confidential report that *inter alia* included the critical
question of whether an officer appeared 'temperamentally fit' for the
job, itself came to the conclusion that they were not up to it. A few,
too, were dismissed.

The instances of personal disenchantment cited below attracted
attention in and to the Colonial Service because each of the junior
officers (only one of them had been confirmed in his appointment)
went on in his subsequent career to achieve a linked combination of
celebrity and a high literary profile, thereby bringing publicity to his
disappointment with his chosen career in the Colonial Service. Space
is given here to the isolated malcontents rather than the countless
contents on grounds of the intellectual credibility of this study.
Because their dissatisfaction was so publicized (because, in turn, they
became public figures), to imply that there was no unfavourable
comment — a feature common to every institution or organization
one can think of — on the Colonial Service as a career in what has
been conceived here as an authoritative history of the Colonial
Service could be to run the risk of this study being viewed as nothing

more substantial than a celebratory in-house publicity product, glossy and glossing over.

Leonard Barnes, whose condemnatory *Skeleton of Empire* appeared in 1937, was the stormy petrel of the Colonial Office. He called for the League of Nations to assume greater responsibility for Britain's colonial empire, to include mandated peoples on its commission, and to open the Colonial Service to non-British citizens. The 1930s, too, were to witness one of the most scathing and far-reaching insider attacks of all. It came from the pen of a colonial policeman, an old Etonian, Eric Blair. He wrote of his disgust at what he saw as the hypocrisy and pettiness of the British community in an upcountry town of Burma. Better known as George Orwell, his condemnation took the form of a powerful novel, *Burmese Days* (1934).

Within the Colonial Service proper, three one-time high-flying members each resigned early and published critical testimony on the service, its morality and its morale, as they moved on *en route* to making their name in other professions. Leonard Woolf served as an assistant government agent in the Ceylon civil service from 1904 until his resignation in 1911. In addition to his several short stories (1921) about his life as a junior colonial administrator and the second volume of his autobiography, *Growing*, which covered his years in the Colonial Service, three of his required official diaries for the years 1908–11, when he was assistant government agent in Hambantota district, were published by the Ceylon Historical Society in 1962. Personal testimony is thus abundant. However, while in the self-conscious autobiography, written 50 years later, Woolf claims (despite having chosen to sit for the Eastern civil service examination in 1904) that his decision to resign was conditioned by the fact that 'I had been born in an age of imperialism and I disapproved of imperialism and felt sure that its days were already numbered,' behind — or at least alongside — this possibly retrospective argument of 'I had come to dislike imperialism' was the pressing private affair of his wish to marry Virginia Stephen. Arguing that 'if Virginia would not marry me, I did not want to return to Ceylon and become a successful civil servant in Colombo and end eventually with a governorship and KCMG,' he nevertheless conceded that he would — like many young men in their romantic first years in the Colonial Service — be quite prepared to go back to Ceylon as the government agent of Hambantota district 'for the remainder of my life . . . a final withdrawal, a final solitude, in which, married to a Sinhalese, I would make my district the most efficient, the most prosperous place in Asia'. There are other references in his autobiography to his dissatisfaction, his initial 'feeling of irritation and contempt for the people of Ceylon ... exasperating and distasteful ... annoyance and distrust', his growing 'doubts whether I wanted to rule other people, to be an imperialist and proconsul', and his local unpopularity in Jaffra for being 'too ruthless, too much the "strong man" and displaying the stern Sahib to compensate for or soothe a kind of social conscience which began to condemn and dislike the whole system'. Leonard Woolf went on to become a leading light in the Bloomsbury set and Fabian circles, and was joint editor of the *Political Quarterly*, which published Laski's article cited above.

Before moving on to other critics of colonial rule from the inside, one observation of Leonard Woolf's has a resonance for the critics of empire 60 years on. The politically correct post-colonial generations, in their wonderment at how thousands of well-educated and intelligent graduates — rarely after 1914–18 motivated by any flag-wagging sense of unchallenged 'dominion over palm and pine' — could enthusiastically look to participation in colonial rule as an acceptable, honourable and nationally respected career choice, fail to grasp one significant attitudinal difference between the 'then' and the 'now'. Let the anti-imperialist Woolf answer them himself. 'I had entered Ceylon as an imperialist, one of the white rulers of our Asiatic Empire', he notes. 'The curious thing is that I was not really aware of this.' To this commonplace acceptance he goes on to add: 'The horrible urgency of politics after the 1914 war, which forced every intelligent person to be passionately interested in them, was unknown to my generation at Cambridge. ... *We were not deeply concerned with politics*' (emphasis added).

The second spectacular case of the serving Colonial Service officer as critic took place 25 years later, in Northern Nigeria. Walter Crocker was one of the first Australians to join the Colonial Service, in 1930. He resigned at the end of two rather unhappy tours. His severe disenchantment with the faults of the colonial government, summed up at the end of his first 12 months as 'lack of planning and a hand-to-mouth system of administration', was bluntly set out in his part-diary, part-tract, *Nigeria: A Critique of British Colonial Administration* (1936). Crocker was particularly critical of the senior officers, many of them displaying 'a thread of inferior quality running through the Service'. He found them, particularly among the immediate post-1918 entry, helping to intensify 'that drift towards literalism and clerkliness which all along has been the defect of the Service'. A whole chapter was given over to what he called 'Demoralizing a Service', in which the senior officers were blamed for the poor *esprit de corps* brought about by the system of confidential reports and by victimization over promotions: 'what matters most is not to let a colleague make a better impression than you.' His principal target was the evil of what he called 'careerism'. His views on the deficiencies among his Colonial Service seniors had not softened by the time he came to write his autobiography, *Travelling Back*, 50 years after his first tour. His main target was still careerism and sycophancy. Surveying his seniors in Nigeria, he concluded that 'The loss of the British Empire was due to a variety of reasons, but one was the inadequate behaviour of specific individuals. One official of bad manners or bad judgement or bad standards could undo the work of a dozen good officials.' Sir Walter Crocker, who went on to have a distinguished career in the Australian diplomatic service and in the Australian National University, ended up as Lieutenant-Governor of South Australia.

The third case of public rejection of the Colonial Service from within comes from the divided and internally divisive Palestine mandate. Thomas Hodgkin, having turned down an appointment in the Gold Coast service in 1932, was offered a cadetship in the Palestine administration in 1934. He described his appointment as 'the job I always most wanted'. Yet, within two years he had resigned, filled with bitterness and repudiation of that very job he had so prized. His reasons were a mixture of, on the one hand, the rising community tension between resident Arabs and immigrant Jews, and on the other — in common with other young intellectuals of the time — an inclination to the political left in protest against the rise of the Fascist right in Europe.

Yet his early letters home reflect an idiom recognized and used by most first-tour colonial civil servants, of a modest, interventionist wish 'to alter things a bit' and do some good: 'it is not the glamour of the East particularly that makes me want this job, but the glamour of trying to put beliefs into practice.' A narcoleptic, and cynical where the pomp and circumstance of colonial rule was concerned, Hodgkin was a curious choice for private secretary to the governor, but, in the few months before his resignation, General Wauchope and he struck up a strong if unexpected bond of mutual respect and affection. Liberal rather than a socialist at Oxford, this unusual colonial civil servant now declared himself to be a communist. As he expressed it in a letter to the Chief Secretary over his intended resignation, his 'political opinions' must have seemed controversial, and from his personal correspondence with the governor it is clear that he resented working for a capitalist system. It is interesting, in the context of the preceding paragraphs, that in later life Hodgkin declared that it was the writings of Leonard Barnes, notably his *The Future of Colonies*, published — equally significantly — by Leonard and Virginia Woolf's Hogarth Press in 1936, that led him to 'detest imperialism'. His outstanding characteristic was said by his brother to have been an incurable romanticism: 'he saw people as he thought they ought to be rather than they really were, and so judged them in superlatives.' What Hodgkin missed in the Colonial Service was 'real friends with whom to talk things over', to offset the long hours of loneliness and maybe introspective brooding. That was exactly the sort of potential chink in the emotional make-up of applicants that Furse and his colleagues were on the look out for when selecting young men for the Colonial Service.

If there is a common denominator in explaining why the Colonial Service, like any other institution, be it governmental, corporate or academic, had its share of early resignations (resignation from the top, especially by established colonial governors, was a different matter), it might well be the absence — for whatever reason — of a readiness to conform, the prerequisite of the colonial civil servant as well as of members of virtually every service or formal organization. To require conformity is not the same thing as to demand uniformity. Within the parameters of a basic readiness to conform, the Colonial Service was, as every officer was quick to recognize, a broad enough church to accommodate an array of eccentrics and individualists who would have done credit to any proverbial senior common room.

Today, there are some 20,000 former Colonial Service and HMOCS officers still alive. Each year the Colonial Service is still mentioned in the preacher's prayer, on the authority of the Dean, at the lunch-time service in Westminster Abbey. In 1997, more than 50 territorial associations and groups continued in existence, keeping their members in touch by newsletters and annual reunions. Instrumental in maintaining links with and among former members of the Colonial Service and HMOCS is the Overseas Service Pensioners'

5.7 Overseas Service Pensioners' Association Membership by Territorial Affiliation, 1994

	Number		Number
Aden	107	Malaya	760
Bahamas	23	Malta	4
Barbados	22	Mauritius	64
Bermuda	20	Nigeria	1190
British Guiana	73	North Borneo	97
British Honduras	36	Northern Rhodesia	1000
Central African Federation	117	Nyasaland	485
Ceylon	70	Palestine	182
Cyprus	88	St Helena	10
East Africa	166	Sarawak	116
East African High Commission	86	Seychelles	36
East African Railways	98	Sierra Leone	187
Falklands	16	Somaliland	79
Fiji	142	Southern Rhodesia	374
Gambia	90	Tanganyika	1353
Gibraltar	18	Trinidad	74
Gold Coast	477	Uganda	907
High Commission Territories	248	West Africa	43
Hong Kong	765	West Indies	52
Jamaica	50	West Pacific	118
Kenya	1834	Windward Islands	15
Leeward Islands	16	Zanzibar	98
Total:	9437	(many have services in more than one territory)	

Source: OSPA Records.

Association (OSPA), formed in 1960 from the amalgamation of the Ceylonese, Malayan, West African and East African pensioners' associations. It had more than 9000 members on its books in 1994. Their territorial affiliation is presented in Table 5.7. Unique among these associations is the Corona Club, the social club open to all members of the Colonial Service, HMOCS, the Colonial Office and Crown Agents for the Colonies, and with nearly 1000 active members still on its books when it closed in 1999, its one hundreth year. Yet, by definition, these 'old boys' associations will reduce in numbers and soon pass the usefulness of their keeping-in-touch (not nostalgic) function. It may be that when this last generation of ex-colonial civil servants face the increasingly heard question, 'Grand-father, what did you do in the Colonial Service?', one of the most helpful and telling answers will not lie in pointing the enquirer to the imperial archives in the Public Record Office, Kew, or in the Rhodes House Library, Oxford, but to guide the questioner towards those novels in which the Colonial Service and its work are so centrally depicted (see Bibliography). Fiction has the capacity to offer illus-trative insights into facts which facts alone cannot provide.

To find an epitaph for the Colonial and HMOCS may well call for an amalgam. The plaque in Westminster Abbey, unveiled by Her Majesty the Queen in 1953, is one attempt, with its humbling reminder of the meaning of service: 'Whosoever will be chief among you let him be your servant.' There is, too, Lord Lugard's modest aim engraved on his tombstone at Abinger Hammer: 'All I did was to try and lay my bricks straight.' Then there is the belief of Margery Perham, leading academic authority on colonial administration and personally known to hundreds of Colonial Service officers, that the generic district commissioner could be said to manifest 'one of the supreme types of the [British] nation ... indefatigable, versatile and humane'. Beside this may be set the evaluation of another able historian of the Colonial Service — an American scholar, signifi-cantly — who qualifies his declaration that 'I greatly admire many in its ranks' with the careful proviso of 'My regard for these men does not remove the fact that I salute their *accomplishments* more than their *aims*.' There is, too, the retrospective and reassuring conclusion of Edward Gibbon on the imperial age in his exhaustive *Decline and Fall of the Roman Empire* (1776), that 'every age of the world has increased and still increases the real wealth, the happiness, the knowledge, and perhaps the virtue, of the human race.' Again, there is the tribute paid by Winston Churchill, in his short-lived role as Secretary of State for the Colonies, to the Colonial Service at the 1921 Corona Club dinner, in words strangely anticipatory of his famous utterance 20 years later: 'Never has there been such a varied charge confided to so few.' Finally, there is the novelist Sir Compton Mackenzie's prophetic, regretful reflection in 1951 that from the second half of the twentieth century Britain's youth would no longer be able to read stories about imperial service overseas and then, inspired by the vicarious taste of the larger life, on reaching the last page would decide that here was the career for them. That was perhaps the kind of regret that lay behind Lord Hailey's reflection on his ninetieth birthday when he assured members of the Royal African Society that, under no circumstances, would he think of 'apologizing when I meet my Maker (as soon I must) for having spent some of the best years of my life in India'.

Today, just as there is no Colonial Service nor now no more HMOCS for the young to take up, so too has the concept of a 'career' largely given way to that of a 'job'. Today's graduates do not — some might reasonably argue cannot, in the uncertainties and short term-ness of the employment market — think in terms of a career. Nobody any longer asks them 'What are you going to be?' but merely 'What are you going to do?' Three or four years is now reportedly looked on by graduates as the favourite estimate for remaining in one's first job, with 20 per cent anticipating a move within two years. Changed values over the past half century, prevalent at the time when most of today's survivor generation joined the Colonial Service, mean that the characteristic credo of service and duty as virtues in themselves is no longer as widely or as deeply accepted as it then was. Even the proverbial stiff upper lip, once part and parcel of the public school code and of the ethos of empire, has crumpled before what a societal commentator in *The Times* recently described as the 'feminist demand' for a demonstrative and tactile emotionality.

Reluctant to compose its own epitaph, the Colonial Service has waited for others to write it for them. To their own hopeful belief that the finest memorial to their own service would be for the now independent rural populations to expect from their own civil servants the same standard of honesty and justice as they accorded to their British predecessors, may be added their contentment with their own uncomplicated assessment of 'a worthwhile job well done'. There was, too, often the conviction that, to quote from a letter by the excited young T. E. Fell written to his father as he applied for an administrative appointment in the Gold Coast 100 years ago (1897): 'To get a chance of employment under the Colonial Office seems to me such a capital chance and one not to be missed.' Its Secretaries of State have often tried their hand at it, along the lines of Arthur Creech Jones's inspiring declaration that: 'The Colonial Service is a high responsibility, offering to men and women of commanding quality and character great opportunity and inward satisfaction in an illustrious tradition.'

Perhaps the most valued of all Colonial Service tributes are those coming from the countries in which the Service worked. Personal appreciations and memories apart, two public testimonials in particular are remembered. One is the expression by the Prime Minister of Nigeria in his eloquent Independence Day tribute of his country's gratitude 'to the British officers whom we have known, first as masters and then as leaders and finally as partners, but always as friends'. The other was by the post-colonial Governor-General of Sri Lanka, when he bade the Colonial Service to 'Look on your handiwork and rejoice.'

A Colonial Service Bibliography

This book is not only the first general history of the Colonial Service for more than 60 years, it also contains the first ever attempt at some sort of Colonial Service bibliography. More than 1000 titles are listed. For the convenience of the reader, both generalist and specialist, the bibliography is divided into ten sections:

I   Manuscript Sources
II   British Government Official Publications
III   The Colonial Service (General and Administrative)
IV   The Colonial Service (Departments)
V   The Colonial Office and the Crown Agents for the Colonies
VI   Colonial Governors
VII Women and the Colonial Service
VIII Biographies, Autobiographies and Memoirs
IX   Selected Twentieth-Century Novels about the Colonial Service
X   A Note on Journals

I. Manuscript Sources

The most extensive collection of manuscripts by members of the Colonial Service, totalling more than 10,000 items, is located in the Rhodes House Library, Oxford. These were principally collected under the auspices of the Oxford Colonial Records Project (OCRP, 1963–72) and its successor the Oxford Development Records Project (ODRP, 1977–84). New material continues to be added. Not all holdings are yet open to researchers. Besides diaries, correspondence and unpublished reports, two categories of accession call for separate mention. One is the collection of nearly 100 oral interviews on tape, often with leading figures in the Colonial Service and the Colonial Office. The other is the series of ODRP Project Reports (21 in all), written up and privately published by Rhodes House Library in 1985, relating to the papers of contributors who took part in such special research projects as those on education, medicine and public health, food and cash crops, localization and public service training, women administrative officers, and nursing sisters. There is a substantial Colonial Service oral history archive (Scottish Decolonization Project) in the National Library of Scotland. The Empire Museum at Bristol is currently embarked on an extensive oral history archive. The Royal Commonwealth Society Library at Cambridge University also holds a number of Colonial Service manuscripts.

Five catalogues of manuscript collections in Rhodes House Library have been published since 1970, the last — and largest — by Clare Brown, covering accessions from 1978 to 1994. Other useful guides include the Royal Commission on Historical Manuscripts Guide No. 5, *Private Papers of British Colonial Governors 1782–1900* (1986); vol. 5 in the Institute of Historical Research series on office-holders in modern Britain, *Colonial Office Officials 1794–1870* (1976), compiled by J. C. Sainty; and, as a quick introduction to locations, there are short Colonial Service entries in Chris Cook, *Sources in British Political History 1900–1951*, vol. 2 (1975), and in his *The Making of Modern Africa: A Guide to Archives* (1995).

The best guide to Colonial Office files in the PRO, Kew, is that by Anne Thurston, *Sources for Colonial Studies in the Public Record Office*, vol. I (1995), being a revised and expanded version of R. B. Pugh's *PRO Handbook No. 3* on the Colonial and Dominion Offices' holdings (1964).

Colonial Office files in the PRO dealing with the Colonial Service are not listed in this bibliography. PRO files are not classified under 'Colonial Service' but are scattered across a range of subjects, including patronage (CO 429 and 430), appointments (CO 877 and 918), personnel (CO 850 and 919), establishment (CO 866, 867 and 878), training (CO 1011) and Colonial Service Division (CO 1017), as well as in the correspondence files of the geographical departments. However, many of the most decisive internal Colonial Office and Cabinet memoranda and minutes on the development of the Colonial Service have been valuably reproduced, accompanied by illuminating editorial commentary, in the three general volumes in the *British Documents on the End of Empire* (BDEEP) series: S. R. Ashton and S. E. Stockwell (eds), *Imperial Policy and Colonial Practice, 1925–1945* (1996); R. Hyam (ed.), *The Labour Government and the End of Empire, 1945–1951* (1992); and D. Goldsworthy (ed.), *The Conser-*

vative Government and the End of Empire, 1951–1957 (1994). Others usefully appear in the two volumes edited by A. N. Porter and A. J. Stockwell, *British Imperial Policy and Decolonization, 1938–1964* (1987, 1989).

II. British Government Official Publications

Colonial Service affairs can be conveniently divided into three sections: (i) Parliamentary Papers, also known as White Papers, carrying a serial Command Paper reference (C., Cd., Cmd., Cmnd.) and number; (ii) the non-parliamentary Colonial numbered series, identified as for example, Col. No. 196. Before the introduction of this Colonial series in 1924, and again in the 1950s, these were sometimes titled 'African', for example African No. 973, 1921, *Regulations for the Employment of Officers in [East and Central] Africa*. This series also includes the invaluable annual *Colonial Office List*, colloquially known as the 'Red Book', and the *Colonial Service Lists*, colloquially referred to as the 'Green Books'; and (iii) Colonial Office miscellaneous publications, notably recruitment literature.

(i) Among important Parliamentary Papers (Command series) relating to the Colonial Service are:

C.5828	1889	Correspondence re Appointment of Colonial Governors
Cd.3795	1908	Colonial Office: Despatch re Reorganization
Cmd. 920	1920	West Africa. Vital Statistics of Non-Native Officials
Cmd. 2672	1926	Report of West Indian Conference
Cmd. 2883	1927	Colonial Office Conference: Summary of Proceedings
Cmd. 2884	1927	Colonial Office Conference: Appendices
Cmd. 3049	1928	Report of Committee on Colonial Agricultural Service
Cmd. 3059	1928	Report on Colonial Governors' Pensions
Cmd. 3235	1928	Report on Hon. W. G. A. Ormsby-Gore's Visit to Malaya and Ceylon
Cmd. 3261	1929	Report of Committee on Colonial Veterinary Service
Cmd. 3554	1930	Report of a Committee on the System of Appointment in the Colonial Office and the Colonial Services (Warren Fisher)
Cmd. 3628	1930	Colonial Office Conference: Summary of Proceedings
Cmd. 3629	1930	Colonial Office Conference: Appendices
Cmd. 4556	1933	Report on the Kenya Land Commission (Carter)
Cmd. 4730	1934	Report on Colonial Service Leave and Passage Conditions

Cmd. 5219	1936	Report on Widows and Orphans Scheme
Cmd. 5479	1937	Palestine Royal Commission Report (Peel)
Cmd. 5760	1938	The Colonial Empire, 1937–1938
Cmd. 5784	1938	Correspondence on Welfare of Women in Tropical Africa
Cmd. 6607	1945	West India Royal Commission Report (Moyne)
Cmd. 6647	1945	Report of the Commission on Higher Education in the Colonies (Asquith)
Cmd. 6659	1945	Report of the Commission on Higher Education in West Africa (Elliott)
Cmd. 7167	1947	The Colonial Empire, 1939–1947
Cmd. 8971	1953	Report on Colonial Research
Cmd. 9475	1955	Report of East Africa Royal Commission (Dow)
Cmd. 9768	1956	Her Majesty's Oversea Civil Service: Statement of Policy Regarding Organization
Cmnd. 497	1958	Her Majesty's Overseas Civil Service: Statement of Policy Regarding Overseas Officers Serving in Nigeria
Cmnd. 1193	1960	Service with Overseas Governments
Cmnd. 1308	1961	Technical Assistance from the UK for Overseas Development
Cmnd. 1698	1962	Technical Cooperation
Cmnd. 1740	1962	Recruitment for Service Overseas: Future Policy
Cmnd. 2099	1963	Policy on the Recommendations of the Committee on Training in Public Administration for Overseas Countries

An exhaustive list of colonial parliamentary papers for the period 1870–1920 compiled by A. Taylor Milne is to be found in the bibliography to the *Cambridge History of the British Empire*, Vol. III, 1959. The *Colonial Office List* for 1948 lists all the papers presented to Parliament from 1887 and that for 1951 all those published since 1925. After 1953 the list refers to parliamentary papers published in the preceding year only. A separate volume of the projected *Oxford History of the British Empire* (1997–) will be devoted to bibliographical material.

(ii) Among the most important of the Colonial numbered series (out of the 362 issued between 1924 and 1966) are:

Col.	No. 1	1924	Report on Pensions and Passages
	No. 37	1928	Colonial Regulations
	No. 61	1931	Training of Forestry Service Probationers
	No. 67	1931	Conference of Colonial Directors of Agriculture
	No. 70	1931	Conference of Empire Survey Officers

No. 80	1933	Colonial Administrative Service List
No. 101	1935	Conditions and Cost of Living in the Colonial Empire
No. 106	1935	Colonial Legal Service List
No. 115	1936	Colonial Medical Service List
No. 122	1936	Colonial Forest Service List
No. 132	1937	Colonial Veterinary Service List
No. 143	1937	Colonial Agricultural Service List
No. 156	1938	Conference of Colonial Directors of Agriculture
No. 162	1939	Colonial Audit Service List
No. 168	1939	Colonial Police Service List
No. 194	1944	Report on Sir H. MacMichael's Mission to Malaya
No. 197	1946	Organization of the Colonial Service
No. 198	1946	Postwar Training for the Colonial Service
No. 205	1946	Colonial Office List
No. 207	1947	Report by Sir Harold MacMichael on Malta
No. 209	1947	Report of the Commission on the Civil Services of British West Africa
No. 222	1948	Report of the Commission on the Civil Services of British Central Africa
No. 223	1948	Report of the Commission on the Civil Services of British Central Africa
No. 226	1948	Colonial Office List and Map Supplement
No. 254	1950	Report of the Commission of the Unification of the Public Services in the British Caribbean
No. 264	1950	Report by Major General Sir H. Rance on Development and Welfare in the West Indies
No. 267	1951	Conference of Colonial Government Statisticians
No. 281	1951	Economic Survey of the Colonial Territories
No. 306	1954	Reorganization of the Colonial Service
No. 320	1954	Report by Sir Stephen Luke on Development and Welfare in the West Indies
No. 322	1956	Colonial Regulations
No. 330	1957	Report of the Federation of Malaya Constitutional Commission
No. 343	1960	Report by Sir Bernard Reilly on Aden and the Yemen
No. 347	1960	Report on Colonial Office Public Services Conference

The *Colonial Office List* (from 1926 to 1940 *The Dominions Office and Colonial Office List*) was published annually from 1862 to 1966, except for 1941–5 and 1947. The *Colonial Service Lists* were published between 1933 and 1939, for each branch of the Service as it became unified. Unlike the *Colonial Office List* (but like the territorial *Staff Lists*), they included every member of the service down to the current year's entry. Territorial *Staff Lists* are not cited here, but attention is invited to two articles by A. H. M. Kirk-Greene which discuss these biographical sources in depth: 'Colonial Service Biographical Data: The Published Sources', *African Research and Documentation* No. 46, 1988, 2–16, and 'The Location of Colonial Staff and Civil Service Lists in British Libraries: Preliminary Check-list', *African Research and Documentation*, No. 73, 1997, 8–29.

(iii) Among the Colonial Office Miscellaneous series are the special regulations issued by the Secretary of State for each of the Colonial Services formed on unification in the 1930s, for example Misc. 448 Colonial Forest Service, 465 Colonial Police Service, 479 Colonial Postal Service.

Among the Colonial Office recruitment literature are:

CSR 9	1945	Appointments for Women in His Majesty's Colonial Service
RDW 6	1945	Appointments in the Colonial Service
CSR 1	1950	Appointments in His Majesty's Colonial Service: General
CSR 2–11	1950	[Ditto relating to individual departments]
CSR 1	1954	Appointments in Her Majesty's Colonial Service
OCS 1	1955	Appointments in Her Majesty's Oversea Civil Service
Colonial Office	1955	Her Majesty's Oversea Civil Service: The Administrative Branch
Colonial Office	1960	Appointments Overseas

III. The Colonial Service (General and Administrative)

(For Colonial Service departments/branches, see section IV. For colonial governors, see section VI. For biographies and memoirs, see sections VII and VIII.)

The literature on the Colonial Service is far more extensive than even former members of the Service may anticipate. In this pioneer Colonial Service bibliography, more than 1000 items — many of them post-colonial memoirs — have been recorded, excluding general studies of empire history and colonial policy, journal articles and the hundreds of contributions to the Service's own *Corona* magazine. Yet there is a surprising dearth of books featuring 'the Colonial Service' in their title. The promising *Colonial Administration of Great Britain*, published in 1859 by S. S. Bell, has no reference to the Colonial Service, and A. K. Lowell's more promising *Colonial Civil Service: The Selection and Training of Colonial Officials in England, Holland and France* (1900), deals for the most part with the ICS and the old East India College (1807–57) at Haileybury. In the interwar years, two books appeared in over-quick succession (and from the same publisher), Sir Anton Bertram's rather dull lectures-based *The Colonial Service* (1930) and C. (later Sir Charles) Jeffries's informative *The Colonial Empire and its Civil Service* (1938). The clumsiness of the title was explained by the author's wish not to confuse his book with the more appropriate title pre-empted by Bertram R. Heussler's seminal study, *Yesterday's Rulers* (1963), which relegates mention of the Colonial Service to its subtitle. Jeffries and Heussler count among the most prolific of Colonial Service historians. To Jeffries's authoritative 1936 study he added after the war two recruitment-slanted texts, *Partners for Progress*, subtitled 'The Men and Women of the Colonial Service' (1949), and *Proud Record* (1962), the latter aimed at those contemplating a career in the new HMOCS. His memoir, *Whitehall and the Colonial Service* (1972), offers important insights into how the Colonial Office tried to 'save' the Colonial Service from collapse in the 1950s. As for Heussler (an American scholar), his substantial list of contributions (below) places him in the top rank of historians of the Colonial Administrative Service.

In the absence so far of any history of the Colonial Service as a single entity — and its size and spread has meant that it cannot comfortably compete with the history of more compact civil service units memorialized in Philip Mason's magnificent history of the Indian Civil Service, *The Men Who Ruled India* (1953, 1954), and K. D. D. Henderson's tribute to the Sudan Political Service, *Set Under Authority* (1987) — the history of territorial civil services has taken on a major importance. For instance, there are now available valuable analyses and accounts of the Colonial Service in Malaya (Heussler), the Gold Coast (Kuklick), Uganda (Brown and Brown) and Kenya (Trench), and new initiatives aim at profiles of the post-1945 Hong Kong Civil Service and the Kenya and Eastern Nigeria administrations.

Apart from the *Colonial Office Lists* and the *Colonial Service Lists* noted above, a primary source for establishing who was who over the last 30 years or so of the Colonial Service is A. H. M Kirk-Greene, *A Biographical Dictionary of the British Colonial Service, 1939–1966* (1991). This lists alphabetically all officers who held established posts in that period and who earned an entry in the official *Colonial Office List*, some 15,000 entries in all. For who was who in the Malayan Civil Service, R. Heussler's *British Malaya*, 1981, is useful. Only one *HMOCS Staff List* was ever issued, in 1967. In 1979, the FCO published, for internal use only, a brief list of senior British expatriate officers serving in the dependent territories. Although unpublished Ph.D. theses on the Colonial Service are not recorded in this bibliography, attention is drawn to that by Nile Gardiner entitled 'Sentinels of Empire: The British Colonial Administrative Service, 1919–1954' (Yale, 1998).

The following works are either centrally focused on or contain important discussion of various aspects, institutional and personnel, of the Colonial Service in general or of the Administrative Service.

Allison, P., *Life in the White Man's Grave*, 1988

Austin, R. A., 'The Official Mind of Indirect Rule: Tanganyika, 1916–34', in P. Gifford and W. R. Louis, *Britain and Germany in Africa*, 1967

Barr, Pat, *Taming the Jungle: The Men Who Made British Malaya*, 1977

Berman, Bruce, *Control and Crisis in Colonial Kenya*, 1990

Bradley, K. G., *The Colonial Service as a Career*, 1950

— *A Career in the Overseas Civil Service*, 1955

Brown, D, and Brown, M. V., *Looking Back at the Uganda Protectorate: Recollections of District Officers*, 1996

Burr, E., *Localization and Public Service Training* (ODRP Report, 4) 1985

Carter. T. D., *The Northern Rhodesian Record*, 1992

Chenevix Trench, C. P., *Men Who Ruled Kenya: The Kenya Administration, 1892–1963*, 1993

Cohen, Sir Andrew, *British Policy in Changing Africa*, 1959

Creech Jones, A., 'The Colonial Service' in W. A. Robson, *The Civil Service in Britain and France*, 1956

Crocker, W. R. *Nigeria: A Critique of British Colonial Administration*, 1936

Crowder, M., 'The White Chiefs of Tropical Africa', in L. H. Gann and P. Duignan, *Colonization in Africa*, Vol. 2, 1970

1. *(left)* Joseph Chamberlain, Secretary of State for the Colonies, 1895–1903

2. *(below)* Arthur Creech Jones, Secretary of State for the Colonies, 1946–1950 (left) *(Courtesy of Rhodes House Library, Oxford)*

3. *(left)* Alan Lennox-Boyd, Secretary of State for the Colonies, 1954–1959

4. *(right)* Sir Ralph Furse, responsible for Colonial Service recruitment, 1919–1948 *(Courtesy of the Forestry Institute, Oxford)*

5. *(left)* Dame Margery Perham, 1895–1982, Reader in Colonial Administration, Oxford University

6. *(below)* Officials in the Nigerian Legislature, *c.* 1946

7. *(above)* The District Officer discusses a development problem, North Borneo
8. *(below)* The Divisional Commissioner advises a senior chief in the Gambia

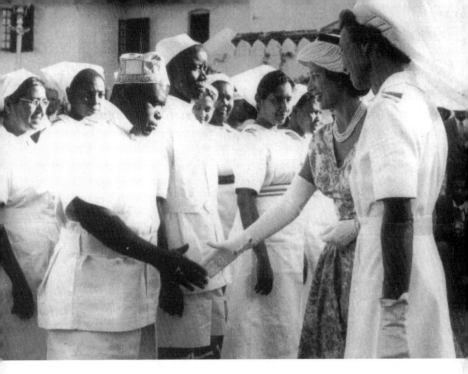

9. *(above)* A member of the Colonial Nursing Service presents the staff of Zanzibar Hospital, 1956
10. *(below)* The Colonial Veterinary Service at work in Uganda

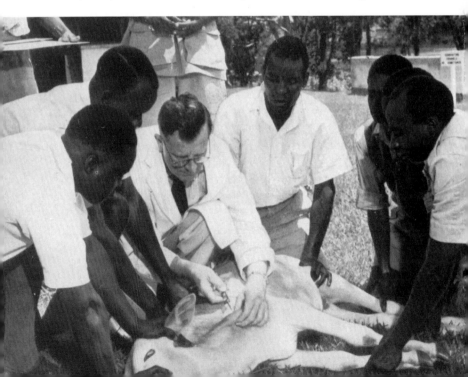

11. *(above)* The Colonial Agricultural Service at work in Sierra Leone
12. *(below)* The Inspector-General of Colonial Police inspects a Guard of Honour in the British Solomon Islands

13. *(above)* Government House, Suva, Fiji, 1938
14. *(below)* The Boma at Mwinilunga, N. Rhodesia *(courtesy of Robin Short)*

15. *(above)* Cambridge University Colonial Service Course, 1934–5
16. *(below)* One of our successors, Northern Nigeria, 1963

Crown Agents, *The West African Pocket Book: A Guide for Newly-Appointed Government Officers*, 1905

Elsman, R. J., *Administration and Development in Malaysia*, 1972

Evans, H., *Men in the Tropics*, 1949

Gann, L. H. and Duignan, Peter, *The Rulers of British Africa 1870–1914*, 1978

Gardiner, N., 'The Colonial Service', in *Daily Telegraph: The British Empire*, 1997

Gill, A., *Ruling Passions: Sex, Race and Empire*, 1995

Gullick, J. M., *Rulers and Residents: Influence and Power in the Malay States, 1970–1920*, 1992

Hailey, Lord, *An African Survey*, 1938

— *Native Administration in the British African Territories*, 1950–3

Heussler, R., *Yesterday's Rulers: The Making of the British Colonial Service*, 1963

— *The British in Northern Nigeria*, 1968

— *British Tanganyika: An Essay and Documents on District Administration*, 1971

— 'British Rule in Africa', in P. Gifford and W. R. Louis, *France and Britain in Africa*, 1971

— *British Rule in Malaya: The Malayan Civil Service and its Predecessors, 1867–1942*, 1981

— *Completing a Stewardship: The Malayan Civil Service, 1942–1957*, 1983

Hyam, R., *Empire and Sexuality: The British Experience*, 1990

Jeffries, Sir Charles, *The Colonial Empire and its Civil Service*, 1930

— *Partners for Progress: The Men and Women of the Colonial Service*, 1949

— *Proud Record*, 1962

— *Whitehall and the Colonial Service: An Administrative Memoir, 1939–1956*, 1972

Johan, K., *The Emergence of the Modern Malay Administrative Elite*, 1984

Kenya Government, *Life and Duties of an Administrative Officer*, 1929

Kirk-Greene, A. H. M., *The Transfer of Power: The Colonial Administrator in the Age of Decolonization*, 1979

— 'The Thin White Line: The Size of the British Colonial Service in Africa', *African Affairs*, 79, 1980

— 'Imperial Administration and the Athletic Imperative: The Case of the District Officer in Africa', in W. J. Baker and J. A. Mangan, *Sport in Africa: Essays in Social History*, 1987

— *A Short History of the Corona Club, 1900–1990*, 1990
— 'Forging a Relationship with the Colonial Administrative Service, 1921–1934', in Alison Smith and Mary Bull (eds), *Margery Perham and British Rule in Africa*, 1991
Kuklick, Henrika, *The Imperial Bureaucrat: The Colonial Administrative Service in the Gold Coast, 1920–1939*, 1979
Lethbridge, H. J., 'Hong Kong Cadets, 1862–1941', in *Hong Kong: Stability and Change*, 1979
Lewis, R. and Foy, Y., *The British in Africa*, 1971
Liebenow, Gus, *Colonial Rule and Political Development in Tanzania*, 1971
Lowell, L. A., *Colonial Civil Service: The Selection and Training of Colonial Officers in England, Holland and France*, 1900
Lugard, Sir Frederick, *Political Memoranda: Revision of Instructions to Political officers, 1919*
— *The Dual Mandate in British Tropical Africa*, 1922
Morris, James, *Pax Britannica: Climax of an Empire*, 1968
— *Heaven's Command: An Imperial Progress*, 1973
— *Farewell the Trumpets: An Imperial Retreat*, 1978
Morris-Hale, W., *British Administration in Tanganyika, 1920–1945*, 1971
Mungeam, G. H., *British Rule in Kenya, 1895–1912*, 1966
Nicolson, I. F., *The Administration of Nigeria, 1900–1960: Men, Methods and Myths*, 1969
Northern Rhodesia Government, *A Career in the Administrative Service of Northern Rhodesia*, 1956
Nuffield Foundation, *Report on a Visit to Nigeria*, 1946
Nyasaland Protectorate, *Hints on Outfit for Officials Appointed to the Nyasaland Government Service*, 1919
Perham, Margery, *Native Administration in Nigeria*, 1937
— *The Colonial Reckoning*, 1961
— *An African Apprenticeship, 1929*, 1974
— *East African Journey, 1929–1930*, 1976
— *West African Passage, 1931–32*, 1983
— *Pacific Prelude, 1929*, 1988
Ridley, F. F., *Specialists and Generalists: A Comparative Study of the Professional Civil Servant at Home and Abroad*, 1968
Roberts, Andrew, 'The Imperial Mind', in *The Colonial Moment in Africa*, 1986
Robinson, K. E., *The Dilemmas of Trusteeship*, 1965

Searight, Sarah, *The British in the Middle East*, 1969

Smith, J. H., 'The Relationship of the British Political Officer to his Chief in Northern Nigeria', in M. Crowder, *West African Chiefs*, 1970

Smith, S., *British Relations with the Malay Rulers, 1930–1957*, 1991

Stigand, C. H., *Administration in Tropical Africa*, 1914

Swaisland, C., *Forty Years of Service: The Women's Corona Society*, 1992

Swettenham, Sir Frank, *British Malaya*, 1948 (1906)

Symonds, R., *The British and their Successors*, 1966

— *Oxford and Empire: The Last Lost Cause?*, 1986

Tanganyika government, *Notes for Newcomers to Tanganyika Territory*, 1946

— *Notes for Newly Appointed Government Officers*, 1957

Tidrick, K., *Empire and the English Character*, 1992

Tilman, R. O., *Bureaucratic Transition in Malaya*, 1964

Winchester, A., *Outposts: Journeys to the Surviving Relics of the British Empire*, 1985

Woodcock, G., *The British in the Far East*, 1969

Younger, K., *The Public Service in New States*, 1960

Though not centrally on the Colonial Service, the 13 volumes written for the *Corona Library* between 1952 and 1971 merit a reference here. They covered Hong Kong, North Borneo; British Guiana, British Honduras, Jamaica; Nyasaland, Sierra Leone, Uganda, Bechuanaland, Basutoland, Swaziland; Fiji, Western Pacific. Their authors were selected for, *inter alia*, 'their experience of colonial administration'. P. J. Marshall's *Cambridge Illustrated History of the British Empire* (1996) is arguably the best single volume reference book.

IV. The Colonial Service (Departments)

Leaving aside the Colonial Administrative Service, which has tended to dominate the studies listed in section III, the Colonial Service was, after its unification in the 1930s, divided into no less than 19 professional services, for example, the Colonial Audit Service, Colonial Forestry Service, Colonial Medical Service, Colonial Police Service, Colonial Survey Service. Often, and especially within territorial governments, these were referred to as departments, for example the Agricultural Department, Education Department, or Public Works

Department. When HMOCS was created in 1954, they were all restyled branches. Once again, if it is surprising that little scholarly attention has been paid to the Colonial Service as a whole, it is even more so that the professional and technical departments have aroused such scant interest, even in the development-oriented 1960s and 1970s. While a number of studies exist on the theme of 'the district commissioner' and 'the colonial administrator' in action, no writer has yet done for the professional departments of the Colonial Service what Maud Diver instigated for their counterparts in British India in her *The Unsung: A Record of British Services in India* (1945).

As with section III, memoirs are considered under sections VII and VIII.

Agricultural Service
Fuggles-Couchman, N. R., *Agricultural Change in Tanganyika, 1945–1960*, 1964
Masefield, G. B., *A History of the Colonial Agricultural Service*, 1972

Education Service
Allen, A. R., *The Colonial Education Service in Northern Nigeria, 1945–60* (ODRP Report No. 9), 1985
Bell, C. V. R., *Education in Uganda Before Independence* (ODRP Report No. 11), 1985
Earle, E. W. D. H., *Development of Education in Pre-Independent Ghana* (ODRP Report No. 10), 1985
Evans, Dorothy, *Schooling in the South Atlantic Islands, 1861–1962*, 1994
Greig, J. C. E., *Education in Northern Rhodesia and Nyasaland Pre-Independence* (ODRP Report No. 13), 1985
Robertson, K. A. *Educational Development in Pre-Independent Tanganyika* (ODRP Report No. 12), 1985
Stevenson, R., *Cultivators and Administrators: British Educational Policy towards Independent Malaya, 1875–1906*, 1976

Forest Service
Collins, W. B., *They Went to Bush*, 1961
Troup, R. S., *Colonial Forest Administration*, 1940

Geological Survey Service
Falconer, J. D., *The Geology and Geography of Northern Nigeria*, 1911

Medical Service

Balfour, A., *Vistas and Visions: Some Aspects of the Colonial Medical Services*, 1924

Beck, Ann, *A History of the British Medical Administration in East Africa, 1900–1950*, 1970

Bull, M., *The Medical Services of Nigeria* (ODRP Report No. 19), 1985

— *The Medical Services of Uganda* (ODRP Report No. 20), 1985

— *The Medical Services of Tanganyika* (ODRP Report No. 21), 1985

Cheverton, R. L., 'The District Medical Officer', in E. E. Sabben-Clare et al., *Health in Tropical Africa during the Colonial Period*, 1980

Clyde, D. F., *History of the Medical Services of Tanganyika*, 1962

Holden, Pat, *Doctors and other Medical Personnel in Nigeria, Uganda and Tanganyika* (ODRP Report No. 17), 1985

Schram, R., *History of the Nigerian Health Services*, 1971

Taylor, S., and Gadsden, P., *Shadows in the Sun*, 1946

Tolmie, P., *Medicine and Public Health in British Tropical Africa* (ODRP Report No. 16), 1985

Nursing Service

Dickson, H. P., *The Badge of Britannia: History and Reminiscences of Queen Elizabeth's Overseas Nursing Service, 1886–1966*, 1990

Holden, Pat, *Nursing Sisters in Nigeria, Uganda and Tanganyika* (ODRP Report No. 18), 1985

Police Service

Anderson, D. M. and Killingray, D., *Policing the Empire, 1830–1940*, 1991

— *Policing and Decolonization, 1917–1965*, 1992

Clayton, A., and Killingray, D., *Khaki and Blue*, 1989

Foran, W. R., *The Kenya Police*, 1962

Gillespie, W. H., *The Gold Coast Police, 1844–1938*, 1955

Horne, E., *A Job Well Done: A History of the Palestine Police Force, 1920–1948*, 1982

Jeffries, Sir Charles, *The Colonial Police*, 1952

Killingray, D., *Guardians of Empire*, 1998

Shirley, W. R., *History of the Nigeria Police*, 1950

Tamuno, T. N., *The Police in Modern Nigeria*, 1970

Wright, T., *A History of the Northern Rhodesia Police*, 1992

Veterinary Service
West, G. P., *A History of the Overseas Veterinary Services*, 1973

V. The Colonial Office and the Crown Agents for the Colonies

Probably because of its role as one of the major — and one of the longer established, its origins going back to the Council of Foreign Plantations in 1660 — institutions of state in what was to become Britain's bureaucratic web of Whitehall ministries, the Colonial Office has attracted more in-depth attention from scholars than has the Colonial Service. Colonial Secretaries' biographies and studies of British political parties in colonial affairs invariably involve consideration of the Colonial Office. Although not made a separate department of state until 1854, a series of detailed studies of its structure and function now exist covering its existence from 1794 to its closure in 1966. They include (see also introduction to section I):

Abbott, A. W., *A Short History of the Crown Agents and their Office*, 1959
Blakeley, B. L., *The Colonial Office, 1868–1892*, 1972
Butler, L. J., *Industrialization and the British Colonial State, 1939–1951*, 1997
Carland, J. M., *The Colonial Office and Nigeria, 1898–1914*, 1985
Crown Agents, *The Crown Agents for the Colonies*, 1933
— *The Crown Agents, 1835–1983*, 1984
Constantine, S., *The Making of British Colonial Development Policy, 1914–1940*, 1984
Fiddes, Sir George, *The Dominions and Colonial Offices*, 1926
Garner, Sir Joe, *The Commonwealth Office, 1925–68*, 1978
Goldsworthy, D., *Colonial Issues in British Politics, 1945–1951*, 1971
Hall, H. L., *The Colonial Office*, 1937
Howe, S., *Anti-Colonialism in British Politics*, 1993
Hyam, R., *Elgin and Churchill at the Colonial Office, 1905–1908*, 1968
Jeffries, Sir Charles, *The Colonial Office*, 1956
Kesner, R. M., *Economic Control and Colonial Development* (Crown Agents), 1981
Kubicek, R. V., *The Administration of Imperialism: Joseph Chamberlain at the Colonial Office*, 1969
Lee, J. M., *Colonial Development and Good Government*, 1967
Lee, J. M., and Petter, M., *The Colonial Office, War and Development Policy*, 1982

Macmillan, W. M. *Warning from the West Indies*, 1936
— *Africa Emergent*, 1938
Morgan, D. J. *The Official History of Colonial Development*, 1980
Murphy, P., *Party Politics and Decolonization*, 1995
Parkinson, Sir Cosmo, *The Colonial Office from Within, 1909–1945*, 1947
Pearce, R. D., *The Turning Point in Africa: British Colonial Policy, 1938–1948*, 1986
Penson, L. M., *The Colonial Agents of the British West Indies*, 1924
Sainty. J. C., *Colonial Office Officials, 1794–1970*, 1986
Shuckburgh, Sir John, *The Colonial Civil History of the War*, 1949
Snelling, R. C., 'The Colonial Office and its Permanent Officials', in G. Sutherland, *Studies in the Growth of 19th Century Government*, 1972
Young, D. M., *The Colonial Office in the Early Nineteenth Century*, 1961

VI. Colonial Governors

While colonial governors, like viceroys and ambassadors, have long indulged in writing their proconsular memoirs of how they reached the top of their profession (*à la* Sir Ralph Williams's title, *How I Became a Governor*) and what it was like there, they — and often their wives — have enjoyed an added prominence in post-colonial studies of imperial administration. Biography is overtaking autobiography as the once popular gubernatorial genre, the latter a fashion that is now set to decline in the face of the sharp falling off in the number of career governorships available since the 1960s. Because of the validity of the separate section VII, the literature by and on governors' wives has been included in that section.

1. General

Cell, J. W., *British Colonial Administration in the Mid-19th Century*, 1970
Francis, N., *Governors and Settlers: Images of Authority in the British Colonies, 1820–60*, 1992
Gann, Lewis, H. and Duignan, Peter, *African Proconsuls: European Governors in Africa*, 1978
Hulugalle, H. A. J., *British Governors of Ceylon*, 1963
Kirk-Greene, A. H. M., 'On Governorship and Governors in British Africa', in Gann and Duignan, *African Proconsuls*, 1978
— *A Biographical Dictionary of the British Colonial Governor, I: Africa*, 1980
— 'Scholastic Attainment and Scholarly Achievement in Britain's

Imperial Civil Services: The Case of the African Governors',
    Oxford Review of Education, 1981
— 'Badge of Office: Sport and His Excellency in the British Empire',
    in J. Mangan, *The Cultural Bond: Sport, Empire, Society*, 1992
Spurr, R., *Excellency: The Governors of Hong Kong*, 1995

2. Biography and Autobiography
Archer, Sir Geoffrey, *Personal and Historical Memoirs of an East
    African Administrator*, 1963
Baker, Colin, *Development Governor: A Biography of Sir Geoffrey
    Colby*, 1994
— *State of Emergency: Crisis in Central Africa, Nyasaland 1959–1960*,
    1997 (Armitage)
— *Retreat from Empire*, 1998 (Armitage)
Bates, Darrell, *A Gust of Plumes: a Biography of Lord Twining of
    Godalming and Tanganyika*, 1972
Bell, Sir Hesketh, *Glimpses of a Governor's Life*, 1946
Bell, Sir Gawain, *Imperial Twilight*, 1989
Blackburne, Sir Kenneth, *Lasting Legacy*, 1976
Boeder, R. B., *Alfred Sharpe of Nyasaland: Builder of Empire*, 1981
Bruce, Sir Charles, *The Broad Stone of Empire*, 1910
Burns, Sir Alan, *Colonial Civil Servant*, 1949
Cameron, Sir Donald, *My Tánganyika Service and Some Nigeria*, 1939
Clifford, Sir Bede, *Proconsul*, 1964
Clifford, Sir Hugh, *In Court and Kampong*, 1897
— *In Days that are Dead*, 1926
— *Bushwhacking*, 1929
Des Voeux, Sir William, *My Colonial Service*, 1903
Dimbleby, Jonathan, *The Last Governor*, 1997 (Patten)
Douglas-Home, Charles, *Evelyn Baring: The Last Proconsul*, 1978
Duignan, P., 'Sir Robert Coryndon', *African Proconsuls*, 1978
Dundas, Sir Charles, *African Crossroads*, 1955
Flint, J. E., 'Sir Frederick Lugard', *African Proconsuls*, 1978
Foot, H. M., *A Start in Freedom*, 1964
Frost, R., *Enigmatic Proconsul: Sir Philip Mitchell and the Twilight of
    Empire*,1992
Gailey, H., *Sir Donald Cameron: Colonial Governor*, 1974
— *Clifford: Imperial Proconsul*, 1982
Garvey, Sir Ronald, *Gentleman Pauper*, 1984
Goodall, H., *'Beloved Imperialist'*, 1998 (Guggisberg)

Grantham, Sir Alexander, *Via Ports*, 1965

Guillemard, Sir Laurence, *Trivial Fond Record*, 1937

Gutch, Sir John, *Colonial Servant*, 1987

Haydon, A. P., *Sir Matthew Nathan: British Colonial Governor and Civil Servant*, 1976

Hickinbotham, Sir Tom, *Aden*, 1958

Hunt, Sir Rex, *My Falklands Days*, 1992

Jackson, Sir Frederick, *Early Days in East Africa*, 1930

Johnston, Sir Charles, *The View from Steamer Point*, 1964

Johnston, Sir Harry H., *The Story of My Life*, 1923

Joyce, R. B., *Sir William MacGregor*, 1971

Lee, Francis, *Fabianism and Colonialism: Life and Political Thought of Lord Sydney Olivier*, 1988

Luke, Sir Harry, *From a South Seas Diary, 1938–1942*, 1945

— *Cities and Men* (3 vols), 1953–6

Maddocks, Sir Kenneth P., *Of No Fixed Abode*, 1988

Mellor, B., *Lugard in Hong Kong*, 1992

Mitchell, Sir Philip, *African Afterthoughts*, 1954

Montgomery, Brian, *Shenton of Singapore: Governor and Prisoner of War*, 1984

Oliver, R. A., *Sir Harry Johnston*, 1957

Pearce, R. D., *Sir Bernard Bourdillon*, 1987

Peel, R. L., *Old Sinister: A Memoir of Sir Arthur Richards*, 1986

Perham, Margery, *Lugard* (2 vols), 1956, 1960

Pope-Hennessy, J., *Verandah: Some Episodes in the Crown Colonies, 1867–1889*, 1964

Rey, Sir Charles, *Monarch of All I Survey: Bechuanaland Diaries, 1929–1937*, 1988

Robertson, Sir James, *Transition in Africa*, 1974

Robinson, R. E., 'Sir Andrew Cohen', *African Proconsuls*, 1978

Rooney, D., *Sir Charles Arden-Clarke*, 1982

Selwyn-Clarke, Sir Selwyn, *Footprints; Memoirs*, 1975

Sharwood-Smith, Sir Bryan, *But Always as Friends*, 1969

St Johnston, Sir Reginald, *From a Colonial Governor's Notebook*, 1936

Stanley, Sir Robert, *King George's Keys*, 1975

Storrs, Sir Ronald, *Orientations*, 1943

Stow, Sir John, *Times Remembered*, 1991

Symes, Sir Stewart, *Tour of Duty*, 1975

Thomas, G., *Last of the Proconsuls: Letters of Sir James Robertson*, 1994

Trevaskis, K., *Shades of Amber*, 1968
Williams, Sir Ralph, *How I Became a Governor*, 1913
Wraith, R. E., *Guggisberg*, 1961
Youé, C. P., *Robert T. Coryndon, 1897–1925*, 1986

VII. Women and the Colonial Service

Among the products of the emergence of feminist studies in the past quarter-century has been a focus on women in the Raj and in the Colonial Service, either as wife or as a career member of one of the branches of the Colonial Service. For ease of identification, the memoirs by such women have been included in this self-contained section rather than subsumed under sections VI or VIII.

Alexander, Joan, *Voices and Echoes: Tales from Colonial Women*, 1983
Bell, Vivienne, *Blown by the Wind of Change*, 1986
Blunt, Alison, *Travel, Gender and Imperialism: Mary Kingsley and West Africa*, 1994
Bose, A. M., *When the Sun Never Set, c.*1982
Boyle, Laura, *Diary of a Colonial Officer's Wife*, 1968
Bradley, Emily, *Dearest Priscilla*, 1950
— *A Household Book for Africa*, 1938
Brownfoot, Janice, 'Memsahibs in Colonial Malaya', in Hilary Callan and Shirley Ardener (eds), *The Incorporated Wife*, 1984
Callaway, Helen, *Gender, Culture and Empire: European Women in Colonial Nigeria*, 1987
Champion, Olive, *Journey of a Lifetime*, 1994
Clifford, Lady, *Our Days on the Gold Coast*, 1919
Corden, Roddy, *Seven Years Island Hopping*, 1997
Craddock, Sally, *Retired Except on Demand: The Life of Dr Cicely Williams*, 1983
Dalton, Heather, *The Gold Coast: The Wives' Experience* (ODRP Report No. 15), 1985
— *The Experience of Colonial Governors' Wives* (Rhodes House Library), 1989
Davidson, Ann, *Real Paradise: Memories of Africa, 1950–1963*, 1985
Evans, Jean, *Not Bad for a Foreigner*, 1996
Falconer, Jean, *Woodsmoke and Temple Flowers*, 1992
Gartrell, Beverley, 'Colonial Wives: Villains or Victims?' in Hilary Callan and Shirley Ardener (eds), *The Incorporated Wife*, 1984

Gaunt, Mary, *Alone in West Africa*, 1912

Gittins, Anne, *Tales from the South Pacific Islands*, 1988

— *Tales of the Fiji Islanders*, 1991

Hoe, Susanne, *The Private Life of Old Hong Kong: Western Women in the British Colony, 1841–1941*, 1991

Holden, Pat, *Women Administrative Officers* (ODRP Report No.5), 1985

— *Nursing Sisters in Nigeria, Uganda and Tanganyika* (ODRP Report No. 18), 1985

Hollis, Rosemary, *A Scorpion for Tea*, 1981

Huggins, Molly, *Too Much to Tell*, 1967

Hutchings, Dora, *Every Road Leads Back Home*, 1986

Kingsley, Mary, *Travels in West Africa*, 1897

— *West African Studies*, 1899

— *The Story of West Africa*, 1900

Knapman, Claudia, *White Women in Fiji, 1835–1930: The Ruin of Empire?*, 1986

Knox-Mawer, June, *The Sultans Came to Tea*, 1961

— *A Gift of Islands: Living in Fiji*, 1965

— *Tales from Paradise*, 1986

Larymore, Constance, *A Resident's Wife in Nigeria*, 1908

Lattimer, Pamela, *A Family of Ginger Griffins*, 1987

Lawrence, Margaret, *The Prophet's Camel Bell*, 1965

Leith-Ross, Sylvia, *Stepping-Stones: Memoirs of Colonial Nigeria, 1907–1960*, 1983

Luce, Margaret, *From Aden to the Gulf: Personal Diaries, 1956–1966*, 1987

Macleod, Olive, *Chiefs and Cities of Central Africa*,1912

Moore, Decima and F. G. Guggisberg, *We Two in West Africa*, 1909

Morley, Patricia, *My Other Family: An Artist-Wife in Singapore*, 1994

Osmaston, Anna, *Uganda Before Amin: Our Family Life, 1949–63*, 1991

Page, Gwendoline, *Coconuts and Coral*, 1993

Powell, Erica, *Private Secretary (Female)/Gold Coast*, 1984

Reece, Alys, *To My Wife 50 Camels*, 1963

Robertson, Bridget M., *Angels in Africa: A Memoir of Nursing with the Colonial Service*, 1993

Ross, M. A., *The Old Third World*, 1977

Rowling, Noel, *Nigerian Memoirs*, 1982

Russell, Elnor, *Bush Life in Nigeria*, 1978

Schofield, Alice Shirley, *The Donas Remember*, 1993

Sharwood-Smith, Joan, *Diary of a Colonial Wife: An African Experience*, 1992
Sitwell, Grace McDonald, *Letters from Far-Away Places*, 1983
Smith, Joan I., *Patch of Africa*, 1991
— *Heart of Africa*, 1993
Strobel, Margaret, *European Women and the Second British Empire*, 1991
Stuart, Wendy, *The Lingering Eye: Recollections of North Borneo*, 1993
Talbot, D. A., *Women's Mysteries of a Primitive People*, 1915
Trollope, Joanna, *Britannia's Daughters: Women of the British Empire*, 1983
Watt, Peggy, *There is Only One Nigeria*, 1985

VIII. Biographies, Autobiographies and Memoirs

Inspired by the realization that here is the last generation of Colonial Service officers, and often motivated by the domestic wish simply to record for children or grandchildren a description of a career and lifestyle beyond their ken and impossible for them ever to replicate, the memoir has constituted a staple of the Colonial Service literature of the 1980s and 1990s. While it has existed almost as long as the modern Colonial Service (Clifford's *In Court and Kampong* was published in 1897, D. W. Carnegie's *Letters from Nigeria* in 1902 and Sir William Des Voeux's *My Colonial Service* in 1903), it is its latterday abundance which has significantly added to the resources of the Colonial Service historian.

Items written by or about colonial governors and women in the Colonial Service appear in sections VI and VII respectively. For ease of reference, the entries are grouped according to their departmental focus. Where the (principal) colony of service is not immediately clear from the title, it has been added in parenthesis.

General

Allen, Charles, *Tales from the Dark Continent*, 1975
— *Tales from the South China Seas*, 1983
Cook, C., *The Lion and the Dragon: British Voices from the China Coast*, 1985
Furse, Sir Ralph, *Aucuparius: Recollections of a Recruiting Officer*, 1962
Hopwood, D., *Tales of Empire: The British in the Middle East*, 1989
Jeffries, Sir Charles, *Whitehall and the Colonial Service: An Administrative Memoir, 1939–1956*, 1972

Knox-Mawer, J., *Tales from Paradise*, 1986
Sherman, A. J., *Mandate Days: British Lives in Palestine, 1918–1948*, 1997

Administrative Service
Allan, Colin, H., *Solomons Safari, 1953–58*, 1989
Arrowsmith, K. V., *Bush Paths*, 1991
Askwith, Tom, *Getting my Knees Brown*, 1996 (Kenya)
— *From Mau Mau to Harambee*, 1995
Atkinson, M. C., *An African Life: Tales of a Colonial Officer*, 1992
    (Western Nigeria)
Bates, Darrell, *A Fly-Switch from the Sultan*, 1961 (Tanganyika)
— *The Mango and the Palm*, 1962 (Tanganyika)
Bazley, Walter, *Bunyoro, Tropical Paradise*, 1993 (Uganda)
Bere, R., *A Cuckoo's Parting Cry*, 1990 (Uganda)
Bevington, E., *The Things We Do for England . . . If England Only
    Knew*, 1990 (Western Pacific)
Blair, J., *Juju and Justice*, 1991 (Western Nigeria)
Blake, C., *A View from Within*, 1989 (Malaya)
Boustead, Sir Hugh, *The Wind of Morning*, 1972 (Aden)
Boyle, D., *With Ardours Manifold*, 1959 (Gold Coast)
Bradley, K., *The Diary of a District Officer*, 1943 (Northern Rhodesia)
— *Once a District Officer*, 1966 (Northern Rhodesia)
Brelsford, W. V. *Generation of Men*, 1965 (Northern Rhodesia)
Bridges, A. F. B., *In the Service of Nigeria*, 1980
— *So We Used To Do*, 1990 (Eastern Nigeria)
Brook, Ian, *The One-Eyed Man is King*, 1966 (Western Nigeria)
Brooks, R. J., *Under Five Flags*, 1995 (North Borneo)
Browne, R., *Beyond the Cape of Good Hope*, 1965 (Tanganyika)
Burkinshaw, P. L., *Alarms and Excursions*, 1991 (Sierra Leone)
Burt, F., *Nakumbuka*, 1989 (Tanganyika)
Butter, J., *Uncivil Servant*, 1989 (Kenya)
Cairns, J. C., *Bush and Boma*, 1959 (Tanganyika)
Cardinall, A. W., *In Ashanti and Beyond*, 1927 (Gold Coast)
Carnegie, D. W., *Letters from Nigeria*, 1902
Carson, J. B., *Sun, Sand and Safari*, 1957 (Kenya)
Coates, Austin, *Myself a Mandarin*, 1968 (Hong Kong)
Collins, D., *A Tear for Somalia*, 1960
Cooke, J., *One White Man in Black Africa*, 1991 (Tanganyika)
Crocker, W. R., *Nigeria: Critique of British Colonial Administration*
    (Part I. Journal of an Administrative Officer), 1936

— *Travelling Back*, 1986 (Nigeria)

Crouch, M., *An Element of Luck: To South Arabia and Beyond*, 1993

Culwick, A. T., *Britannia Waives the Rules*, 1963 (Tanganyika)

Duff, Sir Hector, *African Small Chop*, 1932 (Nyasaland)

Eliot, E. C., *Broken Atoms*, 1938 (Gilbert and Ellice Islands)

Foster, D., *Landscape with Arabs*, 1969 (Aden)

Fowler, W., *This Island's Mine*, 1959 (Solomon Islands)

Forden, K., *The Chittenden Legend*, 1996 (Northern Rhodesia)

Franklin, H., *The Flag Wagger*, 1974 (Northern Rhodesia)

Fremantle, J. M., *Two African Journals and Other Papers*, 1938 (Nigeria)

Gavaghan, T., *Corridors of Wire*, 1994 (Kenya)

Gilmour, A., *An Eastern Cadet's Anecdotage*, 1974 (Malaya)

Golding, J. A., *Colonialism: The Golden Years*, 1987 (Tanganyika)

Griffiths, J. C., *A Welshman Overseas: Requiem for Colonialism*, 1993 (Malaya)

Grimble, Arthur, *A Pattern of Islands*, 1952 (Gilbert and Ellice Islands)

— *Return to the Islands*, 1957

Gunn, Iain, *With a Rod in Four Continents*, 1981 (Northern Nigeria)

Haig, E. F. G., *Nigerian Sketches*, 1931 (Eastern Nigeria)

Harding, C., *In Remotest Barotseland*, 1905 (Northern Rhodesia)

— *Far Bugles*, 1933 (Northern Rhodesia, Gold Coast)

Hastings, A. C. G., *Nigerian Days*, 1925 (Northern Nigeria)

Hennings, R. O., *African Morning*, 1951 (Kenya)

Hives, F., *Juju and Justice in Nigeria*, 1930 (Eastern Nigeria)

Hodgkin, T. L., *Letters from Palestine, 1932–36*, 1986

Horton, D. C., *The Happy Isles: A Diary of the Solomons*, 1965

Ingrams, H., *Arabia and the Isles*, 1942 (Aden)

— *Seven Across the Sahara*, 1950 (Gold Coast)

Jones-Bateman, R., *A Refuge from Civilization*, 1931 (Ceylon)

Keith-Roach, E., *Pasha of Jerusalem: Memoirs of a District Commissioner under the British Mandate*, 1994

Kerslake, R. T., *Time and the Hour*, 1997 (Northern Nigeria)

Kisch, M. S., *Letters and Sketches from Northern Nigeria*, 1910

Langa Langa, *Up Against it in Nigeria*, 1922

Lewis-Barned, J., *A Fanfare of Trumpets*, 1993 (Tanganyika)

Loch, J., *My First Alphabet*, 1994 (Malaya)

Lumley, E. K., *Forgotten Mandate: A British Officer in Tanganyika*, 1976

Lytton, Earl of, *The Desert and the Green*, 1957 (Kenya)

Maciel, M., *Bwana Karani*, 1985 (Kenya)

MacQuarrie, H., *Vouza and the Solomon Islands*, 1945

Marshall, H. H., *Like Father Like Son*, 1980 (Eastern Nigeria)

Maxon, R. M., *John Ainsworth and the Making of Kenya*, 1980

Maybury, M., *Pearl of Africa*, 1991 (Uganda)

McClintock, N. C., *Kingdoms in the Sand and Sun*, 1992 (Northern Nigeria)

Millard, J., *Never a Dull Moment*, 1996 (Tanganyika)

Morley, J., *Colonial Postscript: Diary of a District Officer, 1935–1956*, 1992 (Northern Nigeria)

Mowat, G. S., *The Rainbow through the Rain*, 1995 (Malaya)

Mullins, P., *Retreat from Africa*, 1992 (Nyasaland)

Nemo, (A. C. Douglas), *Niger Memories*, 1937 (Eastern Nigeria)

Nightingale, B., *Seven Rivers to Cross*, 1996 (Northern Nigeria)

Niven, Sir Rex, *Nigerian Kaleidoscope: Memoirs of a Colonial Servant*, 1982

Oakley, R. R., *Treks and Palavers*, 1938 (Northern Nigeria)

O'Regan, J., *From Empire to Commonwealth: Reflections of a Career in Britain's Overseas Service*, 1994 (Ceylon)

Patterson, G., *A Spoonful of Rice with Salt*, 1993 (Malaya)

Pearce, R., *Then the Wind Changed in Africa: Nigerian Letters of R. H. Wright*, 1992

Postlethwaite, J. R. P., *I Look Back*, 1947 (Uganda)

Purcell, V., *The Memoirs of a Malayan Official*, 1965

Rayne, H., *Sun, Sand and Somalis: Leaves from the Note-Book of a District Commissioner*, 1921

Russell, A. C., *Gold Coast to Ghana: A Happy Life in West Africa*, 1996

Russell, J., *Kenya, Beyond the Marich Pass: A District Officer's Story*, 1994

Seaton, H., *Lion in the Morning*, 1963 (Kenya)

Sheppard, M. C., *Taman Budiman: Memoirs of an Unorthodox Civil Servant*, 1979 (Malaya)

Short, R., *African Sunset*, 1973 (Northern Rhodesia)

Skinner, N., *Burden Assumed*, 1985 (Northern Nigeria)

— *Burden at Sunset*, 1996 (Northern Nigeria)

Smith, J. H., *Colonial Cadet in Nigeria*, 1968

Snow, Philip, *The Years of Hope*, 1997 (Fiji)

— *A Time of Renewal*, 1998 (Fiji)

Terrell, R., *West African Interlude*, 1988 (Northern Nigeria)

Trench, C. C., *The Desert's Dusty Face*, 1964 (Kenya)

Turbott, Sir Ian, *Lands of Sun and Spice*, 1996 (Pacific, Caribbean)

Tweedsmuir, Lord, *Always a Countryman*, 1953 (Uganda)

Udoji, J., *Under Three Masters: Memoirs of an African Administrator*, 1995 (Eastern Nigeria)

Ward Price, H. L. *Dark Subjects*, 1939 (Western Nigeria)

Watkins, Elizabeth, *Jomo's Jailor: The Life of Leslie Whitehouse*, 1993 (Kenya)

— *Oscar from Africa: The Biography of O. F. Watkins*, 1995 (Kenya)

White, S., *'Dan Bana': Memoirs of a Nigerian Official*, 1966

Wollocombe, R., *A Passage from India*, 1988 (Northern Nigeria)

Woolf, L., *Growing: An Autobiography of the Years, 1904–1911*, 1961 (Ceylon)

— *Diaries in Ceylon, 1908–1911: Records of a Colonial Administrator*, 1963

Wright, R., *'Strewth So Help Me God: A Tale Told in Twilight*, 1994 (Northern Nigeria)

Agricultural Service

Everard, C., *The Guardian Angel*, 1996

Macdonald, A. S., *Love is a Grapefruit*, 1997 (Sierra Leone)

Ommaney, F. D., *Isle of Cloves*, 1957 (Zanzibar)

— *Eastern Windows*, 1960 (Zanzibar, Malaya)

Audit Service

Boyd, R., *A Colonial Odyssey*, 1997

Education Service

Brown, Ron, *Ex-Africa*, 1996

Clarke, J. D., *Teacher and Friend*, 1993 (Nigeria)

Dorman, T. E., *African Experience: An Education Officer in Northern Rhodesia*, 1993

Hudson, H., *Time Remembered: Reminiscences of Education in Uganda and Nyasaland*, 1996

Hussey. E. R. J., *Tropical Africa: Memoirs of a Period, 1908–1944*, 1959 (Uganda, Nigeria)

Snelson, P., *To Independence and Beyond: Memoirs of a Colonial and Commonwealth Civil Servant*, 1993 (Northern Rhodesia)

Snoxall, R. A., *Peripatetic Pedagogue*, 1985 (Tanganyika)

Engineering Service
Gill, J. M., *Old Bill in the Bush*, 1996 (British Cameroons)
Wells, C., *Six Years in the Malay Jungle*, 1925

Forest Service
Collins, W. B., *They Went to Bush*, 1961 (Gold Coast)
Eggeling, W. J., *When I Was Younger*, 1987 (Uganda)

Legal Service
Alexander, G., *From the Middle Temple to the South Seas*, 1927
— *Tanganyika Memories*, 1936
Knox-Mawer, R., *Tales from a Palm Court*, 1986 (Aden)
— *A Case of Bananas*, 1992 (Fiji)
Williams, J. K., *Black, Amber, White*, 1990 (Tanganyika)

Medical Service
Berry, W. T. C., *Before the Wind of Change*, 1984
Carman, J. A., *A Medical History of Kenya: A Personal Memoir*, 1976
Charters, A. D., *Reminiscences of East Africa ... Milestones of a Doctor's Life*, 1985
Goodall, J., *Goodbye to Empire: A Doctor Remembers*, 1987 (Nyasaland)
Nash, T. A. M., *A Zoo Without Bars*, 1984 (Kenya, Tanganyika)
Nicol, B. M., *Wind of Chance*, 1991 (Nigeria)
Smith, Alec, *Insect Man: A Fight against Malaria in Africa*, 1993
Waddy, B. B., 'A District Medical Officer in N. W. Ghana', in E. E. Sabben-Clare et al., *Health in Tropical Africa during the Colonial Period*, 1980
Willson, L., *A Son of the Raj*, 1966 (Malaya)

Nursing Service
Robertson, Bridget M., *Angels in Africa: A Memoir of Nursing with the Colonial Service*, 1993

Police Service
Boorman, M., *Diamonds are Trumps*, 1997 (Sierra Leone)
Dixon, Alec, *Singapore Patrol*, 1935
Foran, W. R., *A Cuckoo in Kenya*, 1936
Harwich, C., *Red Dust*, 1961 (Uganda)
Imray, C., *Policeman in Palestine*, 1994
— *Policeman in Nigeria*, 1997

Jenkins, A. H., *A Long Beat*, 1995 (British Guiana, Hong Kong)

Macoun, M. J., *Wrong Place, Right Time: Policing the End of Empire*, 1996 (East Africa)

Mellor, F. H., *Sword and Spear*, 1934 (Northern Nigeria)

Murphy, G., *Copper Mandarin*, 1984 (Palestine, Malaya)

Sherwood, Sandy, *It's Been a Pleasure*, 1994 (Nigeria, Jamaica)

Tudor Griffiths, J., *Reminiscences and Observations of a Hong Kong Choi Lo*, 1997

Wild, P. T., *Bwana Polici: Under Three Flags*, 1995 (Kenya)

Postal Service

Dickenson, R., *African Ambit*, 1995 (Nyasaland)

Workman, A., *A Colonial Postmaster-General's Reminiscences*, 1937 (East and West Africa)

Prison Service

Hamilton-Bayly, P. H., *Memoirs of a Colonial Product*, 1994 (Kenya)

Hutchings, S. E. *Life in the Colonial Prison Service*, 1987 (Gold Coast, Malaya)

Survey Service

Bain, A. D. N., *A Geologist in Nigeria, 1920–1940*, 1981

Fairweather, W. G., *A Colonial Surveyor at Work: Field Diary, 1913–14*, (Northern Rhodesia)

Falconer, J. D., *On Horseback Through Nigeria*, 1911

Reeve, W. H., *Hammer, Compass and Traverse Wheel: A Geologist in Africa*, 1992 (Northern Rhodesia, Tanganyika)

Veterinary Service

Smith, J., *Vet in Africa: Life on the Zambezi, 1913–1933*, 1997

Smith, V., *Birds, Beasts and Bature*, 1995 (Northern Nigeria)

Wilde, J. K. H., *Wilde Tales from Africa*, 1990 (Tanganyika)

IX. Selected Twentieth-Century Novels about the Colonial Service

The novel may turn out to be one of the favourite and most enduring sources for a study of the Colonial Service in the field. It already has an ancestry almost as long as that of the Colonial Service: William Thackeray's *Vanity Fair*, with its central character of His Excellency Colonel Crawley, was published in 1848, and Anthony Trollope's novel about the Colonial Office, *Phineas Finn*, appeared in 1869. Besides the novel, there is a strong tradition of Colonial Service 'faction' in short stories by members of the service, often published in *Blackwood's Magazine*, the *Cornhill Magazine* and, throughout the 1950s, in *Corona*. Since the 1990s, the *Overseas Pensioner* has offered a generous and valued outlet for both mini-memoir and shortest of short stories. The subject of verse written by serving Colonial Service officers has been discussed in two articles by A. H. M. Kirk-Greene, 'For Better or for Verse?' in *The Overseas Pensioner*, 72, 1996 and 75, 1998. The resultant collection of Colonial Service verse has been deposited in Rhodes House Library, Oxford.

From the following list of 25 quintessentially Colonial Service novels, it is interesting to note how many well-known novelists have used colonial civil servants as their leading characters. Authors who had been in the Colonial Service are marked with an asterisk. For a discussion of the theme of the Colonial Service in the novel, see Anthony Kirk-Greene, 'The Colonial Service in British Fiction' (forthcoming 1999), complementing a monograph on the French colonial administrator in African fiction, *C'est vous, Monsieur le Commandant? Une certaine image* (1995).

*Bradley, K. G., *The Diary of a District Officer*, 1943 (Northern Rhodesia)
*Cary, Joyce, *An American Visitor*, 1933 (Northern Nigeria)
— *The African Witch*, 1936 (Northern Nigeria)
— *Mister Johnson*, 1939 (Northern Nigeria)
— *Aissa Saved*, 1949 (Northern Nigeria)
— *Cock Jarvis*, (1974) (Northern Nigeria)
*Clifford, Hugh, *Since the Beginning*, 1898 (Malaya)
— *A Freelance of Today*, 1903
— *The Further Side of Silence*, 1916
— *A Prince of Malaya*, 1926
Collins, Norman, *The Governor's Lady*, 1968 (Central Africa)
*Dobson, K. B. A., *District Commissioner*, 1954 (Tanganyika)
*Fowler, Wilfred, *Harama*, 1963 (Nigeria)
Gordimer, Nadine, *A Guest of Honour*, 1971 (Central Africa)
Hanley, Gerald, *The Consul at Sunset*, 1951 (Somaliland)
Huxley, Elspeth, *The Walled City*, 1948 (Northern Nigeria)
— *Murder at Government House*, 1937 (Kenya)

*Kittermaster, M., *The District Officer*, 1957 (Nyasaland)
Maugham, W. Somerset, *The Painted Veil*, 1925 (Hong Kong)
Margery Perham, *Major Dane's Garden*, 1925 (Somaliland)
*Taafe, M., *The Dark Glass*, 1963 (Tanganyika)
Thomas, Alan, *The Governor*, 1961 (East Africa)
Vasanji, M. G., *The Book of Secrets*, 1994 (Tanganyika)
Wallace, Edgar, *The Keepers of the King's Peace*, 1917 (Nigeria)
— *Sanders of the River*, 1926 (Nigeria)

X. A Note on Journals

Articles published in journals are not cited in this bibliography. Articles dealing with Colonial Service matters have appeared from time to time in journals like *Public Administration* (for example A. R. Thomas, 'The Development of the Overseas Civil Service', 36, 1958), *Political Quarterly* (for example, H. J. Laski, 'The Colonial Civil Service', 9, 1938), *African Affairs* (for example, A. H. M. Kirk-Greene, 'The Thin White Line: The Size of the Colonial Service in Africa', 79, 1980), and *Journal of Commonwealth and Imperial History* (for example, I. F. Nicolson and C. Hughes, 'A Provenance of Proconsuls: British Colonial Governors, 1900–1960', 4, 1975; A. H. M. Kirk-Greene, 'The Progress of Proconsuls: Advancement and Migration among the Colonial Governors of British African Territories, 1900–1965', 7, 1979).

On the other hand, specialist journals like *Corona* (1949–62, the Colonial Service house magazine), *Colonial [Office] Journal* (1907–20), *Journal of African Administration*, *Crown Colonist*, *New Commonwealth*, *United Empire* and *Overseas Pensioner* (the Overseas Services Pensioners' Association magazine), carry so many contributions about the Colonial Service that to list the contents would require far more space than is available here. Plans for an anthology from *Corona*, the largest repository of them all, are currently in hand. Certain territorial journals also carried articles relating to Colonial Service experience, for instance *The Journal of the Malayan Branch of the Royal Asiatic Society*, *Tanganyika Notes and Records* and *The Nigerian Field*. The University of Cambridge *Colonial Service Club Magazine* was started in 1928 but it did not survive the war.

Additions of titles central to the focus of this Bibliography will be welcomed by the author.

Colonial Service Documents

I. Guides to Who Was Who in HM Colonial Service/HMOCS

Leaving aside 'the great and the good' who in their lifetime achieved recognition in *Who's Who* or, grander yet, a posthumous entry in the *Dictionary of National Biography*, there are five principal published sources for establishing the career/biographical data of who was who in the Colonial Service.

(a) The Colonial Office List, 1862 and 1962

Published annually from 1862 to 1966 apart from the war years of 1941–5 and 1947, it featured short biographical notes on senior staff. After 1950, a ceiling was imposed of a minimum of ten years' service before qualifying for an entry. Even then, there were more inexplicable omissions than there should have been in such an official document. A handy digest of 15,000 individual entries is provided in A. H. M. Kirk-Greene, *A Biographical Dictionary of the British Colonial Service, 1939–1966* (1991).

Typical entries, selected from the 1862 and 1962 *Lists*, follow.

COLONIAL OFFICE LIST (1862)

MERCER, W. T.— Colonial secretary, Hong Kong; appointed 1854. Salary £1500. Is a member of both councils; entered the colonial service at Hong Kong, 1844; appointed colonial treasurer, 1847; officiating registrar-general, 1849.

MITFORD, E. L.— Appointed a writer to the government of Ceylon, March, 1845; assistant government agent at Ratnapoora, 1847; district judge at Ratnapoora, 1852; acting government agent and fiscal, north-western province of that colony, 1859. Salary £1000.

MOIR, ALEXANDER. — Treasurer and collector of customs, Honduras: appointed 1861. Salary £600. Entered the service in 1843; was for some years in the customs' department, Jamaica; and presiding magistrate of the Bay Islands from Dec. 1855 to the date of his present appointment.

MOODIE, W. J. D.— Was employed in the office of the colonial secretary of the Cape of Good Hope, 1843; in that of the colonial secretary of Natal from 1846 to 1859, in which he became chief clerk of the latter department; was appointed resident magistrate, Lower Umcomas, 1860. Salary £223 and allowances.

MOODY, RICHARD CLEMENT. — Entered the royal engineers, Nov. 1830;

promoted to be captain, March, 1844; lieut.-colonel, Jan. 1855; and colonel, April, 1858; appointed lieut.-governor, June, 1843; which appointment he held until 1847; appointed chief commissioner of lands and works in British Columbia, Sept. 1858; and holds a commission as lieut.-governor. Salary £1200.

COLONIAL OFFICE LIST (1962)

TOWLE, R. P.—b. 1924; ed. King's Coll., Auckland, Univ. of N.Z.; barrister-at-law; mil. serv., 1945–46, sgt; admin. cadet, Uga., 1948; D.O., 1951: p.s. to gov., 1954; dist. comsnr., Kigezi, 1960; courts advr., min. of loc. govt., 1961.

TRAPPES-LOMAX, A. F.—b. 1915; ed. Stonyhurst and Corpus Christi Coll., Oxford; admin. cadet, Nig., 1937; trans. to forest dept., 1947; senr. asst. consvr., forests, 1951; dep. chief consvr., 1957; sec. for forestry, N. Nigeria, 1958; chief consvr., 1960.

TRENCH, D. C. C., C.M.G. (1960), M.C.—b. 1915; ed. Tonbridge Sch. and Jesus Coll., Camb.; mil. serv., 1942–46, lt.-col.; cadet, B.S.I.P., 1938; secon. W. Pac. H.C., 1941; secon., Br. serv., Tonga, 1942; admin. offr., gr. I, 1946; 1st asst. sec., W.Pac. H.C., 1947; sec., govt., B.S.I.P., 1947; att. jt. serv. staff coll., 1949; asst. sec., dep. def. sec., H.K., 1950; clk., councils, 1953; staff gr., 1956; dep. fin. sec., 1956; comsnr., labr., 1957; Imp. Def. Coll., 1958; dep. col. sec., 1959, 1960; redesig. admin. offr., staff gr. A, 1959; high comsnr., W. Pac., 1961.

TROTT, Miss K. J.—ed. Clapham Pk. High Sch., Montessori Train. Coll., Hampstead and St. Gabriel's Train. Coll., Camberwell, London; English mistress, nurses' train. coll., G.C., 1947; educ. offr., 1951; senr. educ. offr., 1954; prin. educ. offr., 1958 (Ghana civil service).

TURNBULL, Sir Richard, K.C.M.G. (1958), C.M.G. (1953).— b.1909; ed. Univ. Coll. Sch., Univ. Coll., Lond., and Magdalene Coll., Camb.; dist. offr., Ken., 1931; civ. liaison offr., h.q., E.A. Cmd., 1947; prov. comsnr., 1948; defence sec., 1954; min. for internal security and defence, 1954; ch. sec., 1955; o.a.g., 1957–58; gov. and c.-in-c., Tang., 1958; gov.-gen., 1961.

(b) HMOCS Records of Service

Following the publication of the final *Colonial Office List* in 1966, the Commonwealth Office issued a list *HMOCS: Records of Service of Senior Staff* in 1967. This initiative was repeated only once in the succeeding 30 years of HMOCS's existence.

A typical page (1967) follows.

HMOCS LIST (1967)

NIELD, J.—b.1911; ed. Dartford Gram. Sch.; mil. serv., 1941-48; maj.; marktg. offr., Fiji, 1953; asst. comm. ind. offr., 1956.

NIELSEN, E. E. E.—b. 1925; ed. gram. schls. Haifa and Jerusalem; mil. serv., 1943-46; contrl. offr., dept. of civil aviat., Pal., 1946; air traffic contrl. offr., gr. 1, Mal., 1948; dep. dir. civil aviat., 1961-63; supt., civil aviat., W.P.H.C., 1963.

NIELSEN, N. H. K.—b. 1907; ed. Folk High Sch., and Royal Vet. and Agric. Coll., Copenhagen; vet. offr., N. Rhod., 1950. (Zambia Govt. service.)

NORMAN-WALKER, Sir Hugh, K.C.M.G. (1966), C.M.G. (1964), O.B.E. (1961).—b. 1916; ed. Sherborne Sch. and Corpus Christi Coll., Camb.; I.C.S., 1938; admin. offr., Nyasa. 1949; asst. sec., 1953; secon. cabinet off., Fed. of Rhod. and Nyasa., 1953; devel. sec., Nyasa., 1954; sec. treasy., 1961; H.M. comsnr., Bech. Prot., 1965; gov. and c.-in-c., Sey., and H.M. comsnr., Br. Indian Ocean Terr., 1967.

NORTH, A. C.—b.1924; ed. Strathallan Sch., Manchester Univ.; mil. serv., 1943-47, lt.; cadet. N. Rhod., 1948; dist. offr., 1950; admin. offr., gr. I, 1962; prin. coll. staff trning., 1963-66. (Zambia Govt. service.)

NORTH, J. D.—b.1926; ed. Acklam Hall Sch., Middlesbrough, Trinity Coll., Camb., and Bham Univ.; mil. serv., 1947-49, R.A.F., f/o; exec. engnr., P.W.D., Nig., 1951; prov. engnr., N. Nig., 1958; senr. exec. engnr., 1961; progress engnr., 1963-65. (Nig. Govt. service.)

NORTHWAY, J. C.—b.1927; ed. Cathedral Choir Sch. and King's Sch., Canterbury; Durham Univ.; mil. serv., 1945-48; asst. audtr., N. Rhod., 1951; audtr., 1953; senr. audtr., H.C.T., 1956; prin. audtr., Fed. Nig., 1960; asst. dir. audit, 1960; senr. audr., Basuto., 1964; dir., audit, Bech., 1964. (Botswana Govt. service.)

(c) Territorial Staff Lists, Civil Service Lists and Staff Biographies
Each territory produced a regular government *Staff List*, with varying amounts of biographical data on every officer in the establishment regardless of juniority or length of service. A few also published a *Civil Service List*, containing detailed personal career data. In the case of Hong Kong, from 1974 the government issued a continuing series of *Staff Biographies*.

The examples that follow are taken from the *Malayan Civil List* (1923), the *Palestine Staff List* (1947) and the *Hong Kong Staff Biographies* (1974).

MALAYAN CIVIL LIST (1923)

MACPHERSON, JOHN STUART. M.A. Edin. Born August 25, 1898.   MALAY.
 Passed Cadet, $375 *p.m.* (Date for seniority, 25-3-21.)   Law.

FEDERATED MALAY STATES.

23 Mar. 1921	Cadet. Attached to the Federal Secretariat, Kuala Lumpur
24 Aug. ,,	Acting Fourth Assistant Secretary to Government, F.M.S.,
to 2 Oct. ,,	Class V
17 Nov. ,,	Acting Fourth Assistant Secretary to Government, F.M.S., Class V
11 July 1922	Passed Cadet
17 Aug. ,,	Acting Assistant District Officer, Kuala Selangor

MARRIOTT, HAYES. B.A. Cantab. Born November 29, 1873.
MALAY.
 General Adviser, Johore, $1,450 *p.m.*

STRAITS SETTLEMENTS.

6 Nov. 1896	Appointed a Cadet by the Secretary of State
6 Dec. ,,	Reported arrival in the Colony. Attached to the Colonial Secretary' Office
25 Mar. 1897	Attached to the Education Office
3 May ,,	Acting Third Magistrate, Singapore
17 Nov. ,,	Acting District Officer, Alor Gajah
7 May 1898	Passed Final Examination in Malay

CLASS V.

14 Feb. 1899	Passed Cadet. District Officer, Malacca
14 Feb. 1903	Acting Second Magistrate, Singapore
2 April 1903	On vacation leave
1 July ,,	On half-pay leave

CLASS IV.

1 Sept. 1903	Appointed to Class IV
1 June 1904	Assistant Postmaster-General, Penang
9 July ,,	Acting Second Magistrate, Penang
1 Dec. ,,	A Coroner for Penang
16 Feb. 1905	Acting Official Assignee, Straits Settlements
16 Feb. ,,	Assistant Superintendent of Indian Immigrants, Singapore, in addition
18 Feb. ,,	Appointed a Commissioner of Currency
15 May 1906	Acting Second Magistrate, Singapore
1 Mar. 1906	Acting Collector of Land Revenue, Singapore

CLASS III.

1 May 1907	Second Assistant Colonial Secretary but continued to act as Collector of Land Revenue, Singapore
8 June 1908	Acting Inspector of Prisons, S.S.
9 April 1909	On vacation leave
2 July „	On half-pay leave

PALESTINE GOVERNMENT: PUBLIC WORKS (1947)

Appointment	Name	Date of Birth	Date of first appt. in Palestine	Date of appt. to present Office	Other Public Service
Director (xix)	(m) C. Wilson Brown, C.B.E., M.C.	6-7-1891	4-3-38	4-3-38	Gold Coast 1920-28; Sierra Leone 1932-37.
Deputy Director (xvi)	(m) H.C.H. Jones	14-3-1898	2-4-36	15-5-46	Kenya 1925-36.
Asst. Director (xiv)	(m) R.F.B. Crook	25-12-1900	31-7-36	10-8-38	Nigeria 1925; 1928-36.
Water Engineer (xiv)	(m) M. Grehan	1-6-1913			
Well Drilling Superintendent (xiv)	(m) J. McWilliams, M.B.E.	21-4-1898	2-11-31	17-2-47	
Chief Accounting Officer	(Vacant)				
(xiv)	(m) (H. Kosloff (Acting))	25-5-1897	16-1-21	1-2-47	
Geologist (xiii)	(m) S.H. Shaw	6-11-1903	11-6-37	11-6-37	Australia 1928-30.
Senior Architect (viii)	(m) P.H. Winter	18-11-1899	13-8-26	13-1-38	
Architect (xiii)	T.A.L. Concannon	3-2-1906	15-7-46	15-7-46	Palestine 1928-33; 1934-38; Nigeria 1938-41; Hong-Kong 1941-46

HONG KONG STAFF BIOGRAPHIES, 1974

HALL, Derick Arnold, B.Sc., C.Eng., F.R.I.N.A., F.I.Mar.E. b. 22.2.38. m. *Senior Surveyor of Ships, Marine Department.*
Surveyor of Ships 22.11.65. Board of Trade Attachment 22.11.65–30.12.66. Arr. 4.2.67. Ag. Sr. of Ships 24.5–7.7.69, 31.7–31.8.69, 1.10.69–28.5.70, 15.1.71–11.1.72. **Sr. Surveyor of Ships 12.10.72.**

HALLAM, John Anthony, A.R.Ae.S., M.I.N. b. 29.4.24. m. *Assistant Director of Civil Aviation. Chmn. of Airport Operations Cttee.*
Royal Navy Lt. 10.42–5.52. **Air Traffic Control Offr., Cl. II 30.5.52.** Arr. 30.6.52. Re-designated **Air Traffic Control Offr., Cl. I 4.1.60. Air Traffic Control Offr., Cl. I 10.12.62.** Ag. Deputy Dir. of Civil Aviation 18–25.2.74, 23.3–14.4.74

HALLIWELL, Peter Robert, B.A. Hons. (Birmingham), P.G.C.E. (Birmingham), F.R.G.S. b. 19.4.27. m. *Senior Principal, Education Department. Royal Hong Kong Auxiliary Police Force (Marine).*

Education Offr. 21.1.52. Arr. 5.1.52. Inspectorate 1.9.59. Ag. Sr. Education Offr. 10.12.62–2.9.63, 12.2.65. **Sr. Education Offr. 1.9.65. Sr. Prin. 7.12.70.**

HAMMOND, Joseph Charles Anthony, M.A. (Oxon.). b. 6.1.34. m. *Administrative Officer, Staff Grade C. Colonial Secretariat.* **C.***
NYASALAND: Adm. Offr. 7.58–11.64. HONG KONG: **Adm. Offr. 8.11.64.** Arr. 9.11.64. Asst. Secy., C. Sect. 19.11.64. Asst. Establishment Offr. & Asst. Colonial Secy, 26.7.68. **Sr. Adm. Offr. 1.10.70.** Clerk of Councils and Asst. Colonial Secy. 13.9.71. **Adm. Offr., Staff Grade C 28.6.72.** Prin. Asst. Colonial Secy. 4.4.73. Deputy Secy for the Civil Service 19.9.73.

HAMPTON, David. b. 2.9.23. m. *Senior Superintendent, Prisons Department.* **C. Prison Offr. 15.12.47.** Ag. Prin. Offr. 5.4–8.12.53. **Prin. Offr. 9.12.53.** Ag. Prin. Industry Offr. 25.5–25.11.55, 31.1–1.4.56. **Asst. Ch. Offr. 3.11.57.** Ag. Ch. Offr. 11.12.58–13.8.60. **Ch. Offr.14.10.60.** Ag. Supt. of Prisons 8.2–12.3.63, 19.5–8.9.64, 7.4–21.5.65, 25.7–31.8.65. **Supt of Prisons 3.3.66. Sr. Supt. of Prisons 1.7.71.** Ag. Deputy Comr. of Prisons 6.8–8.10.72.

(d) Colonial Blue Books

Up to c.1939, the colonial *Blue Books* often carried extensive career information on their staff. In cases where the government also issued a *Civil Service List*, the data were often similar.

Examples follow from Nigeria (1929), Tanganyika (1929) and Ceylon (1931).

NIGERIA, 1929

Charles Edward Jewel Whiting, Lieutenant, Northumberland Fusiliers; Classical Scholar, Haileybury College, Prize Cadet R.M.C. (Sandhurst) B.A. (Oxon). Born 10th June, 1900.
L. Fulani.

Superintendent of Education, £660 p.a.

26 July	1922	Appointed Superintendent of Education.
10 Aug.	1922	Arrived in Nigeria and assumed duty at Yola.
9 May	1924	On leave.
30 Oct.	1924	Returned from leave and resumed duty.
7 May	1926	On leave.
28 Oct.	1926	Returned from leave and resumed duty.
4 May	1928	On leave.
11 Oct.	1928	Returned from leave and resumed duty.

Educated at Haileybury College and St. John's College, Oxford.
R.M.C. Sandhurst. 1st Battalion Northumberland Fusiliers,
April, 1918 to September, 1920.

Rupert Moultrie East, B.A. (Oxon). Born 18th August, 1898.
H. Munshi.
Part "A."
H. Hausa   *Superintendent of Education, £630 p.a.*

11 July	1923	Appointed Superintendent of Education.
25 July	1923	Arrived in Nigeria and assumed duty at Wanune.
9 Aug.	1923	
2 Feb.	1925	On leave.
23 July	1925	Returned from leave and resumed duty.
28 Jan.	1927	On leave.
1 Sept.	1927	Returned from leave and resumed duty.

Educated at St Edward's School, Oxford, Exeter College, Oxford.
Lieutenant R.G.A. May, 1917 to June, 1919.

TANGANYIKA, 1929

m **LEONARD SAXTON WATERALL**, M.A., F.C.Z. Born 20th October, 1884.

District Officer (Seconded as Deputy Labour Commissioner), £840 p.a.

Educated at St. Paul's and Jesus College, Cambridge; 2nd Class Honours Classical Tripos 1907; B.A. 1907; M.A. 1911: Passed Higher Swahili January 1922; Law July 1924; Northern Rhodesia Probationer 1907; Assistant Native Commissioner 1911; Native Commissioner 1912; Inspector of Rhodesian Natives in the Katanga 1914; British Vice-Consul, Katanga 1914; War Service—France 1915-1916; Egypt and Palestine 1917; German East Africa 1918.

24 Mar.	1918	Appointed locally Assistant Political Officer and assumed duty at Malinyi (Mahenge District).
22 Nov.	1919	Transferred to Mahenge.
22 Nov.	1919	Acting District Political Officer.
30 Apr.	1920	Acting District Political Officer.
7 July	1920	On leave.
6 Jan.	1921	Returned from leave and resumed duty at Mikindani.
27 Oct.	1922	On leave.
14 July	1923	Returned from leave and resumed duty at Kilosa.
24 July	1923	Acting Administrative Officer, 1st Grade.
31 July	1924	Acting Administrative Officer, 1st Grade.
1 Aug.	1924	Appointed Administrative Officer, 1st Grade.
4 Aug.	1925	On leave.
21 Feb.	1926	Returned from leave and resumed duty at Morogoro (seconded to Labour Department).
1 Apr.	1926	Appointed Deputy Labour Commissioner.
13 Feb.	1928	On leave.
7 Sept.	1928	Returned from leave and resumed duty at Morogoro.

CEYLON, 1931

Davidson, Gerald Larcom Dean.
Born Feb. 14 1898. £840 (*February* 14,
1931, £880).

Cadet.—Nov. 11, 1921, appointed by
the Secretary of State; Dec. 9, 1921,
arrived in the Colony; Dec. 10, 1921,
attached to the Colombo Kachcheri; Jan.
11, 1922, attached to the Badulla Kachcheri; July 17, 1922, *passed First Examination under the Regulations dated
December* 17, 1920.

Class 4.—Oct. 1, 1922, Officer of
Class IV.; Oct. 19, 1922, *passed Exam-
ination in Riding*; Sept. 29, 1923, Office
Assistant to the Assistant Government
Agent, Hambantota; Jan. 7, 1924, *passed
Second Examination under the Regula-
tions dated December* 17, 1920; Oct. 27,
1924, Office Assistant to the Government
Agent, Province of Sabaraamuwa; June
17, 1926, to Oct. 17, 1926, on commuted
half-pay leave; Oct. 22, 1926, Office
Assistant to the Government Agent,
North-Western Province; Sept. 10, 1927,
Police Magistrate, Gampola.

Class 3.—Feb. 14, 1928, Officer of
Class III.; Jan. 7, 1929, Assistant
Director of Statistics; Mar. 28, 1930, to
July 11, 1930, on commuted half-pay
leave; July 12, 1930, resumed duties as
Assistant Director of Statistics.

Ranasinha, Arthur Godwin, B.A.
London. Born June 24, 1898. £840
(*January* 29, 1931, £880).

Cadet.—Jan. 29, 1921, appointed by the
Secretary of State; Feb. 25, 1921, arrived
in the Colony; Mar. 1, 1921, attached to
the Kegalla Kachcheri; July 17, 1922,
*passed First Examination under the
Regulations dated December* 17, 1920;
Oct. 19, 1922, *passed Examination in
Riding*; Oct. 23, 1922, attached to the
Jaffna Kachcheri; Mar. 14, 1923, Police
Magistrate, Point Pedro.

Class 4.—Nov. 5, 1923, Officer of
Class IV.; Nov. 5, 1923, Police Magistrate, Jaffna.

Class 3.—Jan. 29, 1928. Officer of
Class III., April 21, 1928, District Judge,
Avissawella; Jan. 3, 1930, District Judge,
Badulla.

(e) The Colonial Service Lists

During the 1930s, as part of the unification of the Colonial Services,
each departmental service published its own *List* of officers who were
members. This practice was not revived after the war.

A typical example follows, taken from *The Colonial Forest Service
List* (1939).

CARVER, John Edward Airey. M.A. (Oxon). Diploma in Forestry (Oxon).
B. 1899. Conservator of Forests, Mauritius.
Imperial Forestry Institute refresher courses, 1928 and 1935.
Official service:—Nyasaland: Assistant Conservator of Forests, 1921.
Mauritius: Conservator of Forests, 1936.
Publication:—Memorandum on the intensive management proceeding on
certain divisions of Crown Forests.

CATER, John Charles. B.A. (For.) Oxon. B. 1913. Assistant Conservator of
Forests, Trinidad.

Refresher course at the Imperial Forestry Institute, 1938.
Official service:—Trinidad: Assistant Conservator of Forests, 1935.

CATTERALL, Ralph Drummond. B.Sc. (For.) Edin. B. 1907.
Assistant Conservator of Forests, Nigeria.
Imperial Forestry Institute post-graduate course, 1928-9.

CHAPMAN, Geoffrey Walter. B.A. (Cantab). Diploma in Forestry (Cantab).
B. 1908. Assistant Conservator of Forests, Cyprus.
Imperial Forestry Institute, post-graduate course, 1929-30.
*Publications:—*The importance of Forests in Mountainous countries. (*The Cyprus Agricultural Journal*, 1934). "An investigation in Paphos Forest to determine the accuracy of the Working Plan Enumeration Surveys." "The problem of Aleppo pine regeneration on andesitic soils in Cyprus."

CLARKE-BUTLER-COLE, Robert Falcon. B.Sc. (For.) Edin. B. 1904.
Senior Assistant Conservator of Forests, Nigeria.
Imperial Forestry Institute, post-graduate course, 1926-7.
Official service:—Nigeria: Assistant Conservator of Forests, 1927.
Senior Assistant Conservator of Forests.

II. Colonial Service Guidance

While each territorial government issued its own set of *Laws* and of General Orders (GOs), often supported by *Financial Instructions* and further *Manuals* on bureaucratic procedures, *Colonial Regulations* (col. Regs.) applied to the whole Colonial Service. First published in 1837 (in itself documentary evidence of the existence of a Colonial Service) and revised or reprinted right up to the replacement of the Colonial Service by HMOCS in 1956, there was, as the following lists of contents show, a positive continuity in the format and scope of colonial regulation.

At the more informal level, considerable guidance was offered to newly appointed officers on what to expect in living conditions and what clothing and equipment to take out.

(a) Colonial Regulations, 1837

CONTENTS.

CHAPTER I.
THE GOVERNOR.

Sect.

CHAPTER II.

CIVIL OFFICERS UNDER THE IMMEDIATE CONTROL OF THE SECRETARY OF STATE.

CHAPTER IV.

HONOURS AND DISTINCTIONS.

Sect.

(b) Colonial Regulations, 1956

CONTENTS:
Part I–Public Officers

B. Acting Appointments ... ...
C. Seniority ... ...
D. Salaries and Allowances ... ...
E. Conduct and Discipline ... ...
F. Passages ... ...
G. Leave ... ...
H. Medical Examinations ... ...
I. Transfer Arrangements ... ...
J. Retirement ... ...

(c) Hints for Newly Appointed officers, c.1920

(i) West Africa

While the experience of several generations of service in India and in the Eastern dependencies had built up a corpus of knowledge about health and conditions of living for Europeans in Asia, Africa was very much a novelty when it began to dominate the Colonial Service scene at the turn of the nineteenth century. Consequently, the Colonial Office devoted a lot of attention to the production of booklets containing advice on what to expect. In the early years, individual West African colonies produced guidance along the lines of *Hints for Officers Selected for Service in Northern Nigeria*, published in 1901, Dr A. J. Chambers's *Practical Advice for Colonial Administrators in the Gold Coast* (1903), and W. H. Beverley's *Southern Nigeria Pocket Book and Map* (1911). In the course of time, these became incorporated into guidance for a wider area. *The West African Pocket Book*, from which the following extracts are taken, was published by the Crown Agents for the Colonies and reached its fifth edition in 1920.

The West African
Pocket Book, 1920

CONTENTS.

Voyage Out And Arrival In West Africa

Never be parted from your Mosquito Net.

The systematic use of quinine should be commenced the day before touching the West African coast, and kept up during residence in West Africa and for at least six months after return to Europe, unless an officer is medically advised to do otherwise. Inability to take quinine should be regarded as an absolute bar to residence in tropical Africa.

The systematic use of quinine may be followed in whichever of the four following ways may best suit the individual:—

1. Five grains every day (recommended).

2. Ten grains on Sundays and Wednesdays.

3. Fifteen grains on the 10th and 11th, 20th and 21st, and 30th and 31st (or last two) days in each month. The fifteen grains may be divided into three five-grain doses, each of which may follow one of the main meals of the day.

4. Ten grains on two consecutive days weekly, by preference Saturdays and Sundays.

Most people find that the best time to take the five-grain doses is just before the "big" breakfast or lunch. When the larger doses are adopted it is best to take them after dinner, so that the buzzing in the ears and deafness which are likely to follow may occur during sleep and rest, and not during the day, when they might prove troublesome. Quinine "tabloids" are commonly used, and it should be ascertained by experiment that such tabloids are capable of breaking up easily and dissolving when placed in water. Anyone who finds that the quinine disagrees with him should consult a Medical Officer. If the daily dose of quinine is taken in solution it prevents the symptoms of dyspepsia, which are often brought on by taking of quinine in tablet form.

Food and Drink

Never eat tinned food if you can get fresh.

Avoid all over-ripe fruit, and meat or fish which is the least bit tainted.

When a tin of provisions – animal or vegetable – has been opened, its contents must at once be emptied into a glass or earthenware vessel. Neglect to do this is a frequent source of ptomaine poisoning, and one's servants have to be constantly kept up to the mark in this respect, as they cannot see the necessity for the precaution.

In some parts of West Africa chickens are the chief fresh animal food, but they are very small. A good plan is to buy a number of live chickens, according to the size of the place they are to be kept in, and to give them a small feed once a day of rice, maize, or other grain. In a month they are much better eating, and will repay the trouble.

Beef, mutton, and goat-flesh can generally be obtained.

West African yams are large potato-like tubers and are of two kinds. Both are of a yellowish white inside, and the smaller of the two kinds has a pink layer just below the skin. The larger are called yams simply, and the smaller coco-yams; the former are the better eating.

On the coast potatoes may sometimes be bought from the steamers.

The pawpaw looks like a small vegetable marrow, but grows on a tree. When ripe it is eaten as a fruit; and when unripe it can be boiled and served like a vegetable marrow, from which when properly cooked it is practically indistinguishable.

Certain kinds of leaves, such as the young leaves of the coco-yam, can be chopped up fine and served like spinach.

Banana, orange, pineapple, and certain kinds of plum, are common. Mango, guava, &c., grow in some places.

When travelling, biscuits may be used in the place of bread, but, when stationary, bread is easy to make (see recipes in Appendix D).

Beef should be firm, of a deep red colour, not flabby, sodden, or watery. The flesh should consist only of meat fibres, fat, and gristle. There must be no minute white spots on or between the meat fibres.

Goat meat is paler in colour than beef and there is not much fat as a rule.

It is very important to know that a beast intended for food was slaughtered and that it did not die from disease.

A humane way to kill a bullock is to have the animal tied up by the head close to a tree or post, and then to shoot it with a revolver. The revolver should be held about six inches from the centre point of the frontal bone, *i.e.,* midway between the upper border of the eye socket and the lower border of the horn of the opposite side. The animal falls unconscious at once. It should be bled five minutes afterwards.

Fish is usually plentiful and good on the coast.

With regard to drink, water and palm wine are the two beverages of the country. Palm wine should not be drunk unless it has been seen collected, otherwise it is very likely to have been mixed with water from some infected pool or stream.

Water should be filtered, and must always be boiled. It is important to use a filter of the best kind, and to keep it clean. "Stand filters" are supplied for use in bungalows or station houses, and the "candles" of these should be thoroughly scrubbed and boiled once every week; on the least suspicion of a crack in it, a candle should be at once condemned and replaced by a new one. The Doulton, Pasteur-Chamberland, or Brownlow filters can be recommended, but the ordinary carbon filters are worse than useless. The filtering can be left to a servant, but the European should always go daily and *see that the water is actually boiled.* The vessel of boiled drinking water should then be covered up and placed to cool on a piece of wood in a soup plate full of water, to keep it free from ants.

In addition to a filter, a water cooler is almost a necessity, as lukewarm or tepid water is a very un-inviting drink. Water coolers can be obtained in most towns, and when filled with water (filtered and boiled) and hung up in a breeze, the water becomes quite cold by evaporation. Any liquid in a bottle may be cooled in much the same way by wrapping a piece of wet flannel round the bottle and placing it in a breeze half-an-hour before it is required.

A thermos flask is also a useful article to have on patrol, but, owing to its being so fragile, it is necessary to stuff it with cloth or paper when not in use, so that it is not cracked by excessive vibration.

Water, if muddy, should first be strained through a piece of linen, such as a handkerchief. If it is still thick and difficult to filter, it can be placed is a large basin and a little alum added to it, six grains to the gallon being the usual quantity. The alum causes all the fine particles in the water to sink to the bottom of the basin in about six or eight hours. The addition of a little lime is occasionally an advantage.

WORK AND AMUSEMENT

The working hours in West Africa vary greatly in the different Colonies and Protectorates, but a good plan is to get up early and do as much work as possible before 11 a.m. This leaves the hotter part of the day for what is usually the smaller half of the work.

An early breakfast of, say, a rasher of bacon or an egg, with tea, is usually taken on first getting up in the morning, about 6.15. It is of importance never to go out without having first eaten at least a biscuit. The remaining meals vary according to the Colony, and the work that has to be done.

A day's work in West Africa is much the same as a fair average day's work in England. If what has to be done is done regularly and with method, an officer will rarely have any serious difficulty in performing his duties.

Officers who have to travel should always arrange their journeys so that the in-coming and out-going official mails are not neglected.

Every officer should use a diary or some other means of bringing to mind duties which require to be discharged periodically, and things which should be done on particular days.

Games, chiefly golf, bowls, cricket, and. tennis, are played in the late afternoon from about half-past four, at all events at the larger stations. Polo is played at Bathurst, Accra, Kumasi, and at several stations in Nigeria. In any case Europeans should always take brisk exercise every day equal at least to a two-mile walk. Exercise readily causes sweating, and it is essential that those who indulge in games should immediately afterwards take off wet clothes, dry the body, and put on dry underwear before sitting down outside in the cool of the evening.

APPENDIX A.

OUTFIT.

All officers are recommended to provide themselves with the following articles:–

Mosquito net.

*White pith sun hat, with puggaree.

White umbrellas, lined.

Large kettle or camp saucepan, to hold at least five pints, for boiling
water.

Lantern, to burn candles or vegetable oil.

A few Medicines, &c., as described on page 49.

Two cases of provisions.

The most recent map, or maps, of the Colony or Protectorate to which
they are proceeding.

Clothing.—With regard to clothing, several flannel tennis or khaki drill
suits, an old serge or tweed suit, and a light waterproof are required, and also an
overcoat for use chiefly on the voyages. The seams of the waterproof must be
sewn and not stuck together. Waistcoats are not worn except on the voyages,
but kummerbunds are useful. In Nigeria there is a special (optional) dinner
dress (see Appendix C). Officers of the higher grades going to other parts of
West Africa should take out a dress suit, with dinner jacket. This will also be
wanted on the voyages.

Plenty of thin summer woollen underclothing should be taken out, and also
heavy underclothing for the voyages.

It is unwise to wear cotton next to the skin; and a flannel shirt, or linen or
cotton shirt with woollen undervest, should be worn. Shirts, vests, and drawers
should, when possible, be changed once every day, and at least eight, of each
are needed. Shirts with turn-down collars are suitable. Needles, thread, buttons,
&c., will be wanted for repairs.

Two pairs at least of stout brown leather boots are recommended, and dubbin
should not be forgotten. For the Northern Provinces of Nigeria, a third pair
should be taken. For the bush, boots should be well nailed. Mosquito boots
should be bought in England when an official comes out on his first tour;
subsequently he can have similar boots made locally on the Coast at less
expense, but it **is** important that the new comer should be provided with them in
the first instance. Boots give greater protection than shoes against mosquitoes
and tsetse flies. When on trek the end of the trousers should be tucked into the
socks as tsetse flies seek the ankle so as to get in under the open end of the
trousers. Shoes should only be worn when playing tennis, cricket or other
games.

All clothing, more especially if woollen or merino, must be kept in air-tight
steel trunks to preserve them from moth and mould. A few naphthalene balls or
camphor squares should always be placed amongst the clothes to help in
preserving them. In case of woollen clothes it is necessary to take them out of
the boxes at least once a fortnight, examine them for mould, brush them
thoroughly if necessary, to remove any traces of mould, place them in a bright

sun for a couple of hours to remove dampness, then replace in the box, which should also have been put out into the sun, not forgetting to replace the camphor and naphthalene among the clothes.

Miscellaneous.—All officers should take out towels, blankets, sheets (if used), pillow and pillow cases, crockery, cutlery, table linen, saucepans, kettle, frying pan, and kitchen cloths.

Valuable watches should not be taken as they are likely to be spoiled, but several, two or three, good and fairly cheap watches are useful. Spare glasses should be taken out for each watch.

Officers going to Hausa-speaking districts should take Robinson and Burdon's Hausa Grammar (Kegan Paul, 5/-). Other useful books on Hausa are Miller's Hausa Notes (Oxford University Press), and Robinson's Hausa Dictionary (2 vols., Cambridge University Press).

Camp Outfit.—Medical and military officers, all officers going to Nigeria (except, those who will remain in Lagos town or on the Railway), and all officers whose duties may require them to travel inland otherwise than by railway in any of the other West African Colonies should take out camp outfit, except tents. Tents will be supplied by the Government when required.

In addition to the articles mentioned in the preceding list as necessary for all officers whether they will travel or not, travellers will require most of the following articles:—

> Pump filter, with stirrup and six spare candles, in case, or a
>   small size portable drip filter with at least three spare candles.
> "Compacaum" (or other) camp bed, mosquito rods, mosquito
>   net, three blankets, pillow and two pillow cases, in waterproof
>   canvas bag.
> Waterproof sheet, about 8 ft. by 6 ft.
> Bath and washstand (combined).
> Canvas bucket.
> Camp table and camp chair or deck chair.
> Water bottle, large, felt-covered, of enamelled iron or aluminium.
> Cooking and eating utensils.
> 20 yards of muslin, for making houses mosquito proof.
> Indiarubber boots, reaching to the knees, not lined with felt.
> Two sir-tight metal uniform cases, not larger than 44 ins. by 16
>   ins. by 11 ins., with name of officer painted on.
> Revolver and ammunition.
> Small compass.
> Hammer, nails, case opener.

The following list will serve as a guide to the cooking and eating utensils needed. Some of the articles are the same as have already been mentioned

under the heads "General" and "Miscellaneous." These need not, of course, be
duplicated.

> Two kettles.
> Nest of three steel or aluminium saucepans with detachable
>   handles.
> Frying pan.
> Small mincing machine for preparing tough meat.
> Three pots, for salt, pepper, and mustard.
> Metal tea-pot.
> Two block tin or aluminium provision boxes, about 9 ins. by 6
>   ins., for sugar, and bread or biscuits.
> Enamelled iron (or stout crockery) plates, cups, saucers, knives,
>   forks, tea-spoons (two of each article); table-spoon, soup-spoon,
>   enamelled iron (or stout crockery) meat dish, two metal tumblers.
> Cook's knives, forks and spoons, two of each.
> Small metal "Sparklet" bottle and "Sparklets."

At a slightly increased cost, some of the articles may be got in the form of a
small luncheon basket, and one of the bottles may be replaced by a copper
kettle with a screw lid and a screw stopper to the spout. This kettle will serve
instead of a teapot, and also to hold water during marches.

A portable lamp and a lantern or hurricane lamp are also necessary.

The bed, bedding, mosquito net, etc., should be made up with special care as
a single load, which must be thoroughly waterproof. A cork mattress may be
added if desired, and three good blankets are recommended as a great comfort,
particularly in those parts of Nigeria where the temperature falls at night to
anything between 40º and 55º F.

Some officers prefer to take, instead of a canvas bath, a metal hip bath, with
a wicker lining, which serves to pack things in.

All clothing must be packed in the air-tight uniform cases for travelling.

If the eyes are likely to be sensitive to the glare of the sun, smoked goggles
should be taken. Men who can shoot for the pot will like to take a shot-gun and
cartridges.

Northern Nigeria.—Officers going to the Northern Provinces of Nigeria
must also take saddlery and horse requisites, suited to ponies not usually
exceeding 14 hands, and riding breeches and gaiters.

A drip filter, in addition to the pump filter, is often useful. Two or three
water bottles should be taken for marches.

Officers of the Political and Medical Departments, and others whose work
may involve their travelling in the interior of Nigeria, are also required to
provide themselves with a brown leather belt, ammunition pouch, holster, and
lanyard, and a revolver of ·455 bore (to take Government ammunition).

In the Northern Provinces of Nigeria a shot gun with about 500 cartridges (say, 100 No 2 for geese, 200 No. 3 or 4 for guinea-fowl, &c., and 200 No. 5 for partridges, &c.) will be found almost indispensable if an officer is quartered in the bush. Each 100 cartridges should be soldered in tin. A small bore single shot carbine is good enough for the smaller antelope. For the larger antelope and dangerous game a larger bore is more effective, but so very few opportunities occur of hunting the latter that expensive double-barrel rifles of large bore are seldom used. Officers will, of course make themselves acquainted with the restrictions imposed by law in regard to the shooting of game.

MEDICINES, &c.

Bi-hydrochloride of Quinine, 500 tablets of 5 grains each.
Sulphate of Soda, in crystals, 11 lb. weight.
Bottle of Chlorodyne, ½-oz.
Boracic Acid, 2 lbs. weight.
Bi-carbonate of Soda, 2 ozs., in tabloids of grains x. each.
Clinical Thermometer (to be used only if there is no doctor at
    the Station).
6 First Aid Dressings.
Alum, for clearing water, 1 lb., in tabloids of grains iii. each.
Permanganate of Potash, ½ lb.
Vaseline, for protecting knives and razors from rust, 1 lb.
Sulphate of Magnesia, 1 lb., in 1 oz. packets.
Large tube of Hazeline cream.

The sulphate of soda is intended for use as an aperient, in doses of one heaped-up teaspoonful. Other aperients may be substituted if preferred. Directions for the use of the rest of the drugs are given in Appendix E and other parts of this book.

Officers likely to be stationed in any place where a Medical Officer is not available should apply, on the Coast, for a small bottle of the following tabloids:—

Vegetable Laxative.
Lead and Opium Pills.
Compound Phenacetin.

Directions for use to be put on bottle.

PROVISIONS.

It will usually be found cheaper to take out the less perishable kinds of provisions from England rather than to buy them locally. Good fresh provisions when obtained are much preferable to tinned, but almost every officer will require some of the latter. Except in the cases mentioned in the footnotes on page 42, it is suggested that at least three months' supply of provisions should be taken out, and officers going to bush stations may find it expedient to take out a larger supply. Provisions should be packed in cases with hinged lids and a padlock and key, and not in nailed-up cases. Suitable cases are obtainable ready packed. Some of the cases weigh 60 lbs., but this will not be too heavy for a strong carrier, although 50 lbs. is better.

The following list of articles for one case will serve as a guide to those who prefer to select their own provisions:—

½-lb. tin Tea.
½-lb. tin Coffee.
½-lb. tin Cocoa.
7 small tins "Ideal" or "Green Butterfly" Milk.
1 bottle Saxin Tabloids.
1 2-lb. tin Rolled Oats.
2¼-lb. tins Sardines in oil or Tomato Sauce.
6 tins assorted Meats.
2 1-lb. tins of Marmalade.
6 4-oz. tins of Jam.
2½ lb. tins of Butter.
2 1-lb. tins of Plain Biscuits.
1 bottle Salt.
1¼-lb. tin Pepper.
1¼-lb. tin Mustard.

2 boxes Sparklets, if Sparklet Syphon is taken.
6 tins assorted Soups or 6 Soup Squares.
1½-lb. tin Curry Powder.
1 2-lb. tin Rice.
2 1-lb. tins Beef Dripping.
4 tins assorted Vegetables.
4 tins fruit.
1 bottle Pickles.
1 small bottle Worcestershire Sauce.
2 1-1b. tins Tongue.
3 tins assorted Tinned Meats or Army Rations.
1 bottle Lime Juice.
1 Tin-opener.

This will more than suffice for a week even where nothing can be got locally, and ordinarily, where some fresh provisions are obtainable, it will last a good deal longer.

APPENDIX B.

FURNITURE.

The Government of the Gambia provides all European officers with furnished quarters.

In the Gold Coast the following is a list of the articles of furniture usually supplied to single officers:—

DINING ROOM.

Table, Dining	1	Cupboard	1
Sideboard	1	Table, Writing	1
Wagon, Dinner	1	Chairs, Bentwood	6

Chair, Bentwood, Arm 1

BED-ROOM.

(NOTE THAT MOSQUITO NETS ARE NOT SUPPLIED.)

Bedstead	1	Pillows	2
Canvas Sit	1	Press	1
Mattress, Wire	1	Table, Dressing	1
Mattress, Hair	1	Toilet Glass	1
Bolster	1	Chairs	2

BATHROOM.

Washstand	1	Towel Horse	1
Toilet Ware (5 pieces)	1	Bath Tub	1

VERANDAH.

Madeira Couch	1	Madeira Centre Table	1
Madeira Lounge	1	Madeira Tea Table	1
Madeira Chairs	4	Filter	1

Filter, Stand 1

LATRINE.

Latrine Pan	1	Latrine Cover	1
Latrine Rim	1	Sand Box	1

Sand Scoop 1

PANTRY.

Meat Safe 1

KITCHEN.

Stove	1	Water Drum	1
Table	1	Water Bucket	1

(ii) Nyasaland

Like West Africa, East and Central Africa too had their hints for newly appointed government staff, for example *Hints on the Preservation of Health in Eastern Africa*. This booklet was impregnated with a solution 'specially prepared to render the work impervious to the ravages of insects'. The excerpts that follow are taken from *Hints on Outfit for Officials Appointed to the Nyasaland Government Service* (1919).

Important.

Every one who comes to Nyasaland runs the risk of contracting malarial fever. Many of these infections are incurred during the up-river journey from the Coast, and the attacks of fever develop from ten to fourteen days later.

It has been incontestably proved that the malarial fever germ is introduced into the human body by the bite of the mosquito.

Therefore, the plain duty of every official from the day of arrival at Chinde is to avoid, as far as lies in his power, getting bitten by mosquitoes. Even though, in the dry season, very few may be noticeable, the mosquito (*Anopheles*) lurks about human dwellings and the cabins of river boats, the whole year round.

It has been found that quinine, IF TAKEN IN TIME, will to a very great extent, prevent the malarial germ, when introduced into the human body by the mosquito bite, developing or multiplying.

Quinine is both a *preventive* and a *cure* of malaria.

It is therefore a necessary and wise precaution to take quinine immediately on arrival at Chinde; a daily dose of 5 grains should be regularly taken before breakfast. Every official during his residence in the Tropics should take quinine regularly. At river stations a daily dose of 5 grains is required. If this daily dose tends to produce digestive troubles, a system which is effective is to take 7½ grains every fifth day. It, has been recently stated that the latter method, if systematically adhered to, is an almost certain prophylactic against attacks of "Blackwater Fever."

5-grain tabloids of quinine bi-hydrochl. are the best. They are convenient and easily digested. The tabloids must be fresh as in the Tropics they deteriorate rapidly, becoming hard and insoluble. Their solubility can be tested by placing one out of a freshly opened bottle in water when it should immediately begin to dissolve.

Very Important.

NEVER SLEEP WITHOUT A MOSQUITO NET WHILE IN AFRICA.

Mosquito Net–The following are the characteristics of a good net:—

It should be strong, with small meshes, have no holes, be closed all round, be roomy, and rectangular, not bell shaped. The top should be of net, so as to allow of a maximum of ventilation, and the lower edges should be lined with calico for tucking in under the mattress, and extended upwards for a foot. The net should be white in colour, so as to better see mosquitoes which may have penetrated inside. It is of little use having a net so small that any part of the body lies in contact with it during sleep, so that mosquitoes can easily gorge themselves through it. Take especial care of this point in the narrow bunks of the river steamers.

Before leaving England see that your bottle of 5-grain quinine tabloids (Burroughs & Wellcome), your net and mosquito boots, are packed in your light baggage where they can easily be got at directly you arrive at Chinde, as you should use your own net in preference to those supplied by the Transport and Hotel Companies, which are usually small, and which often have holes them.

See that your net is carefully tucked in *under the mattress before sunset,* and that no mosquitoes have been imprisoned. Do not allow it to hang down loose on the floor, even if the ends are weighted.

Another important point.– The mosquito is more active at sunset and an hour or two after, than at any other period of the day or night, therefore take care not to get bitten during the evening before the time comes for getting under your mosquito net. The ankles are specially liable to get bitten; to avoid this wear mosquito boots, and do not indulge in deck shoes or slippers.

Mosquito boots, procurable from the Army and Navy Stores, Westminster, London, will be found invaluable.

NEVER SLEEP WITHOUT A MOSQUITO NET.

THE OFFICIAL SHOULD BRING HIS OWN MOSQUITO NET FROM ENGLAND.

Food and Drink.

In order to guard against stomach and bowel complaints, not infrequent during the river journey, abstain from partaking of tinned foods, particularly preserved fish and meat.

While in Africa there is seldom need to eat tinned food. Fresh food is easily obtainable, and should always be eaten in preference to tinned.

Water for drinking purposes should be first filtered and afterwards boiled. It is important to use a filter of the best kind, either Doulton or Pasteur-Chamberland, and to keep it clean. The "candles" and fittings should be thoroughly scrubbed and boiled once every week, and re-assembled under the supervision of the European, who should at once discard a candle that has the least suspicion of a crack in it, or any loose part that is worn or ill fitting. Do not rely upon water which has been filtered only, as the best filters are useless unless thoroughly and periodically cleaned by boiling. The filtering can be left to a servant, but the European should see for himself that the water is actually boiled.

A kettle should be brought specially for boiling drinking water while in Africa, and the habit acquired of drinking water which has been boiled.

The less alcohol the official drinks in Africa the better his health will be.

Exposure to the sun should be avoided at all times, even when the sky is cloudy and the temperature appears cool. A sun helmet should be invariably worn when out of doors: a cap or straw hat only after sunset.

When travelling during the rainy season officials should see they have a good waterproof cover to their machillas, and a great coat or rug should also be taken in the machilla, as the temperature varies greatly, and every care should be taken to avoid getting wet or contracting a chill. Two pillows are necessary in a machilla.

Climate.

The country is not suited for the prolonged residence of ladies and, except in the Highlands, is unhealthy for children, who soon feel the effects of the climate.

Officers on first appointment who are married, and who are uncertain where they will be stationed, are advised not to bring their wives until they have become conversant with local conditions after their arrival in Nyasaland.

Household.

There is no general Mess for officials, who are quartered in brick houses, which, in Zomba, are lit by electricity, and generally each official has his separate establishment. The following, therefore, are suggested—small breakfast and dinner service; knives, forks, spoons, table linen, napkins, etc.; glasses and tumblers; a few strong cooking utensils (those of aluminium in "nest" form are convenient), and good stout iron kettle (not enamel ware), candlesticks and lamps with duplex or incandescent burners (oil can be obtained locally); Hitchcock clockwork lamps are very satisfactory as no glass chimney is required; small filter (Pasteur-Chamberland or Doulton is perhaps the best); a good comfortable bed (ordinary iron one) with spring mattress, for those who are permanently settled in one place; blankets, sheets, horsehair mattress, pillows, etc.

As there is no necessity for any one to live in any but a comfortable manner, such articles as small pictures, brackets, travelling clock, etc., etc., may be brought.

A convenient form of bath is the ordinary travelling bath with strap, lid, and lock, and inner basket; for clothes, etc. Baths are liable to damage during transport by steamer, etc., and it is advisable to have an outer covering of wicker, or else have them packed in a crate.

A scheme is in progress whereby Government is furnishing Officers' houses free with the bulkier articles of furniture, and most are now provided for. In addition to the articles already enumerated the following are suggested:—

A couple of easy chairs with cushions, or Roorkhee folding chairs, Erdgington's canvas folding chairs and a square of carpet, a, rug or two, or Indian dhurries, from Army and Navy Stores, together with some light Indian curtains, and table covers. Such trifles add to one's comfort and health, and can invariably be sold for good prices when leaving the country.

Clothing.

The temperature of the Protectorate ranges from great heat on the Shire River and Lake Nyasa, to a temperature in the Highlands where fires and warmish clothing are essential during part of the year. It is necessary, therefore, to include in the outfit clothes of a character to suit both extremes, if the official is liable to be stationed anywhere in the Protectorate.

The following articles are suggested – plenty of white or coloured or soft fronted tennis shirts and soft collars; a good supply of thinnish grey or white flannel trousers; two or three suits of thinnish tweed or serge; a thin dark blue serge suit; evening dress clothes and a few white shirts; some very thin and some moderately thick pyjamas; khaki and white drill suits will be found useful (they can generally be made up in the country); a good supply of boots; putties; leather gaiters; a great coat, travelling rug; waterproof with sewed seams; a stout umbrella; tennis shoes, racket, hockey stick, golf clubs and balls, cricket bat, etc. There are Government billiard tables at Zomba, Blantyre, and Fort Johnston. A large rectangular mosquito net and mosquito boots are absolutely essential.

Headgear.

The ordinary Elwood "shikar" hats are suitable (Army and Navy Stores and elsewhere), also a pith helmet (solar topee, obtainable at Port Said on the voyage out), double terai hat, ordinary cloth caps and straw hat.

Baggage.

Clothing should be packed in moderately sized tin cases; a useful size is 26" x 13" x 10." It should be remembered that transport up country is often on men's heads, and loads therefore should be light, not over 60 pounds.

A good way of packing bedding (blankets, sheets, mosquito net, etc.), is to use an ordinary green rot-proof canvas bag fitted with a hasp and padlock. This keeps the bedding dry even in the heaviest rain, and prevents theft; whereas the ordinary folding bed valise can be opened with little difficulty by thieves, and in rainy weather the contents are liable to become wet.

Officials are allowed, on the ocean steamers, 80 cubic feet of baggage free, on the river steamer and railway, by Government, one ton (40 cubic feet), and in addition by the Transport Company on the river only a quarter of a ton (10 cubic feet) free. Any excess has to be paid for by the official. The present rate from Chinde to Limbe is £5 14s. 11d. per ton.

Officials are warned that only cabin and personal baggage of moderate dimensions when labelled "CABIN" or "WANTED ON VOYAGE" are unshipped off Chinde with the passengers. The heavier baggage is generally taken on to Beira, and the owner does not see it again until three or four weeks afterwards.

Miscellaneous.

If in possession of a bicycle, bring it. It should have tropical tyres, a good brake, and extra valve and pump, tobes, etc.

There are very few places where a bicycle will not be found very useful. Good roads are found nearly everywhere in the country.

There are many motor cycles in use: petrol and spares can be obtained from the Motor Union of Nyasaland at Zomba, etc. Motor cycles can be used in most districts. An allowance is made by Government to officials using their motor or push bicycles on Government service, and details of this will he found on pages 12-14 under the head of Travelling and Passage Allowances.

Saddlery is not required, and should on no account be brought as horses cannot be used in the Protectorate.

If in possession of fishing gear bring it, though there is only rough fishing to be had at a few places.

Dogs imported from England, as a rule, do not do well in Nyasaland;

many die of "tick" or red-water fever or are killed by leopards and hyænas.

A Medical Officer is stationed in the chief Districts, but a small medicine case should, nevertheless, be brought for one's private use.

An extra bottle of quinine tabloids (5-gr. Quinine Bi-hydrochl. or Quinine bisulph) Burroughs & Wellcome's, should be brought. Odds and ends, such as looking glasses, small tool chest, stationery, spring balance, measuring tape, flat iron, compass, clinical thermometer, vegetable seeds in hermetically sealed tins, should be brought.

Photographic apparatus, material for Natural History collecting etc., should be brought if the official takes interest in such matters.

There is a good library and a reading room at Zomba. Arrangements should be made for a supply of newspapers from England.

Groceries can he obtained without difficulty in the Protectorate, but at high prices and often of inferior quality; a slight saving is effected by importing one's own stores, and, moreover, a good quality is ensured.

All perishable provisions, such as flour, sugar, etc., should be in soldered tin cases packed in wooden boxes which should not exceed 60 pounds gross weight.

Excellent tea, coffee and rice are grown and are procurable locally. Nyasaland tobacco and cigarettes are retailed locally.

Camp Equipment.

Guns, ammunition, etc., may occasionally be purchased from residents leaving the country, but the supply cannot be depended upon, and it is better and cheaper in the long run to bring them from England, if the official intends to go in for shooting. A ·256 (sporting pattern), or other small bore rifle with ammunition, and cleaning materials for same, will generally be found sufficient. A ·350 sporting rifle is a useful all-round weapon. There is some wild fowl shooting to be obtained, but it is scarcely worth while to bring an expensive shot gun. A cheap one will be found useful to procure guinea fowl, etc. A revolver or pistol (·380 colt) is recommended. The importation of ·303 rifles or ammunition is prohibited.

It is not essential for an official on the Civil Staff to bring a tent, but if he intends to go on shooting excursions he should, of course, have a tent of his own.

(d) Kitting Out for the Colonies, 1930s

Specialist tropical outfitters for those going into the Colonial Service became big business between the wars, not only in London but also, following the establishment of Colonial Service training courses at the two oldest universities in England, in Oxford and Cambridge too.

The following selection of advertisements conveys the flavour of the period *c.*1930 to 1939. Much of it survived into the outfitters' catalogues and display stores of the postwar years.

J. G. PLUMB & SON

VICTORIA HOUSE, 117 VICTORIA STREET, WESTMINSTER, S.W1

Established
1895

Specialists in Colonial Outfits

Phone No.
VICTORIA
3434

MILITARY, NAVAL AND CIVIL TAILORS

Tailors by Appointment to the Royal Military Academy, Woolwich

All garments hand tailored

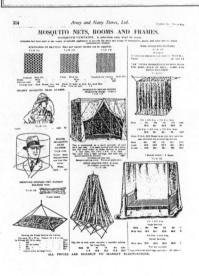

(e) Colonial Service Uniforms: The Governor, 1956

Colonial regulations laid down instructions on the wearing of civil uniform. As early as 1837, it was prescribed that a governor's uniform should be the same as that of a lord lieutenant of a county, only in blue with silver embroidery, scarlet collar and scarlet cuffs. The relevant extract from the final edition of *Colonial Regulations* (1956) is given below.

136. Governors, unless at the time of their appointment they hold the rank of Admiral in the Royal Navy or of General in the Army or of Air Chief Marshal in the Royal Air Force (in which case they will during their tenure of office continue to wear their naval, military, or air force uniform), shall wear the special uniform prescribed for them.

137. The class of the Civil Uniform which may be worn by officers in the Colonial Service under the rank of Governor is regulated in each colony by the Uniform List for that Colony which has received Her Majesty's approval.

138. No person is entitled without the consent of the Queen to wear the uniform attached to any office after he has ceased to hold that office. Such consent can only be obtained on the recommendation of the Governor made through the Secretary of State, and only in cases where an officer has actually worn the uniform during his tenure of the office to which it is attached. No retired officer will be allowed to wear any other uniform than that which was attached to his office during his tenure of it.

139. A white uniform has been approved for use in tropical countries in place of the blue civil uniform. Its adoption in any colony is left to the discretion of the Governor. At outdoor functions in the day-time officers wearing the blue uniform are at liberty to wear with it the white helmet worn with the white uniform.

140. Only Governors may wear the first class of the white uniform, and they may wear with it, if they so desire, the cape forming part of the Governor's special uniform and a helmet bearing a plume similar to that of the cocked hat worn with the Governor's special uniform. On special occasions, however, such as the celebration of the Sovereign's Birthday or the opening or closing of the Legislature, Governors shall wear the special uniform.

The other classes of white uniform shall be worn by persons who are entitled, or have received permission, to wear the corresponding class of the ordinary civil uniform.

141. In lieu of civil uniform, officers may wear, on all occasions when uniform is prescribed, ordinary evening dress with black breeches (with three buttons and black buckles at the knee), black silk hose, and plain court shoes.

III. Colonial Service Recruitment and Appointments

Among the extracts that follow are passages from one of the most influential reports on the evolution of the modern Colonial Service and its management, the Warren Fisher Report of 1930 on the System of Appointment to the Colonial Services (Cmd. 3554).

(a) Recruitment and the Post-Armistice Generation, 1919–26

The following extract is taken from a 'Memorandum on the Recruitment and Training of Colonial Civil Servants' written by the Private Secretary (Appointments) (Major R. D. Furse) for the Colonial Office conference of 1927 and reproduced in the *Appendices to the Summary of Proceedings* (Cmd. 2884).

4. The period since the Armistice has confronted us with certain exceptional difficulties. For our purposes it falls into three main divisions. The first covers the years 1919-21, and was marked by heavy and often urgent demands for men, to make up for lack of recruitment during the war and to meet the needs of the mandated territories. To meet these demands we had to rely almost wholly on the abnormal sources provided by demobilisation and subsequent retrenchments in the fighting Services. The ordinary peace-time sources of supply were practically unproductive, because the Universities, Agricultural Colleges, and so on, required three years or more from the end of the war before they could resume their normal output. As a consequence, although there were very large numbers of ex-service men clamouring for posts, there was a serious and unavoidable shortage of properly trained candidates for all technical and specialised services. Our work in this period mainly consisted in a rather desperate effort to sift out the heterogeneous mass of ex-service candidates and to meet, as rapidly as possible, the urgent demands with which we were bombarded from practically every Colony and Department. It was complicated by the lack of trained material for technical services, such as agriculture; by the fact that the age of so many ex-service candidates was necessarily greater than is normally preferred; and by the difficulty, in many cases, of deciding whether the strain, to which the man had been subjected in the war, rendered the danger of selecting him for tropical service too great. These complications were aggravated by shortage of staff at the end and by the pressure under which the work had to be done.

5. The second period—1922—was marked by a heavy slump in recruitment caused by widespread financial depression. The number of appointments fell and in some Colonies, such as Kenya, retrenchment of existing staff was carried out. The effect, of this slump was very bad. Not

only were better men turned away than some of those selected both before and since, but the confidence of some of the training centres was shaken. In the highly specialised department of Forestry, for example, our recruitment has not yet recovered from this blow.

6. The third period runs from the end of 1922 to the present time. Recovery began in the autumn of 1922, but was only gradual. Demand, therefore, has shown a steady rise up to a figure greatly in excess of the immediate pre-war period. Special features of the last year or two have been (i) increases in the administrative staff in Tropical Africa; (ii) a large increase in the demand for Educational officers and (iii) the creation of a number of scientific posts mainly in connection with agriculture.

During this period the abnormal war-sources of supply have practically dried up. On the other hand, the Universities and training Colleges have resumed their full annual output.

7. It has therefore become possible during the last two or three years to take stock of the position and to get a better idea of the relation between supply and demand, under conditions which might be expected to be fairly permanent. It became clear that definite measures would be needed if the increased demand in regard to both quantity and quality was to be met, and if the higher training required to cope with recent developments was to be provided. I should like to invite attention to certain factors which have considerably influenced recruitment, and which had therefore to be taken into account in considering measures for its improvement.

8. There seems to be a lack of enterprise and a tendency to stay at home amongst the post-war generation. This has been commented on at the Headmasters' Conference and elsewhere, and has, I believe, been noticed by the Civil Service Commissioners, who recruit for different groups of services. This tendency may be largely due to a temperamental reaction from the war, but there appear to be other factors at work; though in discussing them I know that I am on difficult and, possibly, controversial ground, and can only give my opinions for what they are worth. The kind of man who usually proves most fitted for the Services under discussion needs certain personal qualities and an educational background mainly to be found in the type of family which has been most severely hit by the war. The loss of his father or elder brother may strengthen the desire to keep a boy at home. Beyond this we have the undoubted fact of the limitation of families; and it was generally the younger sons of large families who went overseas in the past. Economic pressure has also made it harder for such families to send their sons to a University. Fewer of them, therefore, get the type of education we prefer, and, as for climatic reasons, we cannot usually send a man out till he is 21½, those who cannot go to a University tend to drift into other employment before we can take them. It must also not be forgotten that we lost 30,000 officers

killed in the war. The effect of such a wholesale destruction of leaders cannot be made good in a short time, and it is men with the qualities of leadership whom we especially need. Finally, it is, I think, generally accepted that business firms are far more alive than they used to be to the value of the type of man we seek to attract. We have therefore to face a far stiffer competition from this quarter than in pre-war days, and the greater financial rewards, which a business career offers, are doubly attractive in these times of economic stringency.

9. In the second place, a higher general standard of quality is demanded; and here I may perhaps be permitted to say that the utmost importance has always been attached to obtaining men of the highest quality that circumstances allowed. In pursuance of this policy it has quite often been decided to leave vacancies unfilled for some time, if the available material was unsatisfactory and there was reason to hope that better candidates could be secured by waiting.

The demand for a higher standard has been shown principally in three ways:—

(a) As development progresses there is a growing need for high intellectual ability among recruits for the African Administrative Service, without any relaxation of the necessity for insistence on those qualities of personality and character which are essential to the proper handling of natives.

(b) Whereas in pre-war times the other departments had, on the whole, to be content with a somewhat lower personal standard, it is now recognised that many of them, for example, the Educational, Agricultural, Forestry, and Veterinary Services, need men of similar standing in this respect to the Administrative staff, with the addition of professional qualifications.

(c) It is clear to anyone looking at the whole field that recruitment for scientific departments has entered on a new phase. In a number of important Colonies, particularly in Tropical Africa, Agriculture and the kindred arts of Forestry and Animal Husbandry have reached a stage where their problems call more and more for the application of a higher degree of scientific knowledge and skill. This entails a higher standard of scientific attainment in all officers entering the Service and creates a greatly increased demand for the specialist and the research worker. It is also providing openings for workers in certain specialised branches of science, for which we have hitherto hardly recruited at all; as, for example, bio-chemistry, soil-science, genetics, and various branches of forestry research.

10. As against this increase and intensification of demand, we have to

compete with the adverse general factors which I have tried to outline. Above all we must face the fact that the development of the non-self-governing Dependencies is advancing much faster than is realised by public opinion at home. Neither the young men, who should be our recruits, nor their parents or teachers—perhaps not even we ourselves— yet realise the important part which these Dependencies as a whole already play in the economy of the Empire; still less the far greater part which they are destined to play, if properly developed, even within the official lifetime of any one now entering the Service. The rapidly expanding range of opportunity for responsible and interesting work, which these Services will offer, are by no means fully grasped. Equally apparent is the failure to appreciate the vital part which science and scientific research must play if these territories are to be fully developed.

(b) The System of Appointment in the Colonial Office and the Colonial Services (Warren Fisher Report), 1930

The *Report of a Committee on the System of Appointment in the Colonial Office and the Colonial Services* chaired by the head of the civil service, Sir Warren Fisher, was published as a White Paper in 1930 (Cmd. 3554). It has been called the Magna Carta of the Colonial Service and ranks as one of the service's defining moments.

The following excerpts relate to the committee's recommendations on several key issues.

(i) Appointments to the Administrative Service

The members of the Committee, having already received from the Promotions Branch a statement of particulars of the vacancy and the names of candidates, including any local officer recommended by the Governor, with a summary of the information about each, meet and on a majority vote make a selection for submission to higher authority. If they consider none suitable, they may recommend that the vacancy be remitted to the recruiting authority for an outside candidate. If there are good outside candidates known to be available, the Committee may in any instance be notified of the particulars of such candidates to assist them in their comparative view of the Colonial Service candidates.

In 1929 the number of vacancies considered by the Promotions Committee was 103. The total number of vacancies filled by transfer was recorded in the same year as 70.

On the basis of the evidence we have received we have certain criticisms and proposals to make under this head. As a result of a Report by a Colonial Office Committee, which in 1921 considered the question of the organization of the Department, the Promotions Branch of the Colonial Office was reorganized and its efficiency improved. In particular our evidence suggests that the presence and interest of the several Specialist Advisers appointed during the last few years have had very appreciable results in improving the Promotions work so far as concerns their particular branches. Nevertheless, though we gladly recognize the excellent work which has been done by the existing Promotions staff, there are still improvements which might be effected, but which would require some slight increase of staff for their fulfilment. The provision of such a staff is involved in the proposals of this Report.

We have formed the opinion, from our own investigations and from the statements of many witnesses, that the system of annual confidential reports on officers which are rendered by the several Governors, though adequate in theory, has in practice not always proved satisfactory. We are given to understand that, in the case of certain Colonies, these reports have in the past been received only after a considerable interval of time, and sometimes not at all, and that in some cases only the senior officers of the Administration are thus reported upon. We need hardly emphasize how desirable it is that such Reports should be rendered regularly and fully in the case of all officers who might, however remotely, be considered as possible candidates for promotion or transfer.

It may be convenient at this stage to record a suggestion which we believe to be worthy of support, that the various authorities at home and overseas who have to concern themselves with Promotions work should, in the case of vacant appointments in the Administrative branch, include in their review of possible candidates any suitable officers of technical departments who have shown exceptional capacity of an administrative order, and who would like to be considered for such transfer.

Our attention has been called to the closest co-operation between the Promotions Branch and the other of the Colonial Office, and to the necessity of the Promotions Branch being furnished with very complete information and personal knowledge regarding the officers noted on their lists. We are in full agreement as to the importance of this point.

The Colonial Regulations while requiring all officers of the Colonial Service to report in writing their arrival home do not, on account of the large number of officers coming on leave and of the fact that their homes are scattered all over the country, definitely require such officers to report in person at the Colonial Office, but many senior officers in fact make a practice of doing so. In so far as this is not done already, we think it desirable that with the enlarged Promotions Branch which we propose, it should be the normal procedure for the Geographical Departments of the Colonial Office to keep that Branch informed of the arrival on leave of all officers noted on the lists for promotion or transfer, in order that, if it should be so desired, these officers may be requested to call and interview a member of the Promotions Branch. The Promotions Branch would in this way not have to rely solely on a chance visit from such officers. We are convinced that the more an enlarged Promotions staff is able to obtain information and advice from Governors, Heads of Departments, and other senior officials when they are available in this country in person, the easier will it be to make the best use of the personnel in the Colonial Services. We think that our proposals will enable more to be done in this direction than has been possible with the existing staff.

We are aware of the great difficulties in the way of inter-Colonial promotions due mainly to the fact that each territory maintains its own independent Service. We are also aware that a complete assimilation of the conditions and terms of service in all the several territories has been regarded as impracticable. Some territories are large and rich, others are small and poor; the local climate, local cost of living, and a hundred other circumstances hinder, and to some extent prevent, uniformity throughout the Dependencies. All these difficulties give the central handling in the Colonial Office of the question of inter-Colonial promotions a special importance. The comparatively short career of a European in the Tropical Colonial Services—some 30 years of active service at the most—calls for a policy of the early and rapid promotion of the best officers in whatever Colony they may receive their first appointment, if the fullest use is to be made of them in high positions of responsibility. The constant need to improve the quality and prestige of Colonial service requires that it should offer a career in which the prizes go to merit, and the only value of seniority is the value of the experience which it has brought.

The recommendations which at this stage we make about the Promotions organization are designed to ensure

(1) that there will be no risk of omitting to note officers who are deserving to be considered for promotion in any of the higher appointments in the Dependencies;

(2) that the most complete information may be obtained and recorded about them, so that on the occurrence of any suitable vacancy the work of selection. shall not be hampered;

(3) that individual vacancies are not handled in the Promotions Branch as isolated occurrences, but as part of a large general plan to secure that the most suitable officers of the Colonial Administrations are appointed to such posts as will be to the best advantage of the Service;

(4) that on this special work—special for several of the reasons which we have already mentioned in the case of the Appointments Branch – a sufficient expert personnel may be employed on a scale which will enable considerably more detailed attention to be given to it than can safely be looked for under the existing arrangements.

We recommend that the Promotions Branch in the Colonial Office be separated from the General Division and form a section of the Personnel Division, the creation of which we have proposed. To this Personnel Division we propose elsewhere that, besides the Appointments and Promotions work, there shall also be entrusted certain other business at present allocated to the General Division, which relates particularly to matters of personnel in the Colonial Services, discipline, pension, honours, etc.

Regarding the existing Promotions Committee itself, we suggest that it should be reorganised on a smaller scale. As a standing Committee for its present purpose we believe that a body of 18 persons, with the addition of one of the Specialist Advisers in certain cases, is too large for the effective weighing of the rival merits of candidates. We have been informed that the advantage of having as members the Heads of each of the seven Geographical Departments is that it goes some way to ensure that there is present at the Committee some one person at least who has personal knowledge of each of the candidates under consideration, and that they constitute a valuable "jury" for arriving at a fair selection from the names before them. We believe that the first of these advantages should more properly be looked for from the staff of the Promotions Branch, in so far as it is a case of knowledge pertinent to the candidate's comparative suitability for promotion, and under the new arrangements which we propose we should in due course expect an enlarged Promotions Branch to be in a position to supply it. We recommend that the existing Committee should be replaced by a much smaller body, presided over by the Permanent Under-Secretary of State or his Deputy: and we suggest that the Heads of Departments and Specialist Advisers particularly concerned in any vacancy should, as necessary, be invited to attend the meetings in an advisory capacity.

In concluding this part of our Report we venture to offer an observation on the subject of the appointments to the highest offices in the Colonies.

We have referred to the special method adopted in considering persons for the appointment of Governors of Colonies, and we are aware that in the majority of cases such appointments are the prizes given to the best officers of the Colonial Services as the culminating opportunity of their overseas careers. The outstanding influence and importance of the Governor in his Colony is such that only the most proven and experienced men can be regarded as suitable for such appointments. We therefore recommend that the quest for Governors should first be made among officers holding high appointments in the Colonial Services, and that only after the qualifications of such have been fully considered should the question arise of an appointment from outside the Service. We believe that such a declaration of policy would be a valuable encouragement to, and would increase the prestige of, the whole overseas Service.

(ii) The Appointment of Engineers

We do not recommend any alteration in the system under which such appointments to the Colonial Services are made, but we think it right to take this opportunity to offer certain observations.

The recruitment of qualified technical officers is peculiarly open to competition from private employment, and this has been especially in evidence recently with regard to electrical engineers. The qualifications usually stipulated for by Colonial Governments, for instance in the case of young civil engineers, are both the possession of a University degree, or a similar professional qualification, and some period of practical engineering experience.

We can well understand that often it may not be easy to find candidates satisfying these conditions, who at the same time possess the personal qualities needed for public service in the Colonies. It seems to us possible, however, that sufficient information is not yet available at likely sources, such as Universities and Technical Colleges, where prospective candidates could be informed of the opportunities in the Colonial Services open to young engineers, after qualifying and obtaining some practical experience in their profession. We suggest also that it would be an advantage if a waiting list or pool of applicants found to be qualified and suitable for appointment could be established, from which vacancies could be filled as soon as notified.

We have the further observation to offer that recruitment by Colonial Governments in all of the branches of the Services with which the Crown Agents are concerned seems to be of a spasmodic and irregular character, though its total annual volume is considerable. It is beyond doubt that the field of candidates might be improved and enlarged if it were possible for the

Colonies to indicate their requirements, even if only their minimum require-ments, in a bulk requisition, presented some months before the actual selection of candidates was imperative.

In particular branches of engineering work—for example, railway con-struction—where experience is not generally to be obtained in this country, we recommend that Colonial Governments should offer appointments of a cadet type. This would make it possible to engage young engineers on the completion of their professional studies, and then send them overseas to acquire a practical knowledge of the particular branch of engineering required.

Apart, however, from these special observations, we do not hesitate to give it as our opinion that any real improvement in the quantity and quality of the fully-trained engineering personnel required for the Colonial Services must depend on an improvement in the general rate of emoluments offered. Our evidence shows clearly that in view of the cost and duration of an engineer's training and financial inducements usually offered by the Colonial Services are not adequate.

(c) Major Furse's Secret: Interviewing Colonial Service Applicants

Among the recommendations of the Warren Fisher Report (1930) was the abolition of the post of Private Secretary (Appointments) in the Secretary of State's Office and the establishment of a Director of Recruitment (Colonial Service) in the Colonial Office. At the same time, the Colonial Service Appointments Board was created. The key figure in Colonial Service recruitment from 1910 to 1950 was Major R. D. (later Sir Ralph) Furse. With the aid of a small staff in the Colonial Office, he developed a detailed procedure for interviews and reporting on candidates. Some of his methods can be deduced from reading his autobiography, *Aucuparius* (1962). In 1948, Furse's code of selection principles and procedures (what he sometimes referred to as his 'hunches') were gathered together in the Colonial Office as an *Appointments Handbook*, a confidential guide for the use of the appointments staff. The following excerpts are taken from this in-house handbook, compiled by Furse's deputy, F. Newbolt.

On the Process of Interviewing

THE STORY GOES that in Alfred Lyttelton's time his Private Secretary was once asked if he would say how selections for appointments in the Colonies were made. "Ah!" he replied, "that is one of the secrets of the Empire." Since those far-off days of "patronage" much water has flowed under the bridge and the method of selection is now described in official pamphlets available to the public for the asking: before this war several thousands were distributed each year. In these it is explained that a candidate must fill in the proper application form with detailed particulars of his career; that he must supply certain testimonials and the names of referees; and that he may have to attend for interview at the Colonial Office. It is stated that "the selection of candidates depends on the general educational attainments, the professional or other subsequent training and experience (if any) and on the character and personal fitness of the applicants"; and that selections are made by the Secretary of State, on the advice of the Colonial Service Appointments Board. But what is not explained is that, in the normal case, success depends more than anything else on the outcome of the individual interview at the Colonial Office. That, and the operation of the interview itself, has remained a well-guarded secret.

No-one nowadays expects to be considered seriously for a responsible appointment without at some stage having to be "seen" personally. He probably supposes that he will either appear before a formal Board or, if he is lucky, undergo the lesser ordeal of a short or perfunctory interview with, say, two or three selectors. The candidate for the Colonial Service may or may not appear at some time before a Board, depending on his qualifications or on the class of appointment for which he is applying. He is almost certain, if he is any good at all, to be given at least one informal interview—but closeted with one man only, tête-à-tête. As he shakes hands and takes his seat in a comfortable chair he may experience a feeling of relief: the man is obviously friendly, even glad to see him. When, as often happens, he is invited to smoke he may think to himself "This is going to be simple. What could be easier than to talk things over quietly in this unofficial way?" Then the interview begins.

For the interviewer it is not, of course, a simple matter at all. The claim, often lightly made, to be able to "size a fellow up the moment he comes into the room" is inapplicable here, and might be positively dangerous. Immediate impressions are sometimes right: they sometimes prove wholly wrong. An interview may move in totally unforeseen directions. One is seldom in the least like another. Ideally, there should be no circumscribed time limit; it is fatal to hurry. Sound interviewing is, indeed—and should be—an exacting, not to say exhausting, process.

The first principle, as we have seen, is to put the candidate at his ease: the atmosphere must be very antithesis of "third-degree" inquisition. Most men of intelligence will respond and come into rapport quickly enough. Some may take a considerable time to "thaw": these sometimes call for infinite patience—often well rewarded. A few, the difficult or purely dense, may remain almost impervious to the end, like thaw-refusing snow men. The tempo of the interview may well be in itself the first indication of character. You have before you a complete paper record of the young man's history since early schooldays. You have read the judgements of those who have handled him at every stage and you know, or can sense, the value of each of those judgements. No time need be wasted therefore in recapitulation of historical facts. Nor, if he is a "specialist", need you concern yourself unduly about his technical equipment, for that will be assessed independently by professional experts.[*] But your eye may have spotted some unusual or arresting entry, or some underlined passage in a report; these may be valuable signposts which you have noted for use later on. For an opening subject it is not a bad idea to probe his general knowledge of the career for which he is applying, and the sincerity of his motives. The modern generation has no links with that dim past when a common conception of "the Colonies" was of remote red patches on the map, the hunting-ground of the adventurer or the purgatory of the prodigal son. The old catchwords "White man's grave" and "White man's burden" have lost their currency and meaning, and to-day "the Colonial Service" is esteemed as an honourable career of public service second to none in importance and prestige.

Your candidate will be conscious that he is competing with the best youth of the nation for a popular profession, but when you ask what attracts him personally to it you will meet with a wide variety of answers. Even now, of course, he may be uninformed and empty-headed, and the appeal may be simply to the vague prospect of a pleasant "open-air" life or of "going abroad" and "seeing the world". Even now he may prove to be little more than a budding careerist, concerned about material rewards. On the other hand you may well find, especially if he has imagination and a strain of the Elizabethan, that the "Colonial Empire" struck some chord in his mind even as a boy; that he fostered this at school with tales of discovery and adventure; and that he has since persevered with a few standard works on Colonial history, systems of British administration, anthropology and so on. You may find that he has discussed these sort of things with a critical circle of his contemporaries, or with friends or relations who have spent their lives in the Service. You may be surprised not only by his intelligent interest but by his genuine sense of vocation to work amongst native races——a consequent perhaps of holidays devoted to boys' or men's clubs, camps for the unemployed or other kinds of social service. Or again, you may find that he has few of these assets, or none. At any rate their presence will rarely be detected in application forms or by any formal methods. Yet they may count for much.

By now your candidate will have revealed something of the nature of his mind and of the size of his intellect. If he should be manifestly below par this will be seen already, and your task will be simplified. If he has scholarly ability of a high order this will be quickly obvious in conversation—which you may be tempted to enjoy unduly for its own sake! But the average case will show wide variations of the subtle, the shrewd, the original, the slow-but-sure type of brain, and for a true and fair estimate of his capacity you will probably rely to a large extent on the opinions of tutors who have watched and been intimately concerned with his intellectual growth. Wherever there is doubt such opinions,

---

[*] This and the following paragraphs relate in the main to the case of the would-be Administrative Officer, though much of what is said is of general application.

frankly given, will be more trustworthy than any you may form yourself during an hour's talk—or, as many think, than the hazardous test of a special written examination. A man's brain is a continually progressive organ and cannot be measured, like his bones, at a fixed point of final maturity. Your calculation must take into account not only its performance of to-day but the probable pace and direction of its future development.

By now, too, you will have begun to form an estimate of his "character and personal fitness". It is, of course, a major and constant aim of your enquiry to discover character, relating what you find to the needs of the career in view and to the special conditions under which that career will be followed. If a man is going to spend his working life far from home in an alien or inimical climate, if he is to carry successfully the multiple and often lonely responsibilities of a Government official in a colonial country, living on terms of mutual friendliness and respect alike with the native citizens and with his imported colleagues, it stands to reason that he must possess, in fullest possible measure, qualities of a special order which are not necessarily requisite to success in many other professions. In considering some of these qualities and the process by which you will assess your candidate's share of them it will be convenient to classify them broadly into those that may be described as "natural" and those that are "acquired".

His physical appearance will, of course, have been noted at once; the cut of his face and the extent, if any, to which he has the indefinable quality of "presence". Colouring, build, movement, poise will have come under review, and even such superficialities as style of dress and hair, health of skin and fingers. But your scrutiny will be directed chiefly to eyes and mouth for they, whether in repose or in action combined with speech and gesture, may tell you much. You will have in mind the truism that weakness of various kinds may lurk in a flabby lip or in averted eyes, just as single-mindedness and purpose are commonly reflected in a steady gaze and a firm set of mouth and jaw. If need be you will search for any signs of nervous disorder, in the knowledge that an even temperament counts at least equally with a sound physique as a bulwark against the strains of a tropical or solitary existence. You will note whether he is by nature a man of physical activity, accustomed to playing games or enjoying other exercise; and, of course, whether there are any tendencies to over-indulgence. In short, you will set great store by the quality of Balance. In the same classification may be included the question of Background. A man's natural qualities, in the sense here implied, derive partly from inheritance and home environment, and partly from school or academic training. If he comes of stock that has proved its worth, generation by generation, in the professions or in public service, if he has been reared in the faith that duty and chivalry are of more account an ambition and self-seeking, if his education has broadened his mind in that faith and taught him the meaning of responsibility and the value of comradeship, then he has been blessed with such a foundation as should ensure his possession of many of the qualities for which you are looking. The truth of this is incontestable, and accounts for the fact that a preponderance of men of this stamp, trained at the universities, come forward as candidates for the Colonial Administrative Service, and are successful. On the other hand it may be that your candidate has had a modicum of these endowments and you will yet find much and enough of what you are seeking. Whatever his origins, humble or noble, whatever his schooling, it is not they that you are judging but the man he has now become and the man he is likely to become later on.

In the course of growing from boyhood to manhood he will have developed various individual qualities, tastes and interests, and it is these which are here classified loosely as "acquired". The quality of leadership is popularly, perhaps especially in time of war, associated in the mind with the Fighting Services. Yet there can be few professions which demand a greater measure of this quality, in its widest sense, than that of the colonial administrator. It is largely by his powers of personal authority and example, his patience and tact, his human relationships, that he will be able to play his allotted part successfully in furtherance of general policy. Allusion to some of these virtues will probably have been made in written reports on your candidate, and you will have noted the extent to which he was a leader or organizer at school or university in games, clubs, societies and so on; for his role even in these youthful activities may indicate much. To be head of one's House Captain of Boats or a cricket Blue is in the long run a fleeting distinction, yet it may be at once a test and a presage of character. But here again you will rely in part on your own observation and instinct. In cases of doubt or immaturity you will probably consider whether allowance should be made for "late development". If, on the other hand, you should be dealing with a "born leader" your task will be easy, for it will be written on his face and in his manner.

You will also have in mind that the duties of the appointment in view may be undertaken, at least in part, in the vast stretches of an agricultural district or in the wilds of forest or bush or perhaps in a network of small islands, far from the ordered civilization of towns and, as has already been suggested, under conditions of prolonged loneliness. You will therefore think it well to discover whether your candidate is by preference a *townsman or a countryman*, whether his tastes are for the pleasures of the crowd or for the pursuits of the field, and whether his hobbies, if any, are of a kind that will stand him in good stead when he is thrown on his own resources. It may be that he has been *brought up on a farm or country estate* and learnt something of the management of live-stock or crops; or he may have studied the habits of birds or the science of flowers; he may be at home with gun or rod, or sailing-boat or. saddle, or a carpenter or mechanic, photographer or draughtsman. It may be that, through lack of opportunity or disposition, he has few interests of this sort. Or again, you may find that, having some absorbing hobby, he has not appreciated its possible usefulness in this context. You will perhaps also take stock of any experience he has gained of foreign countries and foreign peoples, from the point of view both of the interest he may have shown in observing the customs and habits of other races, and of his aptitude for picking up new languages. Here may be mentioned the advantage of a good musical "ear"—though this, being a natural gift, hardly belongs to the present category. Here too may be mentioned the unusual item which caught your eye at the start of the interview: a life-saving medal, perhaps, an archaeological expedition, a love entangle-ment, a trip in the stoke-hole of a tramp steamer, a published volume of verse. Any such experience is worth exploring, as indeed is every facet of a candidate's composition if there is a chance that it will contribute in some way to a just estimate of his fitness for the particular work.

This, it must be said in conclusion, is no more than a sketch of a process of infinite variations and almost indefinable essence. Intuition, which must be its guiding principle, is a faculty that cannot be translated into words. The story goes that not many years ago another Private Secretary, the founder of to-day's system of interviewing and now Director of Recruitment for the Colonial Service, was asked if he would define by what methods he proceeded to judge a candidate. "Well," he replied, "it is difficult to say. But if I had to choose a hunter for work in a particular type of country I should have a pretty good idea which would be the best animal to pick, though I might not be able to tell you how I went about it."

(d) Appointments for Women in the Colonial Service, 1945

While women had long been recruited into the Colonial Service, first for the Colonial Nursing Service, then for the Colonial Education and Colonial Medical Services, and more recently to social welfare appointments, it was not until the end of the Second World War that administrative appointments were open to women. These were mostly in East and West Africa. A lower age limit of 24 was set.

The following extract is taken from Colonial Service Recruitment Pamphlet No. 9 (March 1945), *Information Regarding Appointments for Women*.

Types of Appointments Available.

The majority of posts for women in the Colonial Service are likely to occur in the Colonial Medical, Education and Nursing Services and in Social Welfare appointments. Special appointments to other Departments are made from time to time. A number of senior executive posts have been filled by women during the war but many of the posts are directly connected with war-time activities and are therefore of a temporary character. There is also a small but growing demand for women to fill administrative posts in the Colonial Service. For these appointments a high standard of general education and per-sonal qualities will be essential, and experience in administrative work in the Home Civil Service or other public services is a desirable qualification.

The total number of permanent appointments filled by women in the Colonies in the past has not been large. Women will, however, play an increasingly important part in the Colonial Service in post-war years. There are many problems (not exclusively feminine) with which women are particularly qualified to deal. The traditions and customs of many Colonial peoples have tended to keep their womenfolk in the background, but such prejudices are gradually disintegrating under the impact of modern ideas. Responsible leaders of Colonial opinion now realise that the progress of the Colonies depends to a large extent on their giving women the advantage of modern education. In many Colonies women of the country are already taking a part in public life undreamt of by their mothers and grandmothers. The whole process of their emancipation has needed and will still need careful and sympathetic guidance and assistance. To achieve this aim there will be considerable scope in the Colonial Service for women of both European and Colonial origin with high professional attainments and personal qualifications.

Conditions of Life in the Colonies.

European women who feel a desire to take up a Government post in the Colonies should carefully study the problems and conditions of Colonial life through books and personal contacts. The spirit of adventure is an asset to anyone who contemplates working in the Colonies. But the essential qualification is a deep interest in humanity, in men, women and children of all races, colours and creeds. Without this, and without a spirit of sympathetic understanding, no work in the Colonial Service can he really successful. Naturally all people away from their homeland must have much in common with one another, but they must also find common interests and take real pleasure in getting to know the people of the country and entering into their lives. A woman should go out feeling that she has a great responsibility and a worthy object in giving to the women of the country the best of our civilisation, and in learning to understand and encourage all that is valuable in their own ideas and civilisation. Women all the world over have much in common and in these common interests, outside the administrative, educational, medical, nursing or social service duties of a post, the most valuable contacts can be made. The home, housekeeping, dress, music, art, literature, sport—all these give an opening for real friendship and understanding among women of all races.

It is difficult to present a vivid picture of Colonial life to women whose families have not served in the Empire overseas and who have not been outside these islands or beyond the continent of Europe. It is possible, however, to assess certain advantages and dis-advantages. The separation from relatives and friends is probably the disadvantage that weighs heaviest with many people. The fear that Tropical climates are unhealthy may discourage some women from going to the Colonies. In these days of prophylactic medicine, however, it is possible to keep as well in the Tropics as in temperate climates, provided that certain rules of health are strictly observed and the advice of "old hands" is not disregarded. In addition there are certain times of year in the Tropics when the climate is delightful. In Tropical countries women will still find willing and usually devoted domestic service, which leaves them leisure for recreation. Games and sport are usually easy to come by and social life is more informal than in England. There is naturally a lack of plays and concerts, but radio carries good music round the world and in every Colony there is a nucleus of people who are interested in books, art and music. Everything depends on the temperament of the woman who accepts a post in the Colonies—"the mind is its own place". She has not only the opportunity of being a member of the European community, which offers more variety than the groove in which she would normally find herself in England, but she also has the chance to enter into the life of other races, to learn their traditions and customs and to win their lasting friendship.

IV. Colonial Service Training

With the introduction of the Tropical African Administrative Services (TAAS) courses at Oxford and Cambridge universities in 1926 and the professionalization of training for the agricultural, forestry, veterinary and education services in the 1920s, Colonial Service training became a priority in the Colonial Office. It received a further boost from the appointment of the Devonshire Committee in 1943 to consider the training of a postwar Colonial Service and from the Colonial Office memorandum to that committee.

(a) Interchange between the Colonial Service and the Colonial Office, 1930

Interchange between the separately recruited Colonial Service and Colonial Office staffs grew out of suggestions for a single combined service which from time to time was discussed in both institutions. Within the Colonial Office the practice came to be known as 'beachcombing'. It was finally accepted as one of the Warren Fisher reforms of 1930.

The extract is from the Warren Fisher Committee on *The System of Appointment in the Colonial Office and the Colonial Services*, 1930 (Cmd. 3554).

System of Appointment.

The Colonial Office staff is interchangeable with that of the Dominions Office up to and including the rank of Assistant Secretary. The Administrative staffs of both Offices are recruited by means of the open competitive examination common to such appointments in all Departments of the Home Civil Service, but in these particular Offices, as also in the case of the Foreign Office, there is now a liability to undertake periods of service overseas. The examination includes a competitive interview, for which marks are allotted, and by means of which the candidates' personal qualities, not necessarily tested by the literary part of the examination, may influence the result.

We recognize that in respect of most branches of the Public Service—and perhaps in a rather special degree a Department such as the Colonial Office with its close contact with the Colonial Services and with the administration of native races—a not inconsiderable weight of opinion exists in favour of a system of appointment which will attach greater value to personal qualities, such as the system of appointment to the Foreign Office and Diplomatic Service.

But we do not advocate any change in the customary system of entry—either in the direction of selecting all or part of the permanent administrative staff of the Office from the members of the Colonial Services, since the work of the Colonial Office is in its essentials different from the work of Colonial Administrations; or in the direction of creating a distinct form of examination or other system of appointment to the Colonial Office separate from the general arrangements for the Home Civil Service.

(b) Postwar Training for the Colonial Service, 1943

The following summary of R. D. Furse's memorandum to the Devonshire Committee is reproduced from *Postwar Training for the Colonial Service*, 1946 (Col. No. 198).

SUMMARY OF MEMORANDUM ON TRAINING

Memorandum is in two parts.

Part I is called for short "The Case for Reform," but it is more accurately a case for expanding the scope of the training we give our officers rather than for reforming such training as we give already.

Part II outlines a plan for reform.

PART I.

Paras. 1-5.—Need of bold plans to meet probable post-war conditions.

Paras. 6-8.—Outline of development of present system of training.

*Para.*9.—Six main defects in present system.

Paras. 10-28.—*The main objectives to be aimed at namely:*–

Para. 10.—Training adapted both to probable exigencies of post-war era and to structure proposed for the post-war Service.

Para. 11.—The maintenance of contact between serving officers and informed public opinion not only on Colonial affairs, but also on general questions of the day, and on such subjects as Economics, Welfare, etc.

Para. 12.—A training related not only to the needs of particular colonies or areas but built upon a broader understanding of the relevant background of colonial and world affairs generally.

Paras. 13-14—A foundation for a better understanding and liaison between the various branches of the Service, and with the unofficial elements in the colony.

Para. 15.—The fusion of the Service into a whole – example of the Armed Forces.

Para. 16.—Training "the whole man" instead of merely imparting professional knowledge.

Para. 17.—The fortification of "morale" and the breeding of confidence based on knowledge.

Para. 18.—To lay the foundation on which every officer can develop his full potentialities, and to make him effective as soon as possible.

Paras. 19-20.—Facilities for sabbatical leave at a later stage. Also to arrange, if possible, so that part of the training for cadets could serve by itself as an introductory course for certain other officers and possibly un-officials. See also paragraph 98.

Para. 21.—A fuller appreciation of the spiritual and artistic background of colonial peoples.

Paras. 22-24.—A better understanding of the educated native.

Paras. 25-28.—To cater for the special needs of a new type of white Officer.

PART II.

In making concrete proposals a complete scheme of training for Administrative Officers is outlined and used as a "master plan"; certain aspects of the training of officers in other Services being interwoven with it (see para. 29 (3), (5) and (6) and paras. 80-83).

Para, 29.—Outlines six main proposals, which are detailed in the next following paragraphs.

Paras. 30-32 deal with the *preliminary course* for Administrative Orders.

Paras. 33-37 deal with their *Apprentice Period.*

Para. 33 is meant to show that an officer during his apprentice period is intended to take as much, and as early, responsibility as he now does when on probation in Africa.

Paras. 35-37 make suggestions for early contact between white officers and educated natives at centres such as Achimota.

Paras. 38-44 deal with their *Second Course,* its objects and outline being given in 38-41.

In 42 it is suggested that any mistakes of selection be corrected by weeding out misfits at the end of the preliminary course, apprentice tour, and second course respectively.

43 touches on the date of confirmation. N.B.—The attached graph shows the length of time between selection and confirmation under these proposals compared with that now ruling in the case of certain types of officer.

Paras. 45-49 deal with the *Advanced Course* or as it might be better termed *"Sabbatical Leave."*

Extreme flexibility in choice of subject and of where it should be studied is advocated (para. 45, first part) but suggestions are made (second part of same para.) for getting the fullest advantage out of what officers have learned, and (in 47) from the presence of some of them in training centres.

Paras. 50-67 discuss the question where the theoretical part of the training can best be given, vide the four alternatives stated in para 51.

Para. 68 recommends the use of the Universities of Oxford, Cambridge and London as a team for the conduct of the preliminary and secondary courses.

Paras. 69-71 discuss this particular choice, which *inter alia* would enable us to send any cadet, who had not been to a public school or residential university, to Oxford or Cambridge for a period; and conversely anyone with such a background to a "modern" university (para. 71).

Paras. 72-76 discuss various practical difficulties involved in the choice of these universities; and in

Paras. 77-85 some suggestions for meeting these difficulties are made, in relation to the preliminary and second courses for Administrative Officers and such parts of these as are applicable to other branches.

Paras. 86-89 discuss the problem of finding suitable staff for courses conducted at three centres.

Paras. 90-100 suggest ways in which the training so far outlined which is primarily designed for officers recruited from this country, could be used for the benefit of locally recruited staff, officers of the Services of Dominion Mandated Territories, etc., and certain unofficials.

The danger of the "uninstructed white" in "plural communities" (see also para. 20) is discussed and suggestions for introductory "regional background courses" made (paras. 98-100).

Para. 101.—"Conclusion."

(c) The Second Devonshire Course Syllabus, 1943

Whereas Colonial Administrative Service probationers had since *c.*1910 been required to attend some sort of basic orientation course before proceeding overseas, later (1926) upgraded to an academic year at a university, and departmental officers had been expected to attend various professional courses since the 1920s, these were all pre-posting courses. The Devonshire Committee (1943) proposals for a mid-career course imaginatively broke new ground. Not only was the Second Devonshire, as it came to be known, to be open to all officers, departmental as well as administrative. It also took account of the significant shift in what fields the postwar Colonial Service officer should be expected to have some understanding.

Psychologically, too, the Second Devonshire course was designed to

> *check, criticize and clarify the experience the cadet had gained; to counteract those 'bolshevist' tendencies, which are said to be most common about the fifth to seventh year of service, by teaching him where he fits into the general scheme of colonial government and how to understand and cooperate with other departments and with the Secretariat; to deflate his conceit if he thinks he knows too much; and to fortify his morale after any shocks which his idealism has received during his apprentice tour.*

The extract is from *Postwar Training for the Colonial Service*, 1946 (Col. No. 198).

(a) GENERAL

(1) *British Colonial Aims.*

(2) *Comparative Colonial Administration.*– The theories of colonial rule of the various colonial powers and the differences in their methods of dealing with the various problems common to all colonial administrations, such as political development, the place of native institutions in the administrative system, law and justice, education, the place of European settlement and capitalist enterprise, the "colour bar."

(3) *Social Administration.*– In the future it seems likely that most colonial administrators will be largely occupied in developing forms of Local Government and also in co-ordinating the social services engaged in joint welfare development problems. For this reason it seems important that they should make a survey of the principles and practice of modern Public Administration, exemplified mainly by British experience, but also by comparison with that of other countries.

(4) *Economics and Statistics.*– There would be options within this compulsory subject, viz.: –

(a) *Trade.*– Domestic markets; the marketing of local and imported produce; export marketing; arrangements in consumer countries; international commodity agreements; trade treaties; imperial preference; economic aspects of transport problems.

(b) *Labour.*– Fluctuations in demand and supply; population density and distribution; migration; recruitment; training; methods of paying wages; profit sharing; terms and conditions of labour; trade unions; labour legislation; the I.L.O.

(c) *Agricultural Economics.–* Long and short term price movements; varying forms and scales of production; agricultural finance; research and education; organisation of producers and marketing, including co-operation.

(d) *Public Finance.–* Central, municipal and native authorities; central and local taxation; borrowing; objects of public enterprises; public finance and development; currency; trade agreements; public accounts.

(b) OPTIONAL

(5) A special study of one or more subjects in the following fields: –
Anthropology.
Colonial History.
Law.
Colonial Economics.
Colonial Education.
Agriculture and Rural Economy.
Language.

The following are among the topics which might be chosen: –

Anthropology of a particular area: Detailed study of indigenous political systems and their adaptation to modern conditions.

Diplomatic history with special reference to history of international relations in the Colonial field: The study of Colonial records.

Common Law: Land Tenure: Local Government: Legal systems and their adaptation to the needs of Colonial peoples:

Adaptation of British and indigenous systems of law.

Currency and finance: Labour: Commodities and markets: Colonial peasant economic systems and their adaptation to modern conditions.

Soil fertility: Peasant economy: Animal husbandry

(d) The Postwar Reconstruction of HM Colonial Service, 1946

In 1946 His Majesty's government published a fundamental White Paper outlining the structure and measures which it proposed 'to improve the quality and efficiency of the Colonial Service' now that the war was over.

The excerpts are from *Organization of the Colonial Service*, 1946 (Col. No. 197).

A PLAN OF ACTION.

5. The succeeding sections of this paper set out in some detail the measures which are proposed to improve the quality and efficiency of the Colonial Service. But it is perhaps as well to begin by stating broadly and as simply as possible the main points of the programme.

6. **The first is that the Colonial Service needs large reinforcements.** They will have to come from two main sources; the Colonies themselves and the United Kingdom and the Dominions.

The second point is that **the reinforcements must be fully equipped for their task.** This means, that Colonial candidates must be given opportunities which they have hitherto lacked for obtaining qualifications to enter the higher grades of the Service; also that selected candidates, from whatever source, must be given better and broader training than has been thought sufficient in the past.

Thirdly, the structure of the Colonial Service must be adapted to modern conditions. It must provide a framework in which the right man or woman can be put in the right place, irrespective of race or colour; in which there is equality of treatment and opportunity for all on the basis of merit and efficiency, in which the "passenger" can be disposed of without undue hardship; in which the poorer Colonies stand the best possible chance of getting the staff which they need.

7. Those are the requirements. They can be met only by co-operative action on the part of His Majesty's Government in the United Kingdom and the Colonial Governments, legislatures and people. His Majesty's Government can and will do its part: –

By contributing to the cost and providing opportunities for increasing the supply of qualified Colonial candidates for posts in their own service;

By recruiting qualified staffs as may be necessary in the United Kingdom and the Dominions,'

By organising and contributing to the cost of training courses;

By giving financial help to Colonies to secure the services of expert staff which they could not otherwise afford;

By co-ordinating the distribution of staff so that the available resources are disposed to the best advantage of the colonies as a whole.

8. For their part, the Colonial legislatures will be invited to adjust their service regulations, legislation and budgetary provision to conform to the general principles of organisation which are desirable if the Colonial Service is to function at the highest level of efficiency.

RECRUITMENT AND TRAINING.

(i) Improvement of opportunities for Colonial candidates.

9. The potentialities of the Colonial peoples themselves for public service have not yet been anything like fully used. The future of each Colony rests ultimately in the hands of its own people, and substantial progress must depend upon the people themselves supplying the administrative and technical staffs which the needs of each territory demand. There is no doubt that given the necessary conditions the Colonial peoples can eventually meet these needs. The first objective of post-war organisation will, then, be to provide those necessary conditions.

10. Fundamentally, this means that education facilities must be provided to create, amongst other things, a wide field of qualified candidates from whom the best can be attracted to the public service. There are potential candidates in the Colonies, both inside and outside the Civil Service, who have hitherto had

no opportunity of acquiring the same standard of education as candidates from the United Kingdom or the Dominions, but who if granted that opportunity, would be fully capable of reaching that standard. The opportunity must be provided, in existing or projected higher education institutions in the Colonies and, to the extent that and so long as these are not fully developed, in this country or elsewhere overseas. A generous gift from the Nuffield Foundation has enabled a start to be made in meeting this need, but the problem is of such importance and magnitude as to call for a broad and comprehensive measure of help from United Kingdom funds.

11. The first practical measure in this programme of action bas been taken by allocating over the next ten years from the money provided under the Colonial Development and Welfare Act a sum of £1,000,000 for the purpose of enabling carefully selected Colonial candidates to receive professional and vocational training which would qualify them for appointment to the higher grades of the Colonial Service.

(ii) Recruitment from the United Kingdom and Dominions.

12. At the same time, the Colonies need to recruit candidates on a very considerable scale for a wide variety of posts from the United Kingdom and the Dominions.– The Colonial Service still requires large reinforcements to restore establishments to the pre-war level and to afford some relief to those who have borne the burden under most exacting conditions during the years of war. Apart from this the post-war development of the Colonies demands quickly expanded staffs and will greatly increase the scope and variety of opportunities offered by the Colonial Service. The broadening activities of Government, especially in the field of social and economic services, call for staffs with a great diversity of qualifications. In particular there are more openings for qualified women than were available before the war. Without therefore prejudicing in any way the plans and opportunities for the recruitment of Colonial people for their own services, there are numerous openings for candidates from this country and the Dominions who have the desire to serve in the Colonies and the qualifications which the Colonial Service demands.

13. So far as the urgent need for reinforcing the Colonial Service allows, recruitment for these openings is being spread over the demobilisation period so that a fair and equal chance is given to all. In addition to appointments on the usual permanent basis, there are appointments on contract for a term of years, with a gratuity at the end, available for candidates who may prefer this form of service or to whom on account of their age or other circumstances it may be more suitable.

(iii) Training after Selection.

14. With the most generous and valuable co-operation of the University authorities concerned, a plan has been worked out by which the main

business of post-selection training for the Colonial Service will be entrusted to a number of British Universities. For the time being and at the start the three Universities of Oxford, Cambridge and London have been invited and have agreed to assist, and substantial financial assistance has been provided under the Colonial Development and Welfare Act.

15. The pace of development and the widening scope of Government activity make it of the first importance that officers in the higher grades, whether administrative or professional, and whatever the source of their recruitment, should be equipped for their task by the best training that can be given them. The system of post selection training in force before the war for officers recruited in this country for most branches of the service needs to be extended and amplified. It should provide for the common training of both locally and externally recruited officers. It should offer opportunities for study after, as well as before, a period of colonial experience. It must enable officers to equip themselves for the new tasks which the march of events is thrusting upon them, and should extend to professional and technical officers the language and "background" instruction which has been available in the main only to their administrative colleagues. Finally it must assist officers of each branch of the service to understand the problems and functions of their colleagues in the other branches and to co-operate intelligently with them.

16. There have from time to time been advocates of a special "Staff College" for the Colonial Service. Quite apart, however, from the practical difficulties of building, establishing, maintaining and staffing such an institution, it has been concluded that the disadvantages of segregating Colonial studies and their students from workers in other fields of study and experience would outweigh the advantages.

17. It has accordingly been decided, after very full consideration, not to pursue the project of setting up a separate "Staff College," for candidates for the Colonial Service, but instead to base their training, on the existing academic institutions, suitably assisted and reinforced for the purpose with substantial financial aid from funds provided under the Colonial Development and Welfare Act. This training will of course be available for candidates whatever the source from which they are recruited.

The training of selected candidates will fall into four sections:—

(1) Instruction designed to supplement the candidate's general education and experience, and to assist him in applying his particular skill and knowledge to the needs of the Colonial Service.

In the case of candidates for the administrative service, this instruction will at the outset of the scheme be given at Oxford or Cambridge in a special course lasting from October to June. Candidates for other branches will receive such instruction, at such centres (not limited in any way to the three

Universities mentioned in paragraph 14 above) as may be particularly adapted to their professions and requirements.

(2) A course in languages and social studies on a regional basis. This course, lasting from June to December, will be given by London University, and will be attended, so far as is appropriate and practicable, by candidates for all branches of the Service.

(3) A probationary period of service in the Colony to which the candidate has been assigned. This will as far as possible be timed so as to enable the candidate to return to this country for the final training described in the next section. He will, however, if his services have been satisfactory and he has passed the necessary tests, be confirmed in his appointment on the completion of his probationary period before he returns to this country.

(4) A "summer school" to be held at Oxford and Cambridge, with assistance from London University, in September, followed by a six months' final course devoted to the study of subjects which can be best appreciated in the light of some practical Colonial experience, and in particular to the study of the relationship and interaction between the various departments of government. The organisation of this course will be flexible and will include a wide variety of optional subjects.

In addition to this preliminary training, it is agreed that officers should have at some later stage in their careers the opportunity of study leave or a "sabbatical year" for the purpose of specialising on particular problems or subjects, wherever these can best be studied, or of travelling so as to broaden their experience and compare the methods used in other British and foreign territories for dealing with problems similar to those met with in their own Colonies.

19. In the past, the expense of training Colonial civil servants has in the main been borne by the Colonial Governments, but for many years substantial financial aid has been given by His Majesty's Government to the training of Agricultural, Veterinary and Forest officers by means of scholarship schemes. The present proposals will involve much larger expenditure than was incurred under the pre-war arrangements. Facilities for the instruction described in the previous paragraph, and for the specialist training of medical, agricultural, veterinary, forestry, legal, educational, engineering and other candidates, together with the subsistence allowances of the students of all categories, may be expected to bring the total expenditure up to the region of £300,000 a year.

STRUCTURE OF THE COLONIAL SERVICE.

21. The special conditions under which the Colonial Service does its work make it impossible to lay down a uniform pattern of salaries, grades, and terms of service. There are, however, certain general principles to which it is desirable that local schemes should conform and which, even if they cannot be applied universally or immediately, should be regarded as objectives to be

aimed at by the various Colonial Governments in framing their individual schemes from time to time. These general principles are set out below.

(i) **The salaries of all posts in the public service of a Colony should be determined according to the nature of the work and the relative responsibilities irrespective of the race or domicile of the individuals occupying the posts.**

(ii) **The salaries should be fixed at rates applicable to locally recruited staff, even though there may for the time being be grades in which few or no locally recruited officers are in fact serving.**

(iii) **In fixing these basic salaries regard should be paid to the relevant local circumstances, such as the ruling, income levels in those classes of the community from which the public service is or will be recruited.**

(iv) **Where the salaries so fixed are insufficient to attract and retain officers from overseas, expatriation pay should be provided for such officers.** In determining the rates of expatriation pay it will be relevant to consider such factors as the additional expenses to which an officer may be put by reason of the fact that he is serving away from his own home, especially when his service is in a non-temperate climate; the remuneration and amenities available in alternative careers in the officer's home country; and the general standard of remuneration and conditions in the Colonial Service.

(v) **The practice of providing free quarters far certain classes of officers should be discontinued where it exists.** It is reasonable that where suitable houses are not readily procurable the Government should relieve its officers of the anxiety of finding accommodation for themselves and should provide quarters; but officers may properly be expected to pay rent for such quarters, and their salaries should be fixed on this assumption.

(vi) **Home leave at regular intervals and free or at least assisted passages for themselves and their families on all necessary travelling occasions should be, provided officers whose homes are not in the Colony in which they serve.**

(vii) Generally, the conditions under which officers serve should be reviewed in order to increase the amenities and attractiveness of the Colonial Service and to minimise the discomforts and disadvantages which work in the tropics is liable to entail. For instance, it should be the aim to substitute a system of annual holidays (with the help of air transport) for the system of long "tours". Again, every effort should be made to avoid frequent changes of station, or of quarters within the same station, and officers should be encouraged to make homes for themselves with a reasonable prospect of permanence.

(viii) **The poorer Colonies must not be at a disadvantage in obtaining** the **services of fully qualified staff.** When all necessary adjustments and allowances have been made, there may still remain cases in which a Colony, having made reasonable provision from its own financial resources, cannot afford to pay for the services of an officer whom it needs at a rate which would represent reasonable remuneration from his point of view, or to bear the cost of passage or other expenses involved by the employment of expatriate officers. In such cases, the Colony concerned could properly seek assistance under the Colonial Development and Welfare Act as a part of the scheme relating to the work or department of the officer or officers in question.

(ix) In order to ensure that the standard of qualification required for the higher posts is maintained, and that the resources of the Service as a whole are utilised to the best advantage in the general interest, the Secretary of State will continue to control the appointment of persons to the higher administrative and professional posts in the Colonial Service, in accordance with the provisions laid down, in the Colonial Regulations. Further, while membership of the various functional branches of the Service will be open to all officers without distinction of race or domicile, the Secretary of State will continue to specify such professional or educational qualifications as he may think proper as a condition of his approval of a candidate for appointment to certain designated posts. The Secretary of State will naturally exercise his control solely in the best interests of the Colonies, in order to provide them with the best and most suitable staff possible, the fullest regard being paid to the claims of local candidates. It will also continue to be a part of the understanding between the Secretary of State and candidates whom he selects for appointment to the Colonial Service that the latter accept an obligation to serve in any post in the Colonies to which the Secretary of State may assign them, provided that an officer will not be expected to accept compulsory transfer to a post which in the opinion of the Secretary of State is inferior (due regard being had to climatic and other conditions) to that which he already holds. Opportunities of promotion on transfer will of course be open to locally appointed officers of proved merit who desire them, but they will not be liable to compulsory transfer from their home countries.

(x) While the Service must continue to be organised in distinct professional and functional branches, a rigid departmentalism should be avoided. The aim should be to place officers where their qualifications and experience can best be used. There should be the fullest possible interchange between headquarters and the field, as also between the Colonial Office and the Colonial Service. Opportunities should be given for suitable professional officers to undertake administrative work, and every effort should be made to develop the team spirit and the idea, that all branches of the Service are partners in the same enterprise, each bringing its own special contribution to the common object.

(xi) Public Service Commissions should be established in the Colonies. Subject to the general overriding powers of the Secretary of State, the selection and appointment of candidates in the Colonies to posts in the local service will lie with the Governor of the Colony. It is desirable that the Governor should be advised in these matters by a Public Service Commission appointed by him and so composed as to command the confidence of the Service and the public.

30. The suggestion has been made that it would be simpler and more

convenient for His Majesty's Government to take over the whole cost of the salaries, expenses and pensions of the expatriate officers of the Colonial Service, thus releasing considerable funds which the Colonial Governments could then apply to development purposes. Such a proposal might indeed on a short view make for administrative simplicity, but in principle it is alien to the whole conception of progressive constitutional development on which the structure and organisation of the Colonial Service is based. The effect would be that the higher grades of the Service would be staffed by officers whose conditions of employment would not be controlled by the Colonial legislatures but by His Majesty's Government. From the point of view of political development, such an arrangement would be retrograde; while, from the service point of view, an impassable gulf would be fixed between the expatriate officers and their Colonial colleagues. The spirit of co-operation in a common task, which it is so essential to foster, could not fail to be seriously impaired. The scheme which has been adopted provides for a generous measure of assistance, so planned as to ensure that the Colonies will get a fully equipped Service in which the Colonial peoples themselves will take a progressively increasing share, while retaining the framework of existing institutions and safeguarding the principle of local self-government.

(e) 'The Future of the Colonial Service', 1947

To inaugurate the new postwar Second Devonshire course, a short summer school was held at Oxford University in September 1947. Sir Alan Burns, one of the doyens among Colonial Service governors, was invited to address the members of the courses before they started their academic year at Cambridge, Oxford or London. He was asked by the Colonial Office to talk on 'The Future of the Colonial Service'. The Oxford summer school was to become a regular feature of the Second Devonshire courses.

Sir Alan Burns's comments on indirect rule came six months after the Secretary of State's call for its replacement by a system of local government (see Document Vb).

I HAVE been asked to speak to you this morning of the future of the Colonial Civil Service as I think it must develop if it is to meet the growing demands that will be made on it during the next twenty or thirty years. I shall not attempt to make any detailed suggestions on this subject but shall confine myself to the most important question of all—our relations with the peoples of the colonies on which everything else depends. Before, however, I take on the functions of a minor prophet (not, be it understood, of my own choice), I wish to look backwards for a few minutes to the past of the Service – a past which in my case covers an official lifetime of forty-two years.

In the first place I wish to emphasise that the Colonial Civil Service has little to be ashamed of in its past. Without being unduly complacent, and fully conscious of our many mistakes, I feel that we have done a great job, very often in difficult circumstances, and not seldom in spite of the discouragements we have met from those who should have known better. There has been in recent years a tendency in some quarters to decry our past colonial administration, and to harp unduly on its failures, forgetting, in an orgy of self-depreciation, our very considerable achievements, and the high standard of administrative and judicial integrity which even our critics cannot deny. I think there has been far too much sackcloth and ashes, and I think it has done a great deal of harm. It has given a false idea to our friends of what we have done, and what we are doing, and has provided a handle for our enemies which they can use to attack our so-called Imperialism. It has unduly depressed a number of men in the Colonial Service who have been led to think by these constant apologies that they have perhaps failed in the work to which they have put their hand. But worst of all, in my opinion, is the effect it has had on the people in the Colonies who are only too prone to blame everyone else for their present condition, and to overlook their own failure to take advantage of the chances that have been given them. Let us freely admit that our Colonial Administration has not been perfect, but do not let us for one moment give the impression that we think we have done badly, because I believe we have done very well indeed, and I doubt whether any other nation could have done better.

There have even been suggestions that our Empire is coming to its end, that our Colonies are now ready and anxious to stand by themselves, and there will shortly be no further need for a Colonial Civil Service. I don't believe it. Colonial peoples criticise their governments, but that does not mean that they want any other nation to govern them, or that they think they can yet govern themselves. Only the other day a Gold Coast paper stated (and no one challenged that statement) that that Colony was not yet fit for self-government, and the Gold Coast is far nearer to fitness for self-government than many others. There are, of course, some people in every Colony who would like to see a revolutionary change, but I do not believe that the average Colonial's criticism of Colonial government is anything more serious than the natural desire for improvement. Our Colonial Administration is not perfect. It is run by men and not by archangels, and being human they make mistakes. There is no perfect government anywhere in the world, and there are even Socialists in England today who are dissatisfied with the Socialist Utopia in which we are now living, but would do nothing to throw out the Government.

Believe me, the Colonial Civil Service, with all its imperfections, will be needed for many years to come.

Let me remind you that before the war, if we exclude such fortresses as Gibraltar and Malta, there were practically no white troops in the British Colonies, to hold down, as some people think we hold down, the subject populations. Again in 1940, when we of the British Empire stood alone against the Axis, with our allies overwhelmed by the Germans, and our own armies defeated, when our enemies exulted over our impending ruin, and even our friends had abandoned hope, this was the time when our Colonies stood by us— friends indeed, and true loyal friends.

In the Gold Coast at that time we had few troops and we were surrounded by hostile Vichy territory. Had the people of the Gold Coast wished to push us into the sea there was little to prevent them. But this was the time when the people came forward in their thousands, not with empty protestations of loyalty, but with men to serve in the army (and you know how gallantly the Gold Coast Regiment served in Abyssinia and Burma) and in the Home Guard, and with liberal gifts to war funds and war charities. This was curious conduct for people tired of British rule. And the Gold Coast was one of many Colonies which acted in this curious way...

In its early stages Colonial Administration is a comparatively simple matter. It consists merely of maintaining order, of opening up the country by means of roads and railways, and of giving justice to the people. Colonial Civil Servants in the early days needed physical courage and the ability to live amid great discomfort, the ability also to do any kind of odd job that came along. Above all it was necessary for them to possess a real sympathy for the people among whom they were working. Now that the Colonies are under effective control physical courage is perhaps no longer necessary (but there is still a need for that moral courage which is wanted in every walk of life). Nor is there any need today for the Administrative Officer to be the Jack of all trades that he was in the past, as we have now a number of professional men and technicians of every kind to do the more technical jobs. But there remains of the three things which were needed in the old Service the most important of all—a real sympathy for the people among whom we work. This has always been necessary, and *will* always be necessary however we may develop the Colonies, and however highly and efficiently our Administration may be developed.

When I speak of sympathy I am not suggesting for one moment that we should be sentimental in our treatment of the African. We must be able to see his faults as they exist, for it is a great mistake to regard him always as a "blameless Ethiopian." The African, like ourselves, has lots of faults, but we must help him to overcome them, and we must help him by advice and example, and above all by impressing upon him that we really are his friends and *anxious* to help him. Nor must we be in too much of a hurry to "improve" him, and make him into what we think he ought to be. . . .

Every zealous Officer is seeking for efficiency, and such an Officer may try to force the Africans to be efficient, and if they will not work efficiently will try to do the work himself. This may have satisfactory results from the point of view of the European Officer, but it will not teach the African anything, and it is better to teach them than to do the work oneself. Let the African make his own mistakes, as it is only by making these mistakes that he will learn to avoid them. You yourselves will find it more useful, and more satisfactory, to make your own mistakes, than to make the mistakes imposed on you from Head-quarters. I have myself found it far more satisfactory as a Governor to make my own mistakes than to make the mistakes which the Colonial Office has suggested to me.

Then again don't let us be too sure that we are always right. The local knowledge of the primitive native has its value, and very often he knows a thing to be so, although he could not explain the reason for it. It sometimes gives us a jolt—and a very salutary jolt—when we get the local man's opinion of our bright ideas and of our efficiency. I once opened in British Honduras, with a great flourish of trumpets, a new rice mill of which I was very proud, and I invited the Maya Chiefs of the locality to come and admire this wonderful development. Seeing that one of them did not appear to be impressed I pointed out to him the merits of the mill, and showed him the clean rice emerging at the far end of it. His only comment was that the women of his tribe could do this with a stick.

Now it is clearly better to use the machinery of a rice mill than to use a stick, but he considered that we were making a lot of unnecessary fuss over a very simple thing and he was right. We would have done better if we had taken less trouble over the machinery, and *more* trouble over explaining its uses to the people. And we made that mistake because we did not know enough about the Mayas.

It is, in fact, our first job to learn all we can about the people of the Colonies, to learn their language if possible, and to learn what we can *from* them, including good manners. Above all, do not let us go out to the Colonies crammed with theories and try to make the facts fit into these theories. I speak now with diffidence, but there are perhaps far too many experts today with theories about Colonial Administration, only too ready and willing, from their vast theoretical knowledge, to suggest improvements in the way Colonial peoples should be governed. Sometimes they seem to forget that they are not dealing with abstract principles, but with human beings, and there is a real danger today of some confusion between the means and the end. There is some danger that the Colonies may come to be regarded merely as laboratories in which can be proved some of the magnificent theories evolved by experts. It is no use eliminating the mosquito in the colonies, if into the vacuum thus caused there comes a rush of experts. . . .

The expert in this country is too far away to see life in the Colonies at all, especially when the distant view is obscured by the clouds of theory. Do not misunderstand me. The expert has his uses, provided that he is not regarded as a dictator, and provided that he does not annoy the people of the Colonies with his theories. There is, as I have said, some danger of confusion between the means and the end. There is even a danger in Courses such as this one, lest the

Course be regarded as more important than the Colonies for whose benefit it is devised. And worst of all would it be if anyone began to think that the Colonies existed for the benefit of the Colonial Civil Service. . . .

The main thing in my opinion is to find out first what Colonial peoples want, and if their wants are not too unreasonable to let them have their way. I do not mean by this that we must give way to irresponsible clamour, or to the half-baked proposals of amateur politicians who seldom take the trouble to think out their problems, but where there is a consensus of opinion among reasonable local men (and there are many who could be so described) we should not dismiss their suggestions except for the gravest reasons, and if we do dismiss them we must carefully explain our reasons, with patience and with courtesy. The time is long past when we can get away with the attitude that "Daddy knows best"; and we must remember that children are perverse enough to grow up. We are there in the Colonies to help and to educate, and we can only help by a thorough understanding of the Colonial point of view so far as it is possible for us to understand it. But we certainly will never understand unless we take the trouble to *try* to understand, and we will never get our own motives understood and appreciated unless we make the people believe that we are their friends and that we wish to help them.

Let me refer for a moment to indirect rule. This was an expedient adopted by my old chief, Lord Lugard, in Northern Nigeria, to meet the situation which then existed. He had not a sufficiently large European staff with which to govern the country, and he made use of the existing Native Administrations and governed Northern Nigeria through them. Since that time there have been some who have tried to turn the theory of indirect rule into a mystic religion, and by doing so have made it ridiculous. There is no mystery about indirect rule. It is merely a convenient form in the Colonies of local administration, and the Native Authorities are, or should be, what we in this country call Local Authorities. For those people who are still living a tribal existence I regard indirect rule as the best training in self-government, and we should support it wherever it is possible to do so. But it must really be indirect rule and made more democratic than it is in some places. We must not merely set up autocratic chiefs through whom we can govern, because such rule is just as direct as any rule that a District Officer could administer—and probably less efficient. I am not suggesting that we should take away the power of the Chiefs and give it to men of our own choice. This would be fatal. So long as their own people trust the Chiefs and are willing to be governed by them we should support the Chiefs and help them to work efficiently without regard to the clamour from a certain class of politician, who would like, to satisfy his own ambitions, to replace the Chief as the recognised leader of the people. We must in any case be careful not to move so far ahead of public opinion as to confuse the people, and many of the people would be greatly confused if they lost their Chiefs. But when there is a real demand from the people for greater democracy we should encourage it and persuade the Chiefs to accept the position, and particularly to bring into their Councils more educated men. Let me add that many of the Chiefs realise the need for such a change and are already giving effect to it. In this, as in other matters, let the people decide, and let them if necessary make their own mistakes.

As I have said, I think indirect rule an excellent school in which the difficult art of self-government may be learnt. But indirect rule cannot be applied to all. It cannot be applied, for instance, to those educated people who have become divorced from their tribal life, and have adopted, perhaps with the Christian religion, a form of civilisation which is very much like ours. You cannot set the clock back in Africa or anywhere else, and you cannot expect the educated African to be satisfied with a Native Administration run by men in whom he has no confidence—illiterate men whom in his heart he despises.

One of the troubles has been that these educated Africans are less amenable to our suggestions, less friendly, and less willing to accept us as supermen, and it is not so pleasing to our vanity to be criticised (and perhaps abused) by educated politicians as it is to be treated with courtesy and respect by the members of a primitive community. But I have known a great many Africans, educated Africans, who were very pleasant and intelligent people, with better manners than many Europeans, and ready to co-operate with any of us whom they regarded as their friends. There are, of course, good and bad Africans, as there are good and bad Europeans. But do not be put off because you are criticised or opposed by Colonial politicians or by the Colonial Press. What you must do in such cases is to grin and bear it, and try by your own good manners to shame the others into better behaviour. I have never known such treatment to fail. No man in a responsible position can hope to escape criticism, and sometimes this criticism can be very unfair. But if you are confident in your heart that you have done the right thing, you can afford to ignore such criticism, which can do you no real harm.

Perhaps you will ask me what all this has to do with the future of the Colonial Service. In my view it has everything to do with it. The time has gone when the Colonial Civil Servant could afford to ignore the point of view of Colonial peoples, and indeed of world opinion. In the past we have worked conscientiously, and I think successfully, *for* the people of the Colonies, but now we must work *with* them. In the past we could maintain order, stamp out slave dealing and human sacrifice, and give justice in our courts. We needed no help in distinguishing between right and wrong in such cases, and there were in any case few people in the Colonies of which I am now thinking who were in a position to advise or criticise our actions. Today the position is different. We have to take a far greater interest in the social and economic life of the people, and in these things we must have their co-operation and assistance. We must help them to improve themselves, help them to become more healthy and more wealthy and more wise, and above all we must help them to help themselves. Our function in the future will become increasingly different from what it was in the past.

Our role must in fact change from an executive to an advisory one, and with the acceleration of Africanisation in the Services of the African Colonies, there will be little room for the official who does not regard the training of African staff as his primary responsibility. . . .

The maintenance and development of sound administration in a Colony depends almost entirely on the personal relationship that exists between the officials and the people of the country. The Colonial, like anyone else, is naturally reluctant to admit his shortcomings to unsympathetic persons, but he knows quite well in his own mind that he has much to learn, and he is anxious to learn whatever he can. Like ourselves, while he is willing to be led by a friend, he will not be driven by anybody, and least of all by one whom he does not trust, or who speaks to him in a condescending manner. He is very sensitive and the bad manners, or even the unsympathetic attitude, of one official may be sufficient to undo a great deal of good work done by a number of others. Every Government Officer should bear this constantly in mind. Each has a special and personal responsibility in this matter.

The first thing then that the Colonial Civil Servant has to do is to make friends with the people among whom he is to work, and if he makes friends with them, and gets them to trust him he will have laid the foundation of his life's work, and will find his duties far more pleasing and his work far more effective than otherwise. Our attitude in the future must be one of sympathetic tolerance and unlimited patience. We are there to teach and to help, not to govern by the strong hand. The task is going to get harder and harder each day, but it will become more and more worth while as we see the results of what we are doing. Our main job is to teach the Africans and other Colonials to take our places in the administration of the Colonies. We must try and teach them to do the work that we are doing ourselves, in order that they may replace us. It will be a long time before they are as efficient as we are, because most of them have not got the background of training that we have had over many generations, and we must accept the fact. We must accept a certain amount of inefficiency, a certain amount of criticism even from those we are trying to help, and we must accept cheerfully the fact that we are training the men who in the end must take our places from us. You will get little thanks, but does this really matter?

We must co-operate with the people of the Colonies and we must co-operate with one another. There can be no division of the Colonial Service into water-tight compartments, with the Administrative Officers working separately from the technical men, and the technical men ignoring political repercussions in their professional zeal. As I see the Colonial Service in the future it must consist in each area of a team of men, professional and administrative, working together in close collaboration with one another, meeting frequently in com-mittees, not committees in which there is much talk and little action, but businesslike active bodies of men, realising that they share a common responsibility for getting things done and a common duty to the people of the country. And above all, these Committees must work with the local people, with the local Chiefs and Native Authorities, and get their advice and help.

There is a great deal to be done and you gentlemen are representatives of the men who must do it. But you can only accomplish what you set out to do if you take the people into your confidence, work with them, play with them, and help them to the better life which they should share with us.

Above all, you must have a strong faith in the justness of our policy and confidence in our mission. You belong to a great Service and a Service with great traditions, and I am confident that the Service of the future will maintain those traditions worthily.

V. The Colonial Service and Downing Street: Four Policy Dispatches and Directives

Although not always a Cabinet post, the Secretary of State for the Colonies became an important minister in the two decades following the end of the war, and the Cabinet established its own Colonial Policy Committee. The passages that follow comprise excerpts from a dispatch from the Governor of Uganda on probable political developments in Africa after the war; the Secretary of State's seminal dispatch on local government as the replacement for native administration; and the Prime Minister's call for a balance sheet of empire and likely demands for independence.

(a) Postwar Africa: The Likely Scenario, 1942

Sir Charles Dundas, governor of wartime Uganda, was moved by two events to circulate to his provincial administration and his heads of department a considered memorandum in which he set out his views on Britain's attitude towards social and administrative policy in Africa once the war was over. One of the generating events was Lord Hailey's secret mission of 1940/1, which resulted in his confidential (and restricted until 1979) report *Native Administration and Political Development in British Tropical Africa* (1944). The other was the criticism in the UK of British policy in Malaya following the fall of Singapore in 1942. The Colonial Office, to whom Dundas sent a copy of his memorandum under cover of a dispatch in May 1942, regretted that the Governor had found it necessary to refer to Britain's reverses in the Far East.

Excerpts from the original dispatch are given below.

It is inevitable that in the preoccupations of War the ordinary problems of Civil Administration somewhat recede from mind and for lack of staff and means progress is halted. On the other hand we are asked to plan ahead for post-war conditions and I have myself held that this is the time to study affairs and examine projects for betterment of conditions so that we may go ahead as soon as restored peace permits. I must confess, however, that when I attempt to do this I often seem to be confronted with so much uncertainty as to the future factors to be taken into account as to feel that one is baulked in tackling many, though not all, of the issues that suggest themselves for attention.

There is, however, one presumption on which, to my mind, we can proceed with a good deal of certainty, and for which we ought to prepare ourselves. It is in respect of the post-war attitudes to be expected towards social and administrative policy in Africa. Several forces will combine to impose in these respects reforms that will be in harmony with the spirit of the time.

In the first place there is what I might call the Atlantic Charter spirit, the universal resolve that there shall, so to speak, be no under-dogs, a humanitarian doctrine that is the direct outcome of desperate resistance to tyranny.

There is also the growing sentiment, born in England already before the war, for betterment of all conditions in our Colonies, and elimination of poverty, ignorance and subservient status among backward peoples. It is more than probable that post-war governments in England will be of a very liberal, not to say socialistic, possibility ultra-socialistic character, and we know from previous experience that the Colonial policy of such Administrations is always in the direction of abolition of racial inequalities and emancipation in all directions. But even the most conservative elements look forward to a new social era and will not overlook its extension to Africa. More than ever we shall have to justify our retention of so large a portion of the globe by impeccable and progressive rule over backward races.

Finally our native races, by their fidelity and helpfulness in the war will have a claim to the reward of greater effort and consideration in their behalf. And it will be surprising if the thousands of Africans who have served in many lands remote from their own, and who have seen much and gained many new ideas, will not exert a new influence which will result in demand for new methods and treatment. Even the stay-at-home African has had liberty and equality of opportunity dinned into his ears day in and day out.

All this we must prepare for, not perhaps so much in action as in mind, and we shall do well to shape our present methods so as to fit in with a new order prevailing not so long hence.

It is not easy to cite with clarity and confidence specific instances of the sort of reforms that are to be expected. For myself I should expect general education to be one of them, combined therewith more of rural betterment and improvement of urban native dwellings. I do not believe that existing labour legislation with its penal sanctions can be retained; on the other hand I should expect to see legislation for workmen's compensation and other forms of protection for labour. I think we shall have demand for higher wages, because no housing, education or health service can really raise standards of living in conditions of extreme poverty. I shall expect to hear insistent claims for free admission of educated Africans to higher and better paid positions in public service. The cry for African representation, but not by an European, in the legislature, or at least participation in one form or another in the framing of legislation and administrative controls and for membership in public bodies will be voiced. The younger generation will expect a place in Native Administrations, with a freer hand in their control. The long standing problem of native land tenure must be tackled and a system of ownership devised even if it be still subject to reservations. The system of native taxation will need to be overhauled, and the present burden lightened or its proceeds placed at the disposal of the Native Authorities. In short, the demand will be for more equality and less restraint, for larger scope and fewer barriers, for better conditions of life and the means to make such possible. And it will not come only, and probably not most forcefully, from Africans, nor only from our own nation, it will be universally voiced.

I am convinced that none of these demands, and more of the like, will be regarded as extravagant and to be set aside by arbitrary decision. They must be met at least in a spirit of accommodation. And herein lies the fundamental change to be expected. We can no longer determine according as it seems best to us, in other words dictatorship cannot be perpetuated and if we look for the inner reason it is because we have been waging, and have called upon the coloured races to wage with us, war against dictatorship. Hitherto we have always been actuated by honest belief that what we think good for the African is so. It is an honest well-intentioned motive on the part of the ruler but not always contenting to the ruled. To quote the old saw "Good government is no substitute for self-government". . . .

I have expressed myself in very general terms as above because it seems to me necessary that even now we should think ahead in terms of post-war policy, and keep that before us whenever present practice is under review.

Those of us who knew Africa before and after the last war saw great changes resulting therefrom, chiefly a remarkable awakening of the African, keen desire to advance and appreciation of education, medical service and economic earning power. It is my opinion that the present war will have an even more rousing influence, chiefly political and social, and it will be sheer blindness not to foresee the logical consequences. Unless we are prescient there is a danger that it will be not the Africans but ourselves who are backward and that our outlook and methods will be based on premises that since long have ceased to be valid. It is none to [sic] early now to reflect and consider whether we are up-to-date in our methods and conceptions of Administration.

(b) The Secretary of State's Local Government Dispatch, 1947

A turning point in colonial policy was the dispatch sent by the Secretary of State to the governors of all the African territories in February 1947. By the Colonial Office's introduction of local government to replace native administration, the hallowed Colonial Service policy of indirect rule, in fashion since the 1920s and raised to almost a colonial credo, was brusquely abolished. Local government now became the hoped-for path towards democratization and hence self-government.

Sir,

Since I took office as Secretary of State in October I have been considering some of the basic problems of African administration, and I think it right that I should now address you on this subject, since our success in handling these problems and the extent to which we can secure the active co-operation of the Africans themselves may well determine the measure of our achievement in the programmes of political, social and economic advancement on which we have now embarked. I believe that the key to success lies in the development of an efficient, democratic[1] system of local government. I wish to emphasize the words efficient, democratic and local. I do so, not because they import any new conception into African administration; indeed these have been the aims of our policy for many years. I use these words because they seem to me to contain the kernel of the whole matter; local because the system of government must be close to the common people and their problems, efficient because it must be

---

[1] Later altered to 'representative'.

capable of managing the local services in a way which will help to raise the standard of living, and democratic because it must not only find a place for the growing class of educated men, but at the same time command the respect and support of the mass of the people.

2. In African administration the term local government must not be interpreted narrowly; it covers political questions such as the functions of native authorities, the composition and method of appointment of councils and the constitutional position of chiefs; financial questions such as the working of native treasuries and the relationship between central and local taxation; judicial questions such as the operation of native courts and the development of African law, both traditional and statutory; and economic questions such as the control of land usage and the evolution of systems of land tenure. . . . In urban areas the special problem arises of developing municipal government, or in some places, associating Africans with non-African communities in municipal government where it already exists. In rural areas local government bodies may be native authorities, large or small, or local native councils, as in Kenya. Where native authorities are large and responsible for hundreds of thousands or even millions of people, the problem is one of building up a system of local government below them in close touch with the people themselves; where they are too small to be effective, the problem is one of securing fusion or federation of existing units. The general policy must be applied differently in different areas; the broad aim of securing an efficient and democratic system of local government will, however, be the same everywhere.

3. The African Governments are now beginning to put their ten year development programmes into execution. The stage has been reached when paper plans must be translated into action, and it is in the townships and villages, among the people themselves, that much of this action must take place. There are many development schemes where success, in whole or in part, depends on the active co-operation of the people, and that co-operation can best be secured through the leadership of local authorities. Without an efficient system of local government the great mass of the African population will derive only partial benefits from the monies voted for development by the Colonial Legislatures and the grants made under the Colonial Development and Welfare Act.

4. Local government has an equally important part to play in the sphere of political development. Since 1940 much progress has been made in the granting of increased responsibility to Africans in the central political and administrative machinery of government. In Nigeria and the Gold Coast Africans have been brought onto the Executive Councils and there are now African unofficial majorities on the Legislative Councils. In all the East African territories African members have been appointed to the Legislative Councils for the first time, and such appointments will before long be made in Northern Rhodesia and Nyasaland. Everywhere Africans are playing an increasing part in the making of policy by their service on boards and committees. For the most part these

positions of responsibility are necessarily being filled by men from the educated minority, and in present circumstances almost all the leaders of African society must be drawn from this class. But this very situation, inevitable as it is, carries with it one danger for the future, in that it may result in the creation of a class of professional African politicians absorbed in the activities of the centre and out of direct touch with the people themselves. The problem is fully recognized by the African Governments and is being met in some Territories by the establishment of regional or provincial councils, through which a chain of representation from the people to the Legislative Councils can be secured. The Native Authorities, as the organs of local government, are the most important link in this chain. In countries where literate systems of voting cannot yet be used for the purposes of election, local government bodies must normally provide the electoral machinery so as to ensure that the representatives of the people on provincial, regional and central councils are chosen by the people in accordance with methods which they themselves accept and understand. Local government must at once provide the people with their political education and the channel for the expression of their opinions. An efficient and democratic system of local government is in fact essential to the healthy political development of the African Territories; it is the foundation on which their political progress must be built. But the rate of political progress cannot be regulated according to a pre-arranged plan; the pace over the next generation will be rapid, under the stimulus of our own development programmes, of internal pressure from the people themselves, and of world opinion expressed through the growing international interest in the progress of colonial peoples. If local government is to keep pace with political progress and to exert its due influence on that progress, the Native Authorities must adapt themselves rapidly to the needs of the modern world, and the African Governments will have a major part to play in encouraging that process. In many parts of Africa the development of local government bodies has been held back by the lack of education and the ill health of the people. Where conditions are still primitive they cannot be transformed except through a laborious process of evolution. The political development of the Territories will, however, forge ahead in spite of conditions in the more backward areas, and, if this development is not to be one-sided, it is necessary that local government should everywhere progress as rapidly as possible to the stage at which it can play its effective part in the development of the Territories.

5. I do not intend in this despatch to attempt any general statement of my views on the means by which the policy of local government should be carried forward. Indeed I have not yet reached any final conclusion whether such a statement of policy is required at the present time. It is, I know, widely held that conditions in the African Territories are so diverse as to make difficult, if not impossible, the laying down of any general principles of policy which would be of practical value. As at present advised I do not myself share this

view and I believe that at the appropriate time there would be much advantage
in producing a statement dealing not with the detailed applications of policy,
which vary from territory to territory, but with its objectives, which are
common to all territories, and the manner in which those objectives could best
be approached. Such a statement would, however, demand the greatest care in
preparation and I should wish its terms to be discussed with officers having up-
to-date practical experience of the work of African administration in the field.
As you know I am arranging to hold a summer school on this subject at
Cambridge in August, which I hope will be as representative of the
Administrative Service in Africa as the importance of the subject deserves. I
intend that the minor aspects of local government should be discussed at the
summer school and in particular I hope that attention will be given to the
following points:

(i) Means of securing an effective place in local government for those
Africans who are best qualified to be real leaders of the people.

(ii) Means of developing real financial responsibility in local government
bodies both in relation to the raising of taxation and the control of expenditure.

(iii) The division of functions between local government bodies and the
Central Government and the place of local government bodies in political
systems of the territories.

(iv) The functions of local government bodies in relation to the control of
land usage and the conservation and development of natural resources.

(v) The bearing of African legal systems on social and economic development and their evolution in relation to European law.

(vi) The development of local government for Africans in urban areas.

6. I shall be in a better position after the summer school has taken place to
consider whether any statement of policy is required and, if so, what form it
should take and whether it should be confidential or for publication. I should
not of course regard the exchange of views at the summer school as substitute
for consultation with Governors, and at the appropriate time I should wish to
obtain Governors' views on these points. Meanwhile I shall take the opportunity in this despatch to address you on certain questions of machinery which I
regard as essential to the successful formation and operation of any policy of
African local government. I believe that the knowledge of the subject which
undoubtedly exists throughout Africa must be made more readily available to
all concerned, so that it may exercise the right influence on the formation of
policy. For this purpose we must provide for a much more effective and
continuous exchange of information between individual African Governments
and between the African Governments as a whole and the Colonial Office; and
equally the machinery both of African Governments and the Colonial Office
must be so devised that policy with regard to local government for Africans can
be kept constantly under review. At the same time, in recognition of the pre-
dominant part which the district staffs play in the execution of policy, means

must be found of ensuring that they are enabled to devote the majority of their time and attention to this vital work. . . .

14. The District Staffs.—The principal instrument for putting into effect the policy of African local government is the District Commissioner and it is vital to the success of this policy that the best possible use should be made of his services. I wish to make known to the Service generally my deep concern for the welfare of all staff working in the field. Since I am here discussing the problems of local government, what I say is necessarily addressed to the position of the Administrative Officer, but the principle applies equally to all technical field staff and I should like this to be clearly understood. . . . I regard it as of fundamental importance, and I know that Governors agree, that District Commissioners should be given by Governments the widest possible latitude within the general framework of policy to press on with the development of local government in their district and that full scope should be given for the exercise of individual energy and initiative. For this purpose it is necessary that the district staffs should be kept fully and continuously informed of the broad lines of Government policy within which they must operate; that they should be relieved of the mass of routine which at present often makes it difficult for them to devote enough time and attention to their true work of local government; that every effort should be made, even at some sacrifice of convenience, to leave them in their posts for sufficiently long periods to enable real progress to be made during the term of office of each District Commissioner; and finally that one-man districts should be avoided so that regular touring may take place. I am aware that these problems have been engaging the attention of African Governments for many years. What I have to say is not new. I say it because I believe that the time has come to make renewed efforts to solve these problems of machinery, so as to ensure that the district staffs are in the best position to deal with the exceedingly difficult problems which lie ahead of us in Africa in the immediate future.

15. You will have appreciated from the preceding paragraphs the importance which I attach to keeping the district staffs fully informed of developments both inside and outside the Territory. I suggest that this could be achieved in the following ways:

(a) By providing officers in the field with information regarding current developments in the policy of the Government concerned both while policy is still being formed and after decisions have been taken. Written information should be supplemented by personal contacts between headquarters and the district staff and it should be the special responsibility of the Secretary for African Affairs, or the equivalent officer, to maintain these contacts by frequent touring.

(b) By means of periodic conferences which are a regular feature in some Territories already and undoubtedly fulfil an extremely valuable function.

(c) By arranging for Officers to attend courses, etc., while on leave in this country.

(d) By arranging visits for officers to other British Territories in Africa and to foreign territories.

(e) By encouraging the production of local periodicals whether on an official basis or on the initiative of individual officers of departments.

(f) By ensuring the distribution of important Government publications, e.g., White Papers, etc., published in the United Kingdom.

(g) By ensuring that all important publications affecting their work are made available officially to the district staffs and that they are kept up to date in the general literature of their profession. Arrangements should be made to circulate to them a list of recent publications on all matters affecting their work. In order to assist Governments in this I am examining the possibility of circulating book lists regularly to all Colonial Governments.

(h) By arranging that the district staffs have the means to keep abreast with world affairs and new ideas by means of station or office libraries and central or provincial lending libraries. Library facilities should be renewed and where necessary supplemented.

16. Finally I come to the actual work of District Commissioners and to the complaint which has been heard on all sides for many years, that the district staffs have become increasingly over-burdened with minor routine matters which make it impossible for officers to devote sufficient time and attention to their proper function of local government. You will, I am sure, agree with the view I strongly hold that the development of African local government should be the principal function of district staffs, and I should be glad if this could be laid down emphatically for the guidance of all your officers. This does not of course apply to officers in towns or settled areas who are deputed to deal with the affairs of the non-African communities; nor is it intended to mean that in mixed areas the affairs of these communities should receive less than the attention which they deserve. I do, however, again wish to emphasize that work connected with local government is of greater importance than the submission of returns or the writing of routine reports. I am not suggesting that routine work should be neglected or put aside, but I do consider that it should be subjected to careful scrutiny by Governments to ensure that demands made on District Commissioners by the Secretariat and departments are fully justified and that less important items may, where possible, be eliminated. If any question of priority arises between the two functions, the work of local government must in my view take precedence over all but absolutely essential routine work.

17. Routine work must nevertheless continue, and to help the district staffs to deal with it I suggest, in the first place, that Governments should examine the possibility of increasing the mechanical aids to work at district headquarters and in particular that attention should be given to the increased use of typewriters, stenographers and even possibly dictaphones in the larger centres. I believe that it would be useful for any Government which has not recently done

so to entrust one of its officers with the task of examining the possibility of adopting arrangements to increase office efficiency in the districts. Secondly, and far more important, I consider that arrangements should be made to relieve District Commissioners, and District Officers or Assistant District Commissioners, of the personal responsibility for the handling of routine work. In my view the aim should be to provide every district office with a competent office manager who, while coming under the authority of the District Commissioner, would himself be responsible for such matters as the local Treasury, the issue of licences, the handling of cash, the preparation of returns and such other matters as could be delegated to him. This office manager should himself be recognized as sub-accountant for the district so that he and not the District Commissioner himself could carry the financial responsibility. Such posts should be filled by Africans whenever suitable Africans are available; and, where they are not at present available, by Asians or by Europeans whether male or female. It may be that as a result routine and financial work might in some cases be handled with slightly less efficiency than when dealt with by Administrative Officers themselves, but this could be offset by establishing a system of travelling inspectors of the work of these office managers. In any case, any loss of efficiency involved in the change at first would, in my view, be more than balanced by the advantage of freeing Administrative Officers for the exercise of their proper functions. In permitting highly trained and highly paid Administrative Officers to devote large parts of their time to dealing with minute details of routine administration, I consider that we are acquiescing in an arrangement which is most uneconomical and I feel sure that this state of affairs must be brought to an end at the earliest possible moment. I wish to make it clear that I attach great importance to this point; indeed I regard it as essential that steps should be taken without delay to relieve Administrative Officers of routine work and to ensure that they are able to devote themselves primarily to travelling extensively throughout their districts and to the problems of political, economic, and social development and above all to the development of local government. . . .

(c) The Prime Minister's Minute Calling for a Balance Sheet of Empire, 1957

Prime Minister Harold Macmillan's minute to the Lord President of the Council, written on the eve of independence of both the Gold Coast and Malaya, ranks as a highly realistic signpost in Britain's forward thinking about the timing of her withdrawal from the colonial territories.

LORD PRESIDENT OF THE COUNCIL

It would be helpful if the Colonial Policy Committee could submit to the Cabinet their estimate of the probable course of constitutional development in the Colonies over the years ahead.

It would be good if Ministers could know more clearly which territories are likely to become ripe for independence over the next few years – or, even if they are not ready for it, will demand it so insistently that their claims cannot be denied – and at what date that stage is likely to be reached in each case.

It would also be helpful if this study would distinguish those Colonies which would qualify for full membership of the Commonwealth, and would indicate what constitutional future there is for the others which may attain independence but cannot aspire to full Commonwealth membership.

I should also like to see something like a profit and loss account for each of our Colonial possessions, so that we may be better able to gauge whether, from the financial and economic point of view, we are likely to gain or lose by its departure. This would need, of course, to be weighed against the political and strategic considerations involved in each case. And it might perhaps be better to attempt an estimate of the balance of advantage, taking all these considerations into account, of losing or keeping each particular territory. There are presumably places where it is of vital interest to us that we should maintain our influence, and others where there is no United Kingdom interest in resisting constitutional change even if it seems likely to lead eventually to secession from the Commonwealth.

If your Committee will produce a report on these lines, the Cabinet might well devote the whole of a session to it without other business.

I am sending a copy of this minute to the Colonial Secretary.

H. M.

28th January, 1957

VI. From Her Majesty's Colonial Service to Her Majesty's Overseas Civil Service, 1954–1958

The key documents in this evolution are the three White Papers issued in 1954, 1956 and 1958. Here, these are accompanied by excerpts from the addresses by the Secretary of State to members of the Colonial Service in 1954 (O. Lyttelton) and 1956 (A. Lennox-Boyd) and by the epitaphic reflection on the Service by their immediate predecessor in office, A. Creech Jones, when he learned of the 1954 White Paper.

(a) White Paper on the Reorganization of the Colonial Service, 1954
The first White Paper was titled *Reorganization of the Colonial Service* (Col. No. 306), 1954. Basically, it addressed the issue of HMG's 'special obligation' to members of the Colonial Service and set out six conditions, which HMG believed the members were entitled to expect on a territory attaining self-government. This was also the government statement that announced the new corporate title, Her Majesty's Oversea [not yet Overseas] Civil Service, and the procedure to be followed for acceptance into it.

REORGANISATION OF THE COLONIAL SERVICE, 1954

1. The term "Her Majesty's Colonial Service" has been in use for well over a century to describe the members of the public services of the Colonies, Protectorates and other territories which are dependent upon Her Majesty's Government in the United Kingdom. Originally, the Colonial Service consisted of officers appointed from Britain or recruited locally from amongst British colonists. As time went on, staffs were increasingly built up from the indigenous or resident populations of the territories, but it has always been and still is necessary to recruit large numbers of men and women from Britain and other Commonwealth countries to supply needs which could not be met from local resources, especially in the professional, technical and higher administrative branches.

2. Since 1930, these latter branches have been organised as "unified" Services. Although the members of these Services are directly employed and paid by the territorial governments, they are under the general direction and patronage of the Secretary of State for the Colonies. They have, rightly, regarded themselves and have been regarded as belonging to general service under the Crown as well as to the local civil services of the territories in which they are immediately serving.

3. The political developments now taking place or likely to take place in many of the territories, in pursuance of the declared policy of Her Majesty's Government in the United Kingdom to further their advance towards self-government, make it necessary to review the situation of the Colonial Service. Constitutionally, all officers of the Colonial Service, using this term in the widest sense, are in the same position. They are servants of the Crown, and the

conditions of their employment are embodied in the Colonial Regulations. These Regulations constitute the Secretary of State as the ultimate authority for appointments, discipline, promotions and general conditions of employment. The members of the Service—and more especially those who have been recruited for the unified branches by successive Secretaries of State—are now asking, and are entitled to ask, what will be their position if and when as a result of constitutional changes, Her Majesty's Government in the United Kingdom are no longer able to exercise effective control over their tenure and conditions of employment as hitherto.

4. The debt which the oversea territories owe to the loyal, devoted and efficient work of the men and women in the Colonial Service is inestimable. Their work is far from over. The task of building up fully equipped local public services is progressing fast; it is an evolutionary process which will be completed at different times in different places. But side by side there is going on the evolution of the Colonies and other territories themselves, and while their economies and activities continue to expand a wide field of opportunity and need for the skilled assistance of British staff remains. This fact is fully recognised by responsible leaders in the territories.

5. It is then of the first importance to these countries, and not least to those where a new burden of responsibility is being undertaken by their own government's, that their progress should not be set back by the premature loss of experienced staff or by failure to attract new staff which they may require. There is a problem here which cannot be solved by the territorial governments alone or by Her Majesty's Government in the United Kingdom alone. Both sides must act in partnership.

6. Her Majesty's Government in the United Kingdom recognise that they have a special obligation towards those officers of the Colonial Service who hold their present posts as a result of having been selected for them by the Secretary of State. So long as Her Majesty's Government retains responsibility for the Government of the territory in which they are serving the necessary safeguards are provided by the Colonial Regulations or the constitutional instruments. Should the territory in whose public service they are employed attain self-government, these officers are entitled to expect that the following conditions will be observed: –

(1) So long as they remain in their existing employment, the Government of the territory concerned shall not alter their terms of service so as to make them less favourable than those on which the officers are already serving.

(2) The pensions and other benefits for which they or their dependants may be qualified under existing laws and regulations shall be similarly safeguarded.

(3) They shall continue to be regarded by Her Majesty's Government in the United Kingdom as members of Her Majesty's Service and as such to be eligible for consideration for transfer or promotion to any posts which the Secretary of State may be requested to fill in other territories.

(4) The government by which they are employed will not unreasonably withhold consent to their accepting any such transfer or promotion and will preserve their existing pension rights on transfer.

(5) They will be given adequate notice of any intention to terminate their employment in consequence of constitutional changes and Her Majesty's Government in the United Kingdom will endeavour to find them alternative employment should they so desire.

(6) In the event of premature retirement resulting from constitutional changes they will receive compensation from the government of the territory concerned.

7. Her Majesty's Government in the United Kingdom accordingly make known their intention, if and when a territory attains self-government, to ensure the observance of these conditions by securing their embodiment in a formal agreement, to be entered into between Her Majesty's Government in the United Kingdom and the government of the territory. The agreement will also provide for the continuing payment of pensions already awarded to officers and their dependants.

8. In order that from now on all concerned may be clearly aware of their rights and obligations, a list will be compiled of all officers now in the Colonial Service to whom Her Majesty's Government in the United Kingdom regard the arrangements outlined in the last two paragraphs as applying. The officers included in this list will be given a new corporate title and will be known as Her Majesty's Oversea Civil Service. Regulations constituting this Service and defining the conditions of eligibility for admission to it, are appended to this statement. [. . .]

10. Her Majesty's Government hope that this evidence of their real concern for the present officers of the Colonial Service and of their determination to safeguard the interests of those officers will allay the doubts and anxieties which are now apparent in some quarters.

11. Her Majesty's Government also hope that the establishment of this new form of Service will ensure that qualified men and women may be attracted to come forward in future as in the past, in a spirit of confidence, enthusiasm and partnership, to help the oversea governments and peoples along the path of social, economic and political progress. [. . .]

13. Her Majesty's Government are aware that various proposals have been

put forward for constituting a Commonwealth Service or an Oversea Service directly employed by Her Majesty's Government in the United Kingdom. The decisions embodied in the present statement are not intended to exclude development along some such lines should this be found to be desirable and practicable. But this is a question which needs and will receive very careful examination in the light of changing conditions. It involves complicated administrative and constitutional, as well as financial, problems, and Her Majesty's Government feel that they are not yet ready to reach any conclusions upon them.

(b) The Secretary of State Talks to his Service on the White Paper, 1954

Taking the opportunity of the annual Corona Club dinner on 17 June, Secretary of State Oliver Lyttelton explained to the several hundred members of the Colonial Service present the implications of the change in title to be introduced in the next day's White Paper.

There are many who profess to believe that: the spirit of adventure and of enterprise and of service has departed from the British race. They think that the youth of today is entirely linked to the cinema, the dance hall and the ice-cream barrow, which are the features of so many of our hideous suburbs. No doubt they have their attractions, but if you look at the quality of the young men in the field in the Colonial territories and in the Secretariat, you will see how utterly false such a charge would be and I have in my mind's eye as I stand here more than one District Officer or District Commissioner, young in years but old in wisdom, who are running in an unostentatious way large districts— often in a state of political ferment—and giving once again to the world, if they only knew it, an example of how the great traditions of impartiality, incorruptibility, and, for that matter, of kindness and humour, are still outstanding in our national character. *(Applause.)*

Having said this with the deepest sincerity, let me turn for a few moments to this very subject, the fourth pillar which I mentioned must be preserved, namely the independent nature of the public Service, and first of all, I must pay a tribute to the fact that this necessity has not only been accepted, but vigorously embraced, by those countries and their leaders with whom I have been in negotiation on changes in the constitution and I think particularly this was so of the Gold Coast and Nigeria.

One of the most heartening results of the Nigerian Conference was the far-sighted view which the leaders of all political parties in Nigeria took upon this very subject of the public service.

Nevertheless I am deeply aware of the anxieties which the Colonial Service must entertain as they see or can predict these constitutional changes.

Well, as you know, My Lords and Gentlemen, today we have taken a step forward.

This very day a Colonial Office paper was available to Members of the House of Commons in the Vote Office, and tomorrow morning no doubt it will excite some comment in the Press. The title of that paper is "Reorganisation of the Colonial Service". The paper, which has to be brief, is the result of many months' work. The difficulties which have called for a re-examination of the structure of the Colonial Service arise out of constitutional developments which either have taken place or are expected to take place in certain territories, and, of course, it is quite clear that as progress towards self-government is made, the powers of control conferred upon the Secretary of State must, in practice, be modified.

A territory cannot be given self-government and the Colonial Secretary retain the strings in his own hands.

Therefore two lines of action appear to us to be essential. First, where a new constitution is under discussion, as for example in Nigeria, necessary safeguards for the public service should be embodied in the constitutional instruments. This has been done, and I think the more these arrangements are studied by Colonial Civil Servants the more their confidence in their future in these territories will be underwritten and confirmed. Their skill and advice and experience are, I really believe, recognised by everyone to be necessary if the evolution to self-government is to take place smoothly and if that self-government when it is reached is to fulfil the principles of good government which we have at heart.

There is a second feature in this problem. What is to happen in these countries which in the fairly near future achieve independence of any control of Her Majesty's Government in the United Kingdom? I believe that in all they will want to go on having the help of their friends who have served so well, and that the officers of the Colonial Service too will for the most part be anxious to carry on with the work they know and love. But of course there will be some officers who cannot stay on yet do not want to retire, and Her Majesty's Government, as far as lies in their power, must do their best to find other posts for them. It is, of course, clear that we cannot guarantee other work for them, but we must do our best.

Let me interpolate here that although I regard it as certain and indeed desirable that the proportion or percentage of oversea Civil Servants finding work in the whole of the Colonial territories will decline in relation to those locally recruited, that is not at all the same thing as imagining that the absolute numbers of oversea Civil Servants will decline. They may in particular territories, but it is, of course, well-known to you that we have been recruiting five times as many men and women every year as we did before the war. The rate may not keep up quite to that figure but I don't think it is likely to go down very much for a long time yet. After all, what other conclusion can you reach if you study for a moment some of the figures of the economic development of some of these territories? It bears out my argument when we remember, for instance, that in 1920 the traffic on the Kenya-Uganda Railway was less than a quarter of a million tons, and in 1952 it carried just over 4½ million tons—that is multiplying the freight carried by more than 18 times; and again, Nigeria's total import and export trade in 1920 was no more than £38 m. In 1953 it was £233 m.

But to revert to to-day's statement of policy, we are going to have a new name—Her Majesty's Oversea Civil Service *(Hear, hear)* and this will replace the unified branches of the Colonial Civil Service. The new Service will include members of those branches and other officers who are selected by the Secretary of State.

This does not, of course, in any way imply that we shall overlook the rights and interests of the many pensionable overseas officers who do not fall within this definition. The terms and conditions of their employment vary too much to make it possible to bring them all within a single framework.

Now is this new name to be more than a name? I assure you that it is. The creation of the new Service carries highly important practical implications. The new Service is a definable body, differing from the much more loosely defined body such as is the Colonial Service today. It carries on into the new era the status and traditions of the Colonial Service as one of the great Services of the Crown.

Secondly, once an officer has been enrolled as a member of Her Majesty's Oversea Civil Service, he will be kept on the books and wherever he may be, he can be considered for any suitable employment which Her Majesty's Government may be able to offer and Her Majesty's Government will continue to have an interest in his career and in his welfare. *(Applause.)*

The main object, then, of this new deal is to make clear the position of present members of the unified Colonial Services and to create a firm foundation upon which they can build their future careers. I hope, too, that it will stimulate recruitment, and that it will give the finest possible encouragement to young men and women to come forward and carry on the great tradition which so many of you here have bequeathed or are now bequeathing to posterity.

I might also mention that other Governments do occasionally ask us to lend officers to them for particular tasks, and of course members of Her Majesty's Oversea Civil Service would be among the first to be considered for work like this.

You will have seen, My Lords and Gentlemen, various ideas canvassed in the Press and elsewhere about the possibility of starting some entirely new Commonwealth or Oversea Service. Our statement shows that we do not rule out such a possibility, but, as you well know, there are many constitutional and practical difficulties about such a proposal, and all I can say now is that we have not come to a point at which we could say for certain that it would be wise to embark upon such an adventure today. But the new step we have taken at least clears up the present position of the Colonial Service, and from this vantage point we can study the wider implications which the wider proposals may open up to us.

The new Service has inherited—and I repeat it with a sincerity which I claim is founded upon knowledge and experience of their work—a glorious tradition which I know that it will carry forward and once again embellish in new ways.

It is with great hope and faith that at this moment, I might almost even say this historic moment, I ask you to couple the traditional toast of The Corona Club with the future prosperity of Her Majesty's Oversea Civil Service. *(Loud Applause.)*

(c) White Paper on HMOCS and the Special List, 1956

Following the negative reaction to Her Majesty's Overseas Civil Service in 1954 as a solution to the staffing crisis generated by the rapid exodus of overseas officers from territories approaching self-government, in particular from the four Nigerian governments, HMG introduced a major modification to the structure of HMOCS. In its White Paper, *Her Majesty's Oversea Civil Service* (Cmd. 9768, 1956), it announced the creation of a Special List of officers within HMOCS. These would be in the service of HMG in the UK for secondment to employing governments. The Special List would in the first instance apply to Nigeria only, though it could if necessary be adapted to the requirements of other territorial governments.

HER MAJESTY'S OVERSEA CIVIL SERVICE

Statement of Policy regarding Organisation

1. In 1954 Her Majesty's Government in the United Kingdom outlined in Colonial Paper 306 a reorganisation of the Colonial Service designed to take account of the growth of self-government in the Colonies and of the effect which this was bound to have on members of what became known as Her Majesty's Oversea Civil Service.

2. In this paper the Government indicated that they were ready to consider further developments if changing conditions showed these to be desirable.

3. There is no doubt that such developments are now essential. The problem

is two-fold. In the first place it is clear that as Colonial Territories approach and attain self-government they will from time to time need the assistance of officers who have exceptional administrative or professional qualifications. Various oversea governments have already said that they would like to be able to look to Her Majesty's Government in the United Kingdom for help in finding such officers.

4. In order to meet these prospective needs Her Majesty's Government in the United Kingdom intend to recruit people with the necessary qualifications for secondment to oversea governments as required. Lists will be prepared of those who are ready and available to accept service of this kind, and if the demand rises to substantial proportions and regular employment for a number of years can be foreseen, they will come into the regular employment of the United Kingdom Government for service overseas.

5. This however is only part of the problem. Where constitutional changes take place which fundamentally affect the conditions of serving officers, compensation schemes have been and will be negotiated with the governments concerned. But where, as in the territories which comprise the Federation of Nigeria, acute staffing difficulties exist, special arrangements must also be made to help create conditions which will encourage officers to remain.

6. The Governments in Nigeria have affirmed their desire to retain their experienced staff, whose loss upon any large scale would most gravely prejudice efficient administration and social and economic development. There is an understandable anxiety, however, amongst the expatriate officers, and especially those with families, about their personal future.

7. Recognising this, and attaching, as they do, high importance to these officers continuing to give their invaluable help. Her Majesty's Government in the United Kingdom are prepared, subject to the agreement of the governments concerned, to introduce a new scheme the main features of which are as follows: –

(i) There will be a Special List of Officers of Her Majesty's Oversea Civil Service who will be in the service of Her Majesty's Government in the United Kingdom and be seconded to the employing Government.

(ii) While seconded, officers will serve on salaries and conditions pre-scribed by Her Majesty's Government in the United Kingdom after consultation with the employing Government. Their pensions and any compensation payments for which they may qualify on retirement will be paid to them by Her Majesty's Government in the United Kingdom and recovered from the employing Government.

(iii) The employing Government will be asked to agree not to terminate the secondment of an officer (except in the case of ill-health, misconduct or inefficiency) without giving one year's notice, and to consult with Her Majesty's Government in the United Kingdom before introducing any scheme of reorganisation which might involve terminating the secondment of a considerable number of officers.

(iv) Officers transferred to the Special List will accept an obligation to serve Her Majesty's Government in the United Kingdom up to the age of 50 in any post to which they may be assigned from time to time. They will not, however, be required to accept assignment to a post which, in the opinion of Her Majesty's Government in the United Kingdom, is of less value (due regard being had to climate and other circumstances) than the post in which they are currently serving.

(v) Her Majesty's Government in the United Kingdom hope in the ordinary way to find continuous employment for all officers on the Special List up to at least the age of 50. If, however, any officer should become unemployed through no fault of his own, he will be kept on full pay for as long as may be necessary, up to a maximum of 5 years (or until he reaches the age of 50, if that is earlier), while efforts are being made to place him. If in the last resort he cannot be found suitable employment, he will get his pension, plus any additional compensation for which he would have been eligible if he had remained in his former service, and not transferred to the Special List. An officer who applies and is accepted for transfer to the Special List will not, therefore, lose his compensation by reason of his decision.

8. Her Majesty's Government in the United Kingdom will now approach the Federal and Regional Governments in Nigeria with a view to working out detailed arrangements, if those governments agree, for the transfer on certain conditions of existing expatriate pensionable officers to the Special List.

9. The scheme will be in a form which will make it possible for similar arrangements to be applied to other territories as and when Her Majesty's Government in the United Kingdom are satisfied that circumstances make such action desirable.

(d) The Secretary of State Talks to his Service on the White Paper, 1956

Once again the Secretary of State took the opportunity of the annual Corona Club dinner to explain to members of HMOCS the significance of the new Special List. Passages from Alan Lennox-Boyd's address of 21 June follow.

I have from the start regarded my function as Colonial Secretary as being in large part designed to make it clear to all who work for Her Majesty overseas that the mantle of the United Kingdom is round them and over them in the work they are doing on our behalf and on behalf of the territories where they work.

Last year I said that my hope is to try and convey by practical action the respect we feel, and to watch over the many problems that concern you: and not least the problem of family education, which I know gives constant anxiety to a large number of people.

You will recently have read about our proposals for H.M.O.C.S. We took a step in 1954 towards reorganisation. It was a big step. Now we have taken two steps at once. The 1954 policy statement provided safeguards for officers whose service is cut short owing to constitutional changes. But the really revolutionary thing about it was that for the first time it recognised that H.M.G. in the U.K. had a definite obligation towards certain categories of officers. The whole purpose of setting up this new Service was to define those categories, to separate them from that huge body known as the Colonial Service, and to give them a collective title. Two years ago the categories were originally rather narrowly drawn, and we are now most seriously considering enlarging these categories so as to make sure that they include everyone who ought to be included, so as Lord Chandos said at the Dinner two years ago this was not the end but the beginning of a new deal. During the two years that have followed, we have considered most seriously not only the structure of H.M.O.C.S. but the particular problem of Nigeria, when officers have to be given the right to retire, if they wish, with compensation and yet neither H.M.G. nor the employing government wants them to go. What we have tried to do is to follow the step we took in 1954 with one even more revolutionary. We have decided that, as and when circumstances make it desirable, officers of H.M.O.C.S. should be offered transfer to a Special List. Those on this Special List will be actually in the service of the U.K., and will be seconded to the oversea governments. H.M.G. will determine their salaries and terms of employment after consultation with the governments concerned. H.M.G. will pay their pensions and will look after them if they lose their jobs through no fault of their own. If a displaced officer cannot be found other work immediately H.M.G. will if necessary keep him on full pay for up to five years. I won't go into other details, for they are in the White Paper but what I would like to emphasise is that all the safeguards embodied in the 1954 statement still stand for H.M.O.C.S. as a whole. So long as I remain S. of S. and I know it goes for my likely successor of any Party at all and so long as any of us has it in our constitutional power to look after the interests of members of the service in territories we shall use it. When a territory reaches a constitutional stage at which power passes to a local authority, then the Secretary of State will see that the serving officer gets a fair deal and fair compensation if he does not wish to stay on. Where local circumstances are such as to make it necessary to introduce the Special List arrangements that will be done. But it really is a Special List and involves H.M.G. in special commitments which we cannot undertake except to meet proved need. In other places when the need is proved we shall act likewise.

We have also to look to the future. When countries become self-governing, they may very well want to get British staff, but will wish to decide for themselves whom they will recruit and what terms they will offer. We shall be willing to help them in any way we can. Some governments may wish, for some branches of their public service, to recruit staff on a career basis. If so, and if they offer good enough terms and satisfactory security, they will no doubt be able to get them. The Ministers from the Federation of Malaya who were over here in the spring were very clear about this. They wanted men on secondment but you can only have secondment if there is a parent body from which to second. We have, therefore, taken yet another evolutionary step in taking the initial action to set up a central pool into which people with specially useful qualifications will be recruited for secondment to oversea governments as required. This is a new departure and the details still have to be worked out but H.M.G. is pledged to do it.

It will make a significant contribution towards the problem and I can promise you this is a matter which is not controversial in Parliament. All of us come on the same side in this matter and none of us will ever lose sight of our first need to build a feeling of security in the Service.

I think we can look back on the developments of the last two years with a reasonable degree of satisfaction, and I hope for the continuation over the years of the great work started by the old Colonial Service under the new forms and conditions.

I can promise you, though there are many controversies in Parliament there is no controversy on the need to give to you who are doing this work the sense of security which you so rightly deserve.

Thank you for asking me to come to your Dinner. There is no function I am more pleased to attend. I am delighted to meet you all. I am afraid my rather long speech may somewhat have cut short your talks with old friends and I take it your talks will be eased and smoothed if you feel you can with complete conviction recommend to your children to take up the sort of career which you are so admirably discharging. *(Loud applause.)*

(e) White Paper on Special List 'B', 1958

Recognizing that the Special List initiated in 1956 had failed to stem the exodus of HMOCS officers from Nigeria in the run-up to internal self-government in 1957, HMG now issued a further White Paper, *Her Majesty's Overseas Civil Service: Statement of Policy Regarding Overseas Officers Serving in Nigeria*, 1958 (Cmnd. 497). This created a new list (Special List 'B') alongside the old special list (now renamed Special List 'A'), with terms of compensation purposely redesigned so as to aim at persuading officers to postpone their retirement. Once again, at this stage the new Special List applied only to officers serving in Nigeria.

HER MAJESTY'S OVERSEAS CIVIL SERVICE
Statement of Policy regarding overseas officers serving in Nigeria

1. In the Statement of Policy regarding the organisation of Her Majesty's Overseas Civil Service published in May, 1956, (Cmd. 9768), attention was drawn to the acute staffing difficulties in the territories which comprise the Federation of Nigeria and the need to make special arrangements to help create conditions which would encourage officers to remain in the service of the Nigerian Government.

2. Her Majesty's Government in the United Kingdom announced their readiness to introduce a new scheme to establish a Special List of officers who would be in the service of Her Majesty's Government in the United Kingdom and seconded to the Nigerian Government employing them. After prolonged negotiations Special List Agreements for the introduction of schemes on the lines proposed in the White Paper were signed at the Nigerian Constitutional Conference in June, 1957, and overseas officers in the service of the Nigerian Governments were invited to apply to join the Special List.

3. It is now clear that the terms and conditions of service laid down in these Agreements are not generally attractive to overseas officers serving in Nigeria and less than 400 officers out of the 2,000 eligible to join the Special List have so far applied to do so. Moreover, the great majority of these applications are from officers in the Federal and Northern Regional Public Services who, under the terms of the Agreements with those Governments will have the right to revert to the local Public Services and to retire with lump sum compensation.

4. It seems that the reluctance of overseas officers to join the existing Special List is due in part to political difficulties, actual or apprehended, resulting from the transfer of power to local Governments, partly to the attractions of the lump sum compensation paid to officers who decide to retire from the Nigerian services and partly to dissatisfaction with present emoluments. The terms of the Special List which require an officer to continue serving in Nigeria so long as his services are required deprive him of the right to retire at his own option with lump sum compensation and, because of the uncertainties apprehended from the transfer of power to the local Governments, the loss of this right is not, in the view of the officers concerned, sufficiently offset by the assurances offered in

respect of further employment and by the other benefits conferred by membership of the Special List. Nor has it proved practicable to improve the remuneration of Special List officers so as to remove the dissatisfaction with the level of current emoluments.

5. In these circumstances Her Majesty's Government in the United Kingdom have decided that a fresh approach to the problem is necessary and have made proposals to the Nigerian Governments for the establishment of a Special List B as in the Annex to this Statement. An explanation of these proposals and of the bases on which they have been drawn up is given in paragraphs 6 to 13 below.

6. In the first place an officer's incentive to leave would be much reduced if he could obtain, while continuing to serve in Nigeria, an advance of a substantial proportion of his entitlement to compensation. Officers who did not require to spend the advance on the education of their children or other immediate commitments would be able to invest it and so obtain additional current income to supplement their existing remuneration. Such advances are already granted in certain circumstances by the Government of the Eastern Region. It is therefore proposed that officers should be granted interest-free advances of 90 per cent of their entitlement to lump sum compensation, and that, to alleviate the substantial immediate financial burden which this would otherwise place on Nigerian Governments, half the cost of the advances should be met by Her Majesty's Government until such time as they are repaid when the officers ultimately retire.

7. A system of advances against compensation would not however by itself be sufficient. For elder officers the entitlement to compensation declines year by year, while for younger officers it is small. It is therefore necessary to allow for both situations and Her Majesty's Government's proposals accordingly envisage an extension of the "freezing" device, the operation of which is explained in paragraph 8 below, and a system of abatement of repayment of advances. In both cases financial assistance to the Nigerian Governments would be given by Her Majesty's Government.

8. Without "freezing" an officer's entitlement to compensation normally rises between the ages of 28 and 41 and unless he is promoted then declines year by year until it reaches zero at the age of 55. By "freezing" the entitlement is held at its maximum point for a period of years. It is obvious that this is an attractive arrangement for the older officer, who would otherwise see his entitlement diminish year by year. The longer the term of "freezing" offered, the greater security for officers and therefore the greater their readiness to remain in Nigeria. Such "freezing" on certain conditions and for limited periods has in fact already been introduced in the Western and Eastern Regions.

9. In order to assist Nigerian Governments to make more generous use of the "freezing" provisions, Her Majesty's Government have offered to meet the whole additional cost of "freezing" the compensation of officers on the proposed Special List B for more than three years after the date of introduction of the relevant compensation scheme, on the basis of the formula in the Annex to this Statement. This offer was made on the understanding that no conditions would be attached to the grant of "freezing" privileges regarding the period which the officer in question would continue to serve, save that, in accordance with paragraph 4 of the Annex, each officer would be required to give not less than one year's notice, inclusive of earned leave, of his intention to retire.

10. As regards the younger officers, many of them will not be entitled to substantial

advances in respect of compensation and none under the age of 41 will benefit in any way from "freezing" privileges. It is therefore proposed that they should not be required to repay all of the advances made to them at the cost of Her Majesty's Government and that the amount which an officer would have to repay to Her Majesty's Government would be reduced by 20 per cent of his salary for each year of service under the age of 41 after the introduction of the relevant compensation scheme; there would be a similar but smaller reduction in the amount to be repaid in respect of service between the ages and [*sic*] 41 and 44 since at these ages officers do not benefit so substantially from "freezing" privileges as do older officers. The whole cost of this concession would be met by Her Majesty's Government.

11. Lump sum compensation schemes have not so far been introduced in the North and in the Federation and are not expected to be introduced before Regional self-government in the North and before independence in the Federation. Meanwhile, in order that some immediate benefit may be offered to officers continuing in their Services, it is proposed that, pending the introduction of the full Special List B Scheme in the North and in the Federation, they should receive each year interim advances, also interest-free, equal to one quarter of their annual pensionable emoluments. Half the cost of these would also be reimbursed by Her Majesty's Government. On the coming into force of the compensation schemes, they would receive the full benefit of the concessions proposed above.

12. To summarise therefore Her Majesty's Government propose that overseas pensionable officers admitted to List B should be required to give at least one year's notice of their intention to retire; that they should be entitled to receive interest-free advances of 90 per cent of their entitlement to compensation, the cost to be shared equally between Her Majesty's Government and the Nigerian Government concerned; that Her Majesty's Government should agree to waive repayment of a part of the advance made to each officer under the age of 44, depending on the officer's age and his length of service after the introduction of the relevant compensation scheme; that for older officers there should be a generous extension of "freezing" privileges, the cost of which would be met largely and in some cases wholly by Her Majesty's Government; and that, until the compensation schemes come into force in the North and the Federation, there should be a scheme of interim advances to officers there.

13. The remaining features proposed in the Annex to this Statement for the new Special List require little comment. As in the existing Special List it is proposed that the pensions, gratuities and compensation due to officers or their dependants should be paid by Her Majesty's Government and recovered from the Nigerian Government concerned. It is also proposed that the Nigerian Governments should undertake to provide fair and reasonable conditions of service which would in any case be not less favourable than those at present in force. In all other respects the officers concerned would continue to be members of the Public Service of the Nigerian Government concerned save that an officer would have a right of appeal to Her Majesty's Government against any disciplinary decision which might affect his eligibility for lump sum compensation or pension.

14. The Governments of the Federation of Nigeria and of the Northern Region have indicated their acceptance in principle of these proposals whereas the Governments of the Western and Eastern Regions have proposed certain modifications which are now under consideration.

15. The cost to Her Majesty's Government in the United Kingdom of these proposals, if they were acceptable in full to all the Nigerian Governments and the majority of overseas officers took advantage of them, is estimated to be £1 million in the current financial year and £1½ million in next year; thereafter diminishing sums would be required. It is not yet possible to say what the effect will be of the modifications proposed by the Governments of the Western and Eastern Regions, but it seems likely that, if modifications are made in the sense they propose, the scheme will be less attractive to overseas officers in these Regions and the cost to Her Majesty's Government in the United Kingdom would be reduced.

ANNEX

Special List B

1. All overseas officers who were offered permanent and pensionable appointment to the service of a Nigerian Government before the 31st August, 1957, will be eligible to join Special List B. Officers who are members of the present Special List and who join Special List B will cease to be members of the present Special List.

2. The Nigerian Governments will undertake to accord such officers fair and reasonable salaries, terms and conditions of service which will in any case be not less favourable than those they now enjoy.

3. The pensions, gratuities and compensation due to such officers or their dependants will be paid by Her Majesty's Government and, subject to the other provisions of this Memorandum, will be recovered from the Nigerian Government concerned.

4. Officers on Special List B will be required to give not less than one year's notice, inclusive of earned leave, of their intention to retire.

5. An officer on Special List B will have the right of appeal to Her Majesty's Government against any disciplinary decision which might prejudice his eligibility for pension or compensation.

6. In order to assist the Nigerian Governments in making use of freezing provisions as a means of encouraging officers who would otherwise retire to remain in the service, Her Majesty's Government will meet the additional post of freezing attributable to freezing the compensation of officers on List B for more than three years after the date of introduction of the relevant compensation scheme. Her Majesty's Government's share of the compensation payable to such officers will be

(a) In respect of officers whose age, length of service and salary progression is such that their compensation computed in accordance with the approved table declines at any time during the first three years after the date of introduction of the relevant compensation scheme, the amount by which their entitlement to compensation would have declined, had it not been frozen, between the end of that three year period and the date of their retirement;

(b) In respect of other officers, an amount equal to the difference between the compensation they actually receive under the freezing scheme and the amount to which they would have been entitled had their compensation not been frozen.

7. An officer on Special List B serving in Eastern and Western Nigeria will receive

from the Nigerian Government concerned an interest-free advance of 90 per cent of his entitlement to compensation. Half the cost of such advances will be reimbursed to the Nigerian Government concerned by Her Majesty's Government as an interest-free loan. The advance will be a charge against the compensation, pension, gratuity and death gratuity ultimately payable to or in respect of the officer. The advance will be computed with reference to the officer's pensionable emoluments, age and length of service at the date of his admission to Special List B and will be re-computed annually thereafter. If the advance so re-computed is larger than the amount . . .

(f) A Former Secretary of State Reflects on his Service, 1956

With the legislation of 1954 introducing the new corporate title of HMOCS, Arthur Creech Jones, who had been an innovative and influential Secretary of State for the Colonies from 1946 to 1950, was invited to contribute an essay on the passing Colonial Service for a volume published by the Hogarth Press. The following 'balance sheet' passage of Service credits and debits deserves to be more widely known in the literature on the Colonial Service.

> Its virtues are considerable. Much can be criticized regarding its enlistment and structure, the defects of its conventions and organization, but the massiveness of its contribution and achievement, its sense of responsibility and service to the colonial people, its quality of fair play, tolerance, and patience, are worthy of record. Much of its work is done in exhausting conditions which are not helpful to morale. It is work which provokes anxiety, and involves solitude, danger, and the lassitude of diminished health. It carries considerable and often over-burdening responsibility. It has frequently been a shield of the people against abuses and unjust intervention from whatever quarter. It has sought to guide and persuade rather than to impose the will of government. In places, unhappily, it has sometimes nodded, and lapsed from its high standards, and on occasion a few of its highest officers have been deaf or blind to legitimate aspirations and public needs. A complacency has sometimes afflicted its initiative and energy. But when all is said and done, it has performed a great benevolent work, and thrown up great administrators and social pioneers; it has extended the frontiers of civilization and helped towards the unification of the world. Whatever one may dislike or reject in 'colonization', the great dedication of many of the members of the Colonial Service and the devotion and service rendered deserve our mead of recognition in this present phase when the old habits of imperialism are surrendering to new conceptions of freedom and world order.

VII. HMOCS: Appointments and Work

Although the creation of HMOCS was part and parcel of the accelerating advance towards independence by the colonial territories, paradoxically in its first years its establishment did not call for reduced recruitment. The recruitment literature had to be revised and a fresh spirit of overseas service instilled. The concept of a career was no more, and a different purpose would call for different personnel. Nonetheless, the Colonial Service ethos and experience were often still audible in the undertones of the official literature.

(a) Police Appointments in HMOCS, 1955

The following is an extract from the Colonial Office recruitment pamphlet OCS 1 (1955) dealing with police applicants to HMOCS.

Police Appointments

1. The work of the Police in Colonial territories provides a fine life, but not a soft one. Most of it is carried out in the tropics. Those who join should be prepared in the course of their careers, for the drawbacks as well as the attractions of tropical life, sometimes under primitive conditions. They will be entering a disciplined Service and—as well as the intensely interesting problems, human and other, with which they will deal—must be ready to accept their share of office routine, which is sometimes comparatively dull.

The primary task of the Police Officer is, as elsewhere, the prevention, investigation and detection of crime together with the enforcement and maintenance of law and order within the area under his jurisdiction. He also has wider responsibilities, for on his knowledge of the temper and feeling of the people in his area the other branches of the Service will greatly depend. In common with all Oversea Civil Service Departments his work is to a considerable degree educative and to him will fall the task of training, inspiring and guiding the Police Force to play its part in the general development of the territory. Most Police Forces in Colonial territories are armed and are required to be proficient in drill and to be trained in the use of small-arms.

The duties facing a Police Officer are very varied, from the routine of immigration, passport and licence regulations, and the enforcement of Traffic Laws and Arms acts, to the preparation of cases for presentation to court, and prosecution in minor courts; from the investigation of crime to the training and welfare of the native constable; from working under primitive conditions without any scientific or mechanical aids to the establishment and perfecting of Specialist branches such as C.I.D. finger-print, etc.

The variety of tasks thus gives scope for a diversity of gifts and for many kinds of knowledge and experience. No hard and fast definition of the qualities required can be laid down. What is needed above all is a combination of intelligence, strong personality and common sense.

The life is a mixture of the indoor and the outdoor, of the routine and the unforeseen; but above all it affords a constructive career, variety of opportunity, scope for initiative and responsibility at an early age.

Entry for candidates from overseas is in most Colonial territories at the gazetted rank of Asst. Superintendent. In Kenya, Northern Rhodesia, Nyasaland and Hong Kong, there is a European Inspectorate, and in these territories the gazetted ranks are normally filled by promotion from the Inspectorate.

2. Vacancies.

(a) Vacancies for gazetted ranks occur normally in West Africa, Malaya, Uganda, Tanganyika and occasionally in Kenya.

(b) Vacancies for the Inspectorate in Kenya, Northern Rhodesia, Nyasaland and Hong Kong are dealt with by the Crown Agents for Oversea Governments and Administrations, 4 Millbank, S.W.1, to whom applications should be addressed.

3. Selection Dates.

There is at present no annual selection; vacancies are filled as circumstances require. Completed forms of application may therefore be sent to the Director os [*sic*] Recruitment at any time of the year.

4. Age Limit.

Candidates must be over 20 years of age at the time of applying and normally under 30. Candidates over 30 may sometimes be considered, usually for appointments on agreement or contract terms, if they possess special qualifications or experience.

5. Qualifications.

A good general standard of education is required. The minimum educational qualification is the possession of the School Certificate, or a General Certificate of Education at ordinary level in five subjects which must include English and Mathematics or Science *or* the production of evidence that a candidate has passed some other examination which in the opinion of the Secretary of State for the Colonies is of a standard equivalent to or higher than the above. . . .

7. Training after Selection.

Most candidates who have not had previous Police experience in the Home Forces will be required, before taking up their appointment overseas to undergo a course of training in the United Kingdom for a period of approximately eight months. This training will be undertaken at one of the District Police Recruit Training Centres and also at a specially designed course at the Metropolitan Police Training School, Hendon, and will be followed by a short attachment to one or more of the Home Police Forces. Candidates who have had previous Police experience in the Home Forces will not be required to undertake the first part of the training at a District Police Recruit Training Centre.

During their service, Superintendents and Assistant Superintendents of Police may have opportunities when on leave of attending courses at the Police College, Ryton-on-Dunsmore, near Coventry. In addition certain Police Officers may be able to attend specialised Police Courses, e.g. the C.I.D. Fingerprints, Riot Control, Security and Photography Courses during their leave. There is also a special course at the Metropolitan Police Training School, Hendon for subordinate officers who are suitable for promotion. All the above courses are by arrangement with the Home Office.

(b) The Duties of a District Officer, c.1955

Despite the change from HMCS to HMOCS, the overall responsibility for the good governance of his district remained that of the traditional district officer, regardless of whether he was a local officer or still an expatriate. Yet, as purpose-built programmes for training district officers in local institutes of public administration blossomed in the 1950s and 1960s, the directing staff quickly found that specific manuals on the manifold duties of the district officer were few and far between. A valuable exception was Malaya, where *General Orders* (Chapter XVI) at least furnished a viable summary.

DISTRICT OFFICERS

206. (i) The principal duties of officers in charge of districts are to exercise the powers conferred on them by law, to see that Courts are held regularly at the times and places appointed in their districts, to superintend the District Land Office and, in districts where there is no State Treasurer or specially appointed Sub-Treasurer, to be in charge of the Treasury.

(ii) In districts where there is specially appointed Sub-Treasurer the officer in charge of the district must exercise constant supervision over the books and the cash of the Treasuries, see that the cash book is entered up to date, and that the General Orders regarding financial matters are complied with. *(Note:* The countersigning of cheques is provided for in General Order No. 268 (ii).)

207. District Officers are responsible for the conduct of the general affairs of their district, and should report to the Secretariat any cases of inefficiency in Government matters which are beyond their personal control.

208. (i) Departmental Officers should, as far as possible, keep in touch with, and comply with the wishes of, the District Officer in the execution of their duties. They should report all proposals for new works at the time that such proposals are being made, and keep him informed of the progress of all important works and schemes. They should also advise him of their movements.

(ii) Heads of State and Federal departments when visiting a district should, if possible, inform the District Officer beforehand, and call upon him with a view to discussing any business connected with the district.

209. District Officers should report without delay to the Secretariat all events of importance that may occur in their district.

210. District Officers should periodically inspect all Government institutions and buildings and should make a point of signing the Visitors' Book. Such matters as water supply, hospital accommodation and rations, latrines, burials, safety and ventilation of public buildings should receive their constant attention, and if defects pointed out by them to the officers in charge are not remedied, a report to that effect should be made to Government. They should pay attention to all matters connected with public health and sanitation, and assist the Medical Department in taking all precautions on the outbreak of infectious disease whether among men or animals, and in regard to vaccination. They should visit all English and vernacular schools from time to time, encourage education among the people, and second the efforts of the Inspectors of Schools.

211. In districts where there is a State Treasurer the officer in charge of the district will not be held responsible for the proper working of the Treasury, or for the cash, stamps, securities or other valuables deposited there, or for obtaining and bringing to credit cash imprests from other Treasurers.

(c) General Qualifications for Appointment to the Administrative Branch, 1956

The following notice appeared in the Colonial Office pamphlet *Her Majesty's Oversea Civil Service: The Administrative Branch*, issued in 1955/6.

Qualifications

There is no fixed educational requirement for appointments to the Administrative Branch of the Oversea Civil Service, but a high standard of education is essential. Whilst a university degree is not an absolutely indispensable qualification, candidates selected for Administrative appointments in recent years have nearly all been in possession of a degree, usually with Honours. Exceptions have been in cases where a candidate has acquired some experience (for example, service with a Colonial Force) likely to be of relevance; but in any case evidence is sought of intellectual ability of University Honours standard.

Prospective candidates intending to take a University degree are advised to read for the course in Honours which attracts them most and in which they are most likely to do well. It must, however, be remembered that whatever form of degree a candidate takes no promise can be made that he will eventually be selected. It is therefore also important, in the interests of candidates, that their University education should be such as to be of general value to them in other careers if they fail to obtain a Colonial appointment.

A candidate for any appointment in the Oversea Civil Service must be at least 20 when he submits his form of application. The upper age limit for appointment on permanent and pensionable terms is 35, but in practice the appointment to the Administrative Branch of candidates over 30 is rare and only justified by exceptional experience or qualifications.

(d) The Life of the District Officer, 1956

After both world wars, the Colonial Office, the Crown Agents and several of the territorial governments issued various publications to encourage recruitment. In the 1920s the East and Central African governments produced pamphlets along the lines of *Notes for New-comers* and *Life and Duties of an Administrative Officer*, 1929. K. G. Bradley's semi-fictional *Diary of a District Officer* (1943) inspiringly fulfilled the same recruiting function for the Colonial Service.

Following the establishment of HMOCS in 1954, Bradley's pamphlet *The Colonial Service as a Career* (1950) was reissued as *A Career in the Oversea Civil Service* (1955), and territories like Northern Rhodesia and Tanganyika, where staff shortages remained acute, published their own recruitment propaganda, for example *A Career in the Administrative Service in Northern Rhodesia* (1956) and *The Administrative Officer in Tanganyika: Today and Tomorrow* (c.1958). At the same time, the Colonial Office published its recruitment book-let, *HMOCS: The Administrative Branch* (c.1956), being brief personal sketches of the day-to-day work of the administrative officer in five different territories: Western Pacific, Aden, Hong Kong and Northern Rhodesia. The 'letter home' format was considered to be the most effective style of propaganda for the new, short-term contract opportunities now offered by HMOCS.

Western Pacific

(A description of a typical day on tour of the outlying islands of the Group as seen by an Administrative cadet in the British Solomon Islands Protectorate)

HAVING sailed through the night on one of the small Government ships used by the District Administration we anchored in the early morning in deep water outside the reef. After giving the bosun his instructions for the day, which were to take some cargo and passengers to nearby islands and to send some telegrams to the District Station on the ship's wireless schedule later in the day, I was rowed ashore in the whaleboat. The surf was heavy and I arrived on shore in the middle of a wave.

On the beach I was met by the Headman, the Dresser stationed there by the Medical Department and a crowd of villagers and children. My first duty was to make an inspection of the villages on the island. This provided an opportunity to see if orders given on previous visits had been carried out, and to make further recommendations as to the cleanliness of villages and water supplies, improvement of housing and drainage, &c. A number of complaints and requests were received from the inhabitants, and these were deferred to be dealt with at a meeting in the island's Council house later in the day. A Native Field Assistant of the Agricultural Department was with the touring party and gave detailed advice on operating an improved type of copra drier and, as the soil was suitable, on the planting of a new crop, cocoa. During the course of the day, he and I discussed methods of financing the installation of the new copra drier and the planting of cocoa with the villagers. I visited the Mission School on the Island, giving a short talk to the children, and handing over Public Relations Office literature to the teacher.

At the Council House the clerk to the Island's Native Court was waiting with his court record book which contained the details of the cases heard by the Court since my last visit. I reviewed these cases. Native Courts can deal with minor criminal cases, e.g. petty assaults, thefts, adultery, or civil disputes which may be anything from a quarrel over the ownership of coconut trees to a claim for damages for the destruction of a garden by pigs. Serious criminal cases or major civil disputes are reserved by the Headman for trial by a Deputy Commissioner who may hear them on the spot or remove them for trial at District Headquarters. I did not actually hear any cases during the day.

The villagers' requests, which now came up for attention, included applications for licences for a shot gun, to buy copra and to open a store. One native, as frequently happens, asked me to help him collect a debt owing to him from someone from another Island and several people asked for passages on my ship. I paid the Headman and the Dresser the wages due to them and dealt with some deposits and withdrawals on behalf of the Savings Bank.

Towards the end of the day most of the Islanders had collected under the trees near the Council House to hear what I had to say to them and to discuss matters of general importance. One of these was a community project, the building of a dispensary, which had been making slow progress and I encouraged them to work on it and to complete it. The Native Council held a meeting, which was in public and at which Resolutions were passed for the good government of the Island. These Resolutions have the force of law when approved by the High Commissioner. The Council considered ways of spending its revenue received from native tax and court fines and aired a few political and economic grievances on which I was able to give them advice.

Before I left for the ship the Headman invited me to take food with him in his house, he having prepared fish, yams, coconuts and puddings of taro. It is a local custom here for the eldest son to break each portion of fish and hand it to the guest personally in his fingers (on leave I should probably be fussy about the waiter's thumb in the soup). At such times valuable and often unexpected information emerges. The Island's Headman, a man of long service, in an indiscreet moment explained that the number of petty disputes over money was due to the prevalence of gambling. As this is a criminal offence this rather startling admission was met by a recitation of the penalties that could be imposed under the relevant law. The Headman did not emerge unscathed from the mutual recriminations that followed and himself produced one of the offending dice!

I returned to the ship by canoe after dark and found that the dresser had arranged for his hospital patients to be sent on board and that the police constable had mustered witnesses and the accused for a court case to be held at District Headquarters. During the day a trading and recruiting ship had anchored nearby and the Master came on board in the evening to discuss labour problems with me, to renew his licences, and to exchange news. Later, while still at anchor, I sat down and brought my accounts up to date and drafted reports and memoranda on the day's work. Throughout the day there was of course no distinction between 'office' hours and leisure hours as on tour there is no daily routine.

Each day's conditions make different demands and the nature of the work permits of no sharp distinction between work and play.

Aden

THE great variety in terrain, wealth and political development of the Sultanates and Sheikhdoms of South West Arabia to which an Assistant Adviser in the Aden Protectorate may be posted makes it impossible to generalise about the sort of work which he may expect. Let us however choose three more or less typical areas and see how an Administrative officer will spend his time.

*   *   *

A.B. is Assistant Adviser to one of the more advanced states and he and his wife live in a reasonably civilised manner. Sleeping as they do on the flat roof of their house, they will not want to linger in bed a moment after the sun has risen, but will go down to dress and start the daily round; she to deal with the cook, and he, after spending half an hour or so on his private correspondence or in studying for his Arabic examination, will visit the Headquarters of the Armed Constabulary to see the recruits on their morning parade and to discuss the indents for clothing and equipment with the O.C.

Returning to his comfortable house he has breakfast, and afterwards goes to his office in a nearby building where he interviews callers and deals with his files till 10 o'clock or so when he has an appointment with the State Secretary at the Administrative Building to discuss the draft estimates for the following year; or he may be with some elderly 'Saiyid' to whose house he goes as a matter of courtesy to talk about any of a dozen different subjects. On his way back, he drops in on the Administrative Inspector to arrange details of a tour which they are to undertake the following week to inspect village Councils and the agricultural development scheme on which the State is engaged. He may also call in at the school or the Dispensary. After clearing up his office and signing the remaining letters for the mail he is free to lunch.

A short siesta follows and at 4 p.m. he goes with the Agricultural Officer and the local pump committee on a tour of inspection of the pump scheme, a very important project for the State is in a famine zone and this Scheme has been devised to supplement the annual rainfall in good times and provide a subsistence in bad seasons.

Home for a shower and change and then out again to call on the Sultan who wishes to discuss with him the education of his eldest son, a bright little lad of ten at present attending the local school, He stays on to chat about various matters of interest and then he may hurry off to attend an Arab dinner party at the house of one of the chief merchants of the town, where he finds a dozen guests waiting, or he may return to his house where he and his wife may dine alone or entertain guests from the town or visiting officers of the Administration, or friends from Aden. When they dine in the houses of the leading Arabs the routine is always the same. Greetings are scarcely exchanged before the party is summoned to a magnificent meal laid out on the floor of a balcony. After dinner tea is served and a pleasant hour is passed in conversation and anecdote, the guests reclining on cushions placed around the wall. The party breaks up fairly early and the guests are home before 10 o'clock.

*   *   *

C.D. is attached to a State with which there has been an Advisory Treaty only for a short time and the administration is in a very rudimentary stage. Before he is fully awake his boy comes to tell him that Sheikh Fulan bin Fulan (So and So) is waiting to see him. Smothering a curse he quickly dresses and goes down to his office to meet his visitor, a litigant who believes in the adage of the 'early bird' and is determined to represent well in advance his side of a case in which he is vitally interested. After dealing with him as politely as circumstances permit C.D. breakfasts and then goes over to see the Treaty Chief to whom he has been attached. They have arranged to go together to choose the site of the Administrative Building which is to be built as hitherto the house of the Chief himself has been used for public business. This done, they turn their attention to the draft of a Courts decree and then go to the Treasury to inspect the account books.

Chanting and rifle firing outside announce the arrival of a tribal delegation and the rest of the morning is spent in long and apparently fruitless discussions of trivialities until at last the real purpose of the meeting comes to light. The tribes welcome the advent of Government and thank the Government for its help but want to be assured on one point, namely is their freedom from taxation to be maintained? Considerable tact is needed in dealing with this matter and the Assistant Adviser, feeling perhaps some irritation at the inconclusive nature of the reply which the Chief gives, nonetheless admires the way in which he manages to satisfy his tribes without compromising his future policy.

Today he is entertaining the Chief to lunch and afterwards he must make sure that all is in order for the trek on which he and the Chief are to set out in the cool of the late afternoon. Bedding and stores are loaded on to camels and after inexplicable delays the caravan moves off for a three or four hour stage. Pleasantly tired they encamp for the night near a watering place and after a communal supper the Assistant Adviser sinks on to his camp bed beneath the stars tired and happy.

*　　*　　*

E.F. is a pioneer. He has no particular District of his own but his task is the penetration or pacification of the desert frontier area, getting in touch with the tribes, building forts and generally obtaining all the information possible about the inhabitants of the area, their customs, quarrels and loyalties. Accompanied by an escort of local troops he travels by air, truck, camel or on his feet as the terrain demands, reconnoitring routes as he goes and making a rudimentary map. He carries few possessions with him and faces the extremes of heat and cold, spends endless hours in talk with Bedouin tribes interspersed with long waits for appointments with people to whom time means nothing.

Occasionally he comes down to the coast to get cleaned up and obtain stores. Reports have to be written, matters discussed with the Adviser, and after a quick couple of days' enjoyment of the fleshpots he returns for another month or two to the wilds.

Hong Kong

A NEWCOMER to Hong Kong can normally expect a gentle introduction to it. Arriving usually by sea in July he spends the first three months in finding his feet in the Colony and acquainting himself superficially with the existence, location, activities, and personalities of the various Government Departments to some of which he may be attached. Early in October he begins a course of study in Cantonese at the University lasting one year. Thereafter, he may expect to find himself posted to the Social Welfare Office, the Secretariat for Chinese Affairs, the Labour Department (all three located in the urban area on the island), or the District Administration, New Territories (principally in the rural area). These are all Departments in which he will come into contact with the indigenous population of the Colony through the medium of his work.

In the Social Welfare Office he will find each morning on his desk files with problems ranging from a query by the Director of Audit to a suggestion by the officer in charge of Child Welfare Work that an adopted child is being maltreated and should be removed from its adoptive parents. Soon he will have a number of callers to interview, and later in the morning he may go out to see some of the Department's Relief Centres, or to inspect progress on the construction of an orphanage which is being subsidised by Government.

Back in the office, there will be a conference with the Social Welfare Officer, perhaps arranging the details of a V.I.P.'s tour of inspection of welfare institutions. The sound of a fire-engine or ambulance in the street, followed by a telephone call from the Police, may lead him to drop everything and concentrate on starting relief work for a number of families rendered homeless by a sudden fire or landslide.

In the course of the day more files appear, many with recommendations from his professional colleagues based on expert case-reports. These will sometimes be taken home to be read at leisure, for the future of a child or a family may depend on the decision which has to be taken.

A posting to the Secretariat for Chinese Affairs brings different duties. This is the place to which the ordinary citizens look for impartial mediation or advice whenever their marriages go wrong, their landlords threaten eviction, they themselves are in danger of deportation unless they can prove local birth, or they are about to travel overseas for employment in the Far East and the islands of the Pacific. An Assistant Secretary for Chinese Affairs will have a daily schedule of appointments on all these matters. Matrimonial disputes are certainly the most exciting, as a volatile wife will soon show her anger or dismay if her tale is not believed. Deportation hearings have a more judicial atmosphere as certain statutory questions must be asked, and the replies recorded.

Labour Officers, although specialising in, say, labour relations, workmen's compensation, vocational training or collection of labour statistics, have to be jacks of all trades. Their official day will be partly spent in compiling reports for publication locally or in answer to questionnaires from United Nations agencies such as the International Labour Office. There will be interviews ranging from a full scale meeting between employers' and workers' delegates to an interview with a workman asking for advice in connection with a workmen's compensation case. The Labour Officer may be Secretary to the Labour Advisory Board and will be responsible for arranging meetings and recording the proceedings. Among all his other duties, he will have to find time for regular visits to factories, accompanied by a Labour Inspector, and if he is fortunate he may be able to travel further afield as a member of a delegation at a conference held by one of the United Nations agencies in the Far East.

The life of a District Officer is more urbanised than in colonies with wide-open spaces to deal with. His home will be less than an hour's drive from

Kowloon (the mainland town opposite Hong Kong island), the principal country towns are all accessible by car or launch, and few villages are so remote that they cannot be visited in a single day's outing.

The duties carried out by the Secretariat for Chinese Affairs and Social Welfare Office in the urban areas fall largely on the District Administration in the rural areas. In addition, the District Officer holds land and small debts courts. He can, and usually does, refuse to hear lawyers, which means that he often ends up by being Counsel for both parties. As Land Officer he is responsible for the disposal of Crown land, and for ensuring that it is put to the best use. He will be concerned with anything that affects the well-being of the rural population such as improved irrigation, pig breeding and oyster culture, and the provision of better bus and ferry services.

These interests require close liaison with other Government agencies such as the Public Works, the Marine Department and the Department of Agriculture, Fisheries and Forestry; and it also falls to the District Officer to reconcile the Army's needs for encampments and training areas with those of the local population.

On return from his first leave, the Administrative Officer is likely to be posted to one of the other Departments to gain further experience. In the Commerce and Industry Department he may have to run the Preventive Service which takes the place of a customs service in a theoretically duty free port. He may also be concerned with industrial development or the promotion of trade, and may be attached to a delegation from the Colony at an international trade fair abroad. Whichever branch of the Department he goes to, he will quickly learn the other side of the complaints from Manchester and elsewhere that Hong Kong is dumping cheap cotton goods, umbrellas and gloves on the home market.

In the Urban Services Department he may have to deal with a large staff of Health Inspectors and other subordinate officers who are responsible for the sanitation of the urban areas, or he may be associated with the beginnings of municipal housing. Whichever sphere is his, there will be frequent contacts with unofficial members, both elected and nominated, of the Urban Council and the Housing Authority.

An officer posted to the Colonial Secretariat may find himself engaged on financial, defence, personnel or general duties. From this central position he obtains a wider view of Governmental activities than in a specialised Department.

There is room in Hong Kong for officers with many different types of talents. The essentially urban, commercial and industrial nature of the Colony gives particular scope for the economist and financial expert, while the large Chinese population makes an officer who has a gift for Oriental languages invaluable. There is less scope for one who seeks the more independent and sometimes lonely life of a District Officer in larger territories.

Northern Rhodesia

A day in the life of a Provincial Commissioner

AN early start, before it warms up. On the green lawns the sprinklers are already at work. A string of horses returns to the stables.

Naturally he looks at new mail before he looks again at those three difficult ones left over yesterday (and for some days before that). The first heap contains mainly the 'office work'—necessary but dull, more reading than action: Debit Notes for District Commissioners for example. His factotum (District Assistant or Cadet in his first tour) points out that an order for wheelbarrows has been charged to 'Travelling on Duty'. The P.C. rules that district touring by this means is out of order. A Veterinary note on the campaign against skin disease in cattle, a local scourge. Less usual is a U.N.O. enquiry about the prevalence of Narcotics. Indian Hemp is occasionally cultivated hereabouts.

In a smaller but meatier pile are two Tour reports from District Officers requiring careful reading, directions sent back, and other comment before they go on to the Secretary for Native Affairs. Cases tried by a District Officer for review come next. 'What a sound magistrate this chap is: and how wise his District Commissioner (whose bent is in entirely different directions) to leave to him as much judicial work as he can. Thank Heaven the D.C.'s cases go to a Judge for review and not to me'. An instruction from H.Q. on steps to implement a Boundary Agreement recently made with a neighbouring country follows; and then news of a smallpox outbreak near a labour route. Items for the next monthly meeting of the Development Team, a memorandum on re-afforestation among them; and a report on an attempt to establish rice as an economic crop.

On a side table is laid a cold collation of Secretariat Circulars, with one of them flagged. 'Glory be—this is interesting: what I have been urging for years now comes to pass!' But the rest are a dull meal.

With most of this mail digested, and some replies drafted, the visitors begin.

Two crocodile hunters, cheerful young men out after adventure, are told the few rules which the Native Authority desire to be observed—'bury the corpses to prevent pollution'. Then the District Commissioner with a young African who wants to become a Clerk. He earnestly assures me of his desire to serve the Government 'all my life'. He is engaged as a learner on trial.

Next for discussion is the expected visitor from the New World arriving to 'restore', as someone put it, 'the bank balance of the Old'. He wants first-hand information (and incidentally enjoyment) by making a trip, as the guest of Government, down the river which has always played, and now seems destined to play, such a leading role in the opening up and industrial development of the country. Paddlers and barges to be arranged, and details of camp equipment, commissariat, and timetable. In 50 years' time, possibly, my then successor will merely notify the local branch of the steamer company and the hotel manager.

And now a car brings the Paramount Chief and his advisers, and tea helps the opening amenities. Then trading leases to be approved and cheques to be signed. A question of mineral prospecting: the Chief does not fancy an industrial area in his rural paradise. Should Missions of different denominations adhere to spheres of influence, or shall we allow a free-for-all? A new Education Councillor to be appointed to an outside district: his selection may be due rather to his family connections than to his zeal for Education. Today a new car for the Paramount is another topic. Little cause for argument here: the present one is unsafe to life and limb, and a Landrover vanette is his choice. We fix a date for my return visit, and the party drives away.

By now the plane has arrived with an out-station District Commissioner soon off on leave. Over luncheon, correspondence and time are saved by a chat on the various points he has brought with him. Among them is a judicial enquiry concerning a case of sympathetic magic in which an African practitioner, attending a patient for some arthritic complaint, has made incisions in her infant daughter and caused its death. There are some knotty legal points here and the requirement of policy to be considered. More harm than good might be done if a prosecution failed.

Just time to go and see how the new pumping station for the town water-supply progresses. Not my pigeon, save in so far as everything that happens in my Province is my affair: but I am particularly interested in this because in a country where the excellent rainfall all comes in only four months of the year water is life to crop and cattle and man. And once I have it there is a new horizon in this small part of the Province anyway. Damn it, on the way back there is Schopstein. Both he and I know I have recommended against his request for yet more trading rights. But hope springs eternal and I am delighted to accept his invitation to sundowners on Tuesday week.

Back late to sign the letters now typed. (I will deal with those three difficult ones tomorrow.) Home for tea and a quick look at *The Times,* which has come 6,000 miles in three days. Still time for tennis, or golf, or a swim in the bathing pool, or a potter in the garden. Then a few of the threads handled in the day will be drawn together for a time when guests arrive for a leisurely drink on the lawn looking over the plain, where partridges are calling as the sun goes down.

VIII. The Corona Club: An Abridged History, 1900–99

An Outline History

The Corona Club (1900–99) was the nearest thing there was to a notional Colonial Service club. It was essentially its social club, with an annual highlight of a formal dinner (since the 1950s in the Connaught Rooms) and the Secretary of State as the principal speaker each summer for Colonial Service officers on leave and their colleagues from the Colonial Office. The following pages are an abridgement of A. H. M. Kirk-Greene, *The Corona Club* (1990).

INTRODUCTION

It was at a dinner held on 20 June 1900, in the Hotel Cecil, London, that Joseph Chamberlain, Secretary of State for the Colonies, first proposed the health of the Corona Club. Since then, apart from the ten dark years during two World Wars, members of the Colonial Office and the Colonial Service (and later from the Crown Agents) have gathered in London each summer for a formal dinner or, since 1975, for an informal cocktail-party. The purpose of the Corona Club has been a single and simple one from the very beginning. To quote from the original memorandum drawn up in March 1900:

> It is proposed that an Annual Service Dinner shall be instituted, with a view of affording Officers on leave from the Crown Colonies the opportunity of a social meeting with each other, with the Officers of the Colonial Office, and with past Crown Colony Officers.

ORIGINS AND GROWTH

Although Mr Chamberlain's name is inextricably linked to the inspiration and the fatherhood of the Corona Club, in the classic tradition of the Colonial Office weeks of hard, quiet, preparatory work were put into the planning before the soup and sherry were served at the Hotel Cecil on that midsummer evening. Chamberlain himself acknowledged the primary contribution of Sir William Baillie-Hamilton, who was then Chief Clerk at the Colonial Office. Appropriately enough, he became the Club's first Honorary Secretary. To quote the rather bleak prose of the original CO memorandum, "In pursuance of the foregoing idea [of an annual dinner], a number of gentlemen assembled at the Colonial Office on Tuesday, March 27th [1900], and formed themselves into a committee, with power to add to their number". It was resolved that

> 1. A Club be formed, consisting of Past and Present Members of the Civil Service of the Crown Colonies, or of Protectorates administered under the Colonial Office, and of Past and Present Members of the Colonial Office, and that the Club be called 'The Corona Club'.

> 2. All such officials shall be eligible irrespective of rank.

Later, this aim of the Corona Club was shortened into "to provide a means of social intercourse between past and present members of the Colonial Service and the Colonial Office". Moreover, addressing the Club at its 1912 Dinner, the Secretary of State did more than acknowledge that "our gathering in these rooms is a symbol of and an encouragement to the basic idea of the unity of the Crown Colony Services." The Club, in his opinion, at the same time manifested an aspect "specially distinctive of our race: the desire to eat in common, and in public". And in 1933 the Colonial Secretary proposed to the Club a new motto, "Greatness and Service". He went on:

[It is] that service that wins and keeps gratitude. I can think of no words that better express the tradition and practice of our own Colonial Service. In that spirit rest the justification and the enduring greatness of our Empire.

It is generally accepted that credit for the choice of the Club's name goes to the illustrious Sir Robert Herbert, who had been Permanent Under-Secretary at the Colonial Office from 1871 to 1892. As Sir Kenneth Bradley once remarked in confiding his dislike of the same name without ever being able to come up with a better one for his latter-day 'house magazine' if it was an older generation who connected it with cigars, a younger one linked it with soft drinks of the 'Tizer the Appetizer' variety.

Some three hundred members joined the Corona Club in 1900. The membership rose rapidly, to pass the thousand mark in 1905. The list for 1914 gives 1,988 names. The first list circulated to members was in 1928, "as an experiment . . . a means of renewing old acquaintances", and with a view to making it a quinquennial event. Once recruitment got under way again after the end of World War I, membership expanded, reaching three thousand in 1933. By 1958 the Club's membership was approaching its record of the 4,000 mark. Undoubtedly the most remarkable statistic of all is that in 1990, with 75 per cent of the former colonies independent, no Colonial Office in existence, and no Colonial Service recruitment on permanent and pensionable terms for the past thirty years, the Corona Club still has 2,500 members.

ADMINISTRATION AND OFFICERS

From 1942 to 1966 the Corona Club had a room in the Colonial Office, first in Downing Street and then, after World War II, in Great Smith Street. This was the best possible permanent address for members of a Service who, to borrow the title of a recent autobiography, could for much of their career be described as being "Of No Fixed Abode". The Rt Hon Lewis Harcourt had a similar image in mind when he paid tribute to those attending the 1911 Corona Club Dinner: "You are, by instinct and by profession, rolling stones, yet in spite of the fact that you are in a state of perpetual motion you manage to gather round you the moss of new members, of good-fellowship, and old friends". The Corona Club was very different from London's classical clubland in the Whitehall–St James's Street–Pall Mall enclave. With no Club premises and only the use of the Colonial Office Refreshment Club for tea (and, from 1956, the offer of special temporary membership of the West Indian Club in Whitehall Court to Corona Club members on leave in the UK), it may be wondered what it offered apart from an annual dinner for those who were home on leave, with a free copy of the Secretary of State's speech made thereat.

It is generally conceded that the Club had no regular physical functions, only an intermittent social one. There was one primary Club symbol. This is the Corona Club tie. Despite popular idiom and widespread understanding to the contrary, this is not the Colonial Service or HMOCS tie. There never was a Service tie. Most members will know the present and pleasant dark blue tie with a motif of gold oak leaves. However, this dates only from views put forward in 1948, when ties became "coupon-free" (sic!). It is not the original Club tie. That goes back to 1926, when "a distinctive combination of dark blue, red and white" were adopted as the Club colours authorised by the Secretary of State, and arrangements were made for a Club tie to be manufactured to this design.

Wisely, the administration of the Corona Club was left in the hands of its less nomadic members, those from the Colonial Office and Crown Agents. This included the Chairman (technically, right from 1900 the President was the Secretary of State for the Colonies) and the Hon Sec. As vacancies occur the Committee co-opts new members and elects its own Chairman, Secretary and Treasurer. In the 1920s the Committee, largely made up of retired officers, was widened by the co-option of two 'beachcombers', to have recourse to the Colonial Office vocabulary originally used to describe the secondment of a Colonial Service officer to the Colonial Office for a couple of years, who could be expected to represent the views of serving officers. Although, as every honorary secretary knows and every honourable chairman admits, all the real work is done by the Hon Sec, nobody involved with the history of the Corona Club would want to omit a reference to the work of Morton Jewell, MBE, of the Colonial Office, who for over forty years looked after the administration of the Club's two annual events, registering the names of those attending the Dinner and the despatch of the *Bulletin*. As a historian, I was for a long time curious about the disposal of the portrait and piece of silver plate which the Corona Club gave to Sir William Baillie-Hamilton on his retirement as joint Hon Sec/Treasurer in 1908. Known at the "Corona Cup", it is now a prized possession of the Royal Scots Association. Since 1908, the Club has looked - never in vain - for its Hon Treasurer from among the Crown Agents staff.

OFFICERS OF THE CORONA CLUB, 1900–1997

	CHAIRMAN	HON SEC	HON TREASURER
1900		Sir William Baillie-Hamilton	
1908		F G Butler	E G Antrobus
1921	Sir Arthur Young	C J Jeffries	
1930	Sir Herbert Read		
1947	Sir Cosmo Parkinson		P H Ezechiel
1949		A R Thomas	H F Downie

1954		Sir George Beresford Stooke
1956		Sir George Seel
1959	Sir John Macpherson	
1960		Sir Stephen Luke
1969		E A Morris
1970	G W Thom	
1972	Sir Walter Coutts	
1977	A R Thomas	
1978	G H Clark	
1995	J H Smith	
1997		P C Knights

In 1971 the office of President was personally created, with pre-eminent suitability, for Viscount Boyd of Merton. The office lapsed with his tragic death in 1983. An Hon Assistant Secretary was appointed in 1936. This was J M (later Sir John) Martin, who was succeeded in 1947 by A R Thomas, and then by E R Edmonds.

THE HEART OF THE MATTER

Essentially, it is in the Secretary of State's speech delivered at the annual dinner – as we have seen, the only function which may be said to have characterised the activities of the Club – that the history of the Corona Club emerges at its most palpable. Here, in a sentence, lies the heart of the matter.

The Dinner

First, the Dinner itself, the setting for the speech. The move from the Hotel Cecil to the Connaught Rooms in Great Queen Street took place immediately after World War I. This remained the preferred venue right through to the final Dinner in 1974, save for the year when the Club found them already reserved on the date it required. With anything up to 300 dining (it reached 395 in 1937, 500 in 1960), the Hon Secretary's diplomacy in arranging the placement was matched only by the efficiency of the printers, Messrs Waterlow, who enjoyed much of the Colonial Office publishing business, including the contract for Colonial Regulations and, before World War II, that for the annual Colonial Office List. They, undaunted, received the final proof of the table plan and guest list at noon on the very day of the Dinner and then had it delivered, reputedly with not an initial wrong or a decoration out of order, to the Connaught Rooms well before the first guests arrived. Up to 1914, the guest list was set out alphabetically by colonies grouped regionally: Eastern Colonies, West African Colonies and Protectorates, East African Protectorates, West Indian Colonies, Mediterranean and Miscellaneous Colonies, and the "Colonial Office, Etc." (in 1914 this last identification included the Colonial Audit Department, the Crown Agents for the Colonies and the Imperial Institute). After World War I this was replaced by a single alphabetical index of those dining, without reference to territory. In the 1950s the Hon Sec reverted to seating the larger groups, such as West or East Africa, on a geographical basis. On occasions when a good number of Judges, Attornies-General and Crown Counsel were dining, a separate 'Legal Table' was also arranged. At the same time the innovation was made of the table plan and the list of those dining being printed together in a single booklet, designed as a more worthy souvenir of the evening than just the menu. In later years, space was left in the Dinner application form for a member to indicate his wishes about whom he would like (or, presumably, not like) to sit with.

By tradition there were no guests, though now and again one or two of Malaya's traditional rulers were permitted to breach this rule, eg for the first time in 1924, when the Sultan of Perak and the Regent of Kedah were present or, in 1950, with the Sultans of Perak and of Pahang. While the Dinner was usually held, as it was in 1900, in the second half of June, this was not invariably the case. By tradition, and once again to almost the very end, no ladies were present at the Dinner. Instead, from 1937 a Ladies Dinner was held, simultaneously but separately. The customary lay-out was one long Top Table, graced by some 30 governors pasts and present and top civil servants from the Colonial Office, all seated so as to face a series of E-bar tables numbered from B onwards, each with 29 places.

Many members will recall those splendid (or at least splendiferous) evenings, with white tie, decorations and miniatures, and of course that dazzling Top Table where honorifics and initials averaged a dozen per diner (the rest of us were carefully compensated with "Esq"). CMGs were as frequent at the lower tables as the refilling of the wine glass. Let me quote two participant descriptions of the Corona Club Dinner in its heyday:

> The speech concluded, the applause having died down and the toast having been duly honoured, the company breaks up, and for the rest of the evening there is a free and informal conversation between the members. Old friends whom the Secretary has failed to place near each other at table foregather once more; the young officer on his first leave absorbs the tall stories of those whose job he has taken over; and the Secretary of State is besieged by those who wish to shake him by the hand and engage him in a few minutes' conversation which they will 'remember with advantage' when they get back to the bush. This is the real business of the evening ...

Or, some twenty-five years later:

> For an hour or two each year in the Connaught Rooms old friendships are renewed and fresh ones made (not least with members of the Colonial Office). The former Provincial Commissioner now growing chrysanthemums in Kent can wag his tongue pleasurably at a junior

District Officer and tell him that things aren't half so tough as in the good old days. The serving Agricultural Officer can confound a Director of a previous generation with the complexities of life when those at the receiving end are fast becoming more scientifically inclined. Much is said, much is listened to, with mutual pleasure and profit. But nowadays one overriding question is asked: what of the future? This year one heard not only talk of security for serving officers. 'What the devil can I tell my son?', someone asked, 'he's keen to come in but isn't it a bit of a gamble now?'

One historic break with the tradition of limiting the annual meeting to a dinner deserves to be mentioned. This was in 1960, the year of the Corona Club's diamond jubilee and its 50th Dinner, held in the presence of the Prime Minister. The Club's original hope that either Her Majesty the Queen or HRH the Duke of Edinburgh might consent to be present at the Jubilee Dinner on June 30 in the Connaught Rooms did not fit into the Royal programme. However, the Lord Chamberlain informed the Committee that Her Majesty would be graciously pleased to hold a special reception at Buckingham Palace on 25 May for members of the Corona Club and their wives and for the Women's Corona Society.

While the name, the Corona Club, has remained unchanged, in the 1930s the style of naming the annual Dinner began to alter. While 1932 referred to "The 29th Annual Dinner of the Corona Club", in the two following years the event was signalled as "The Colonial Service Dinner of the Corona Club". In 1933 the Committee announced that –

> While the historic name of the Club should remain unchanged, the dinner should be called in future the "Colonial Service Dinner". It was felt the change would increase the prestige of the Club and its dinner, and would be in accordance with the present tendency to emphasise the corporate aspect of the Colonial Service.

The last Dinner – under any name – took place in 1974. That of 1972 was held, as for the previous fifty years, at the Connaught Rooms, and once more with Lord Boyd (as he had since become) presiding. But by now the dinner was no longer a formal one, and 'White Tie and Glory' had already given way to the quiet sobriety of 'Black Ties' without decorations – as had been the case in the austerity years of 1947–49. Instead, the Connaught Rooms took to providing small round tables seating only eight to twelve guests, and members were encouraged to arrange their own tables of friends in advance. While the dinner remained 'men only', members of the Women's Corona Club, who since 1952 had dined in an adjacent suite, joined the Corona Club at a common bar both before and after dinner. By 1973 things had changed yet further, and for the first time members were invited to bring their wives: the Hon Secretary noted it as 'a turning point in the history of the Club'. For the first time, too, numbers fell below a hundred. They had already dropped to 112 in 1971, 100 in 1972. Now, in the final 1974, 66 members and 30 ladies dined. Quite remarkably, the Committee was still able to hold the cost of the dinner down to £4.75 – a rise of a paltry 600 per cent over 75 years.

The first alternative Corona Club Cocktail Party took place on 19 June, 1975, at the familiar Crown Agents address of 4 Millbank. The cost was £3.25 and 142 people attended: 94 were members of the Club, "the remainder" as the Hon Secretary recorded, "wives, sons and daughters . . . all of drinking age". Ten years after the final Dinner, the Corona Club had to say goodbye to its Cocktail Party venue when the impressive Crown Agents building was sold to private enterprise. After an experimental Cocktail Party at the Royal Over-Seas League in 1985 the annual event has settled down most enjoyably with the hospitality of the East India Club.

The Secretary of State's Speech

At every Dinner throughout the Club's history the Secretary of State for the Colonies presided – with three exceptions. The first was in 1922, when at the last moment Winston Churchill was detained in the House of Commons by urgent Irish business. The second was in 1935, when Mr Malcolm MacDonald, having taken over from Sir Philip Cunliffe-Lister at the Colonial Office in a Cabinet shuffle only a few days before the Dinner, members had "the unusual privilege", as the Hon Sec described it, of hearing a speech from both Ministers. Thirdly, in the Club's Diamond Jubilee year of 1960 when two Royal occasions marked the event, at the Dinner on 30 June members were addressed not only by the Secretary of State, Iain Macleod, but also by the Prime Minister, Harold Macmillan. That was also the year in which more than 500 members sat down to dinner, nearly a fifth of them from the Nigerian Service attending on the eve of the country's independence.

Chamberlain's wish for the Corona Club Dinner to have "a distinctive character . . . [so] that we may know a little more of one another . . . we must not sit in one place around a table . . . we must mix" did no more than reflect his reaction when the idea of holding an "Annual Service Dinner" was put to him in 1900. He had then requested that the dinner be short, "to be followed by a Smoking Conversazione so as to enable those present to move freely about and converse with the Secretary of State or with each other".

Leaving aside the war years, eleven in all (held in mid-June, the 1914 Dinner escaped the cataclysmic interruption brought about in August, while it was not felt possible to hold a Dinner in 1946), the continuity and centrepiece of the annual dinner manifested themselves in the Secretary of State's address and in his proposing the health of the Corona Club. Delivery generally took up something like half an hour. A few were measurably shorter. More often that not, the speech used to take the form of a round-the-world survey of events in the

Colonial Empire and it nearly always included references to colonial governors present or recently retired. While the speeches were, inevitably under the circumstances, aimed in thought and word at men, several Secretaries of State took care to extend their tribute to the role of womenfolk in the Empire. In 1911 Lewis Harcourt added "– and women, too", to those who had to ensure "the rigours" of a life of service overseas, and in 1929 Leo Amery took the opportunity of offering the Club's sympathy to Lord Lugard on the death of his wife to pay a wider tribute to those who married into the Colonial Service:

> I do not think any of us here would disagree as to the greatness of the services which are rendered to the Empire by the wives of those who, whether as Governors or in the junior ranks, have to shape their lives far afield. They have to face the double task, often under heart-breaking difficulties and anxieties, of keeping their flag flying at their husband's side and of preserving a home life. I pay to them my admiring tribute for the work they are doing.

Harcourt gave no less than four Dinner speeches ("Here we are again" was the Harlequinade refrain of the opening of his speech in 1913) as did Alan Lennox-Boyd, against three by the longest-serving Secretary of State, Joseph Chamberlain. The record was held by Leo Amery, who gave five consecutive Corona Club speeches (1925–1929). Three elements may be said to have been constant, warm and welcome, in every speech over the sixty years. One was huge and genuine appreciation of the work of the Colonial Service and of the Colonial Office, carried out always under difficulty and often in dangerous conditions. Another was of pride in the Colonial Empire. The third, as expected as the other two but always the most eagerly appreciated, was a high-profile display of humour. What is clear is how frequently the Secretary of State selected the occasion to announce some milestone event in the history of the Colonial Service and its public servants, often before releasing the news to the press and public.

It was at the Dinner of 11 June 1925 that Leo Amery revealed the fundamental reconstruction of the Colonial Office by the creation of a separate Secretaryship of State for the Dominions along with its own post of Permanent Under-Secretary, "a new and distinct organ of government", albeit housed within the same building and temporarily still held by Amery. This, he promised, would leave the Colonial Office "free to devote itself exclusively and uninterruptedly to your [members of the Corona Club] problems and your requirements". However, it fell to Lord Passfield to speak to the Club in 1930 as the first Secretary of State who was the Secretary of State for the Colonies only, a benefaction which he looked on as "a landmark in the history of the Colonial Empire". At the same dinner, Passfield alluded to two more landmarks. One was "the birth of a new phenomenon, the Colonial Service" – a reference to the proposed unification of the territorial Colonial Services. This had been discussed only a few days before at the Second Colonial Office Conference, and Passfield went on to reveal its details to his audience. The other event was the setting up of a special committee under Sir Warren Fisher to look into the recruitment of the Colonial Service. Its outcome was the abolition of Patronage in favour of a system of record and references. This revolution in Colonial Service appointments again formed the centrepiece of Passfield's address to the Corona Club in the following year, when he announced the establishment, following the Warren Fisher Report, of a Colonial Service Appointments Board (CSAB) linked with the Civil Service Commissioners. It was under Amery's leadership, too, that, as he announced at the 1926 Dinner, the Universities of Oxford and Cambridge had been approached to play a formal role in the training of cadets, not only

> in order to bring our Colonial Service into intimate touch with the life of the universities [but also] to tempt what I hope may be an ever-increasing stream of the best of our young men from the universities to enter what I believe is a great and honourable career.

This transformation and professionalisation of the Colonial Service was the subject of Mr Ormsby-Gore's Dinner speech in 1937. He took the opportunity to announce yet another step, the abolition of the old territorial Treasury staffs, a specialist cadre entrusted with the financial and economic affairs of colonial governments. This arrangement he considered to be out of date. Instead, he offered greater scope for what he saw as the talents now available within the ranks of the better-trained Administrative Service. At the same time he warned against any 'two service' thinking: "I repeat that there must be no divorce between the District administration and the Secretariat administration". On a grimmer note, the 1932 speech from Sir Philip Cunliffe-Lister had focused on retrenchment: "Men taken on, looking forward with a comparative sense of security to a permanent career, have found those careers cut short. We are making the reins as easy as we can, but it is a horrid job to do".

The decision of Cunliffe-Lister in 1933, following King George V's historic broadcast to the Empire the previous year, to enlist the skills of the Empire Programme Service of the still infant BBC for broadcasting his speech to the Empire inspired one Colonial Office listener at the Dinner to conjure up the following dubious image of the impact of this technological revolution on his 'bush and boma' colleagues:

> Before long, no doubt, the development of television will enable the District Officer, sitting down to his meal of stringy chicken and tinned vegetables in the African bush, to behold his more fortunate fellow-members toying with fraises Melba and sipping iced champagne, as well as to hear the hum of their conversation.

This practice of the Secretary of State's frank and personal taking the Club into his confidence during the Dinner speech continued after the Second World War. In 1947 Arthur Creech Jones made the bleak revelation that 168 years of history was coming to an end: "The Colonial Office will soon leave Downing Street". This time there was no *Hear Hear* or *Laughter* recorded, though expression of enthusiasm did greet the Colonial Secretary's subsequent aspirations that "We hope to see, at no distant date, a building rise opposite the Abbey and Westminster Hall worthy of the genius of the British people in their great Commonwealth adventure (*Applause*). Alas! (or maybe hooray?), we never did see that architectural wonder, and for many Club members today it is Sanctuary Buildings and Church House in Great Smith Street rather than Downing Street which the evocative reference to "The Colonial Office", brings to mind. In 1948, besides elaborating on the plans and drawings of the proposed new Colonial Office submitted to the Commission of Fine Arts, Creech Jones referred to the successful inauguration of what was to become the Colonial Office Cambridge Summer School, as well as to the imminent appointment of an editor to launch a Colonial Service Journal designed "to keep members of the Services informed about the recent pronouncements and development in colonial policy and practice". And, on his last appearance in 1949, the year of the imaginative "Colonial Month" in Britain, in one of the shortest Corona Club Dinner speeches on record, Arthur Creech Jones also let his audience into the state secret that when he had presented a copy of the 1948 <u>Colonial Office List</u> (the first full edition since the appearance of the 1940 <u>Dominions Office and Colonial Office List</u>, His Majesty "was most anxious to know that it was up to date".

But it was at the 44th Annual Dinner, held on June 17, 1954, that perhaps the greatest taking-the-Club-into-confidence came, when Oliver Lyttelton made the historical statement about the replacement of the Colonial Service by the creation of Her Majesty's Oversea ["Overseas" from 1956] Civil Service, to take place from October 1, 1954. The historical nature of that speech was followed two years later when, at the Dinner held on 21 June, the Rt Hon Alan Lennox-Boyd unveiled to the Corona Club his "revolutionary" plans for a Special List for work overseas on secondment from HMG. There were no more speeches from the Secretary of State for the Colonies – indeed, no more such Secretaries of State – after 1966, when the last Corona Club Dinner was held.

CONCLUSION

Let me conclude by reminding you of what the Secretary of State for the Colonies, Alfred Lyttelton (father of that successor to the very same office), said to the assembled company at the sixth annual Dinner, held at the Hotel Cecil on June 20, 1905. The British people, he declared, are ignorant of many things, but "there are few things of which they are so ignorant as the Crown Colonies". The challenge, now as then, is to place Britain's colonial aims in their proper prospective and to set our imperial achievements, above all those of our overseas civil servants, in their correct context.

Note: the Corona Club came to a close in 1999.

Index